Rick Steves®

FRENCH

PHRASE BOOK
& DICTIONARY

CONTENTS

Hi, I'm Rick Steves.

I'm the only monolingual speaker I know who's had the nerve to design a series of European phrase books. But that's one of the things that makes them better.

You see, after more than 30 years of travel through Europe, I've learned firsthand: (1) what's essential for communication in another country; and (2) what's not. I've assembled the most important words and phrases in a logical, no-frills format, and I've worked with native Europeans and seasoned travelers to give you the simplest, clearest translation possible.

But this book is more than just a pocket translator. The words and phrases have been carefully selected to help you have a smarter, smoother trip in France. The key to getting more out of every travel dollar is to get closer to the local people, and to rely less on entertainment, restaurants, and hotels that cater only to foreign tourists. This book will not only help you order a meal at a locals-only Parisian restaurant—but also help you talk with the family who runs the place...about their kids, travel dreams, and favorite *fromage*. Long after your memories of châteaux have faded, you'll still treasure the personal encounters you had with your new French friends.

While I've provided plenty of phrases, you'll find it just as effective to use even just a word or two to convey your meaning, and rely on context, gestures, and smiles to help you out. To make harried postal clerks happy, don't say haltingly in French: "I would like to buy three stamps to mail these postcards to the United States." All you really need is *timbres* (stamps), *les Etats-Unis* (USA), and *s'il vous plaît* (please). Smile, point to the postcards, hold up three fingers...and you've got stamps. (For more advice, see the Tips for Hurdling the Language Barrier chapter.)

To get the most out of this book, take the time to internalize and put into practice my French pronunciation tips. But don't worry too much about memorizing grammatical rules, like the gender of a noun—forget about sex, and communicate!

This book has a nifty menu decoder and a handy dictionary. You'll also find tongue twisters, international words, telephone tips, and two handy "cheat sheets." Tear out the sheets and tuck them in your beret, so you can easily memorize key phrases during otherwise idle moments. A good phrase book should help you enjoy your travel experience—not just survive it—so I've added a healthy dose of humor. And as you prepare for your trip, you may want to read the latest edition of one of my many guidebooks on destinations in France.

Adjust those cultural blinders. If you come to France expecting rudeness, you are sure to find it. If you respect the fine points of French culture and make an attempt to use their language, you'll find the French as warm and friendly as anyone in Europe.

Your experience will be enriched by a basic understanding of French etiquette. Here's the situation in a nutshell: The French feel that informality is rude and formality is polite, while Americans feel that informality is friendly and formality is cold. So, ironically, as the Americans and French are both doing their best to be nice, they accidentally offend one another. Remember you're the outsider, so watch the locals and try to incorporate some French-style politeness into your routine. Walk into any shop in France and you will hear a cheery, *"Bonjour, Monsieur / Madame."* As you leave, you'll hear a lilting, *"Au revoir, Monsieur / Madame."* Always address a man as *Monsieur,* a woman as *Madame,* and an unmarried young woman or a girl as *Mademoiselle* (leaving this out is like addressing a French person as "Hey, you!"). For good measure, toss in *s'il vous plaît* (please) whenever you can.

My goal is to help you become a more confident, extroverted traveler. If this phrase book helps make that happen, or if you have suggestions for making it better, I'd love to hear from you at rick@ricksteves .com.

Bon voyage! Have a good trip!

Rick Steves

GETTING
STARTED

hallenging, Romantic French is spoken throughout Europe and thought to be one of the most beautiful languages in the world. Half of Belgium speaks French, and French rivals English as the handiest second language in Spain, Portugal, and Italy. Even your US passport is translated into French. You're probably already familiar with this poetic language. Consider: *bonjour, c'est la vie, bon appétit, merci, au revoir,* and *bon voyage!* The most important phrase is *s'il vous plaît* (please), pronounced see voo play. Use it liberally—the French will notice and love it.

You can communicate a lot with only a few key French words: *ça, ça va, je peux,* and *voilà*. Here's how:

Ça (pronounced "sah") is a tourist's best friend. Meaning "that" or "this," it conveys worlds of meaning when combined with pointing. At the market, *fromagerie,* or *pâtisserie,* just point to what you want and say *Ça, s'il vous plaît,* with a smile.

Ça va (sah vah), meaning roughly "it goes," can fit almost any situation. As a question, *Ça va?* (Does it go?) can mean "Is this OK?" When combined with a gesture, you can use *Ça va?* to ask, "Can I sit here?" or "Can I touch this?" or "Can I take a picture?" or "Will this ticket get me into this museum?"...and much more. As a statement, *Ça va* (which basically means "Yes, it's OK") is almost as versatile. When the waiter asks if you want anything more, say *Ça va* ("I'm good"). If someone's hassling you and you've had enough, you can just say *Ça va* ("That's enough.").

Je peux? (zhuh puh, means "Can I?") can be used in many of the *Ça va?* situations, and more. Instead of saying, "Can I please sit here?", just gesture toward the seat and say *Je peux?* Instead of asking "Do you accept credit cards?" show them your Visa and ask *Je peux?*

While English speakers use *Voilà* (vwah-lah) only for a grand unveiling at a special occasion, the French say it many times each day. It means "Yes" or "Exactly" or "That's it" or "There you go." Unsure of how much your plums cost, you hold a euro coin out to the vendor and say *Ça va?* He responds with a cheery *Voilà*...and you're on your way, plums in hand.

While a number of French people speak fine English, many don't. The language barrier can seem high in France, but locals are happy to give an extra boost to any traveler who makes an effort to communicate. As with any language, the key to communicating is to go for it with a mixture of bravado and humility.

French pronunciation differs from English in some key ways:

Ç sounds like S in sun.
CH sounds like SH in shine.
G usually sounds like G in get.
But G followed by E or I sounds like S in treasure.
GN sounds like NI in onion.
H is always silent.
J sounds like S in treasure.
R sounds like an R being swallowed.
I sounds like EE in seed.
È and **Ê** sound like E in let.
É and **EZ** sound like AY in play.
ER, at the end of a word, sounds like AY in play.
Ô and **EAU** sounds like O in note.

In a Romance language, sex is unavoidable. A man is *content* (happy), a woman is *contente.* In this book, when you see a pair of words like *content / contente,* use the second word when talking about a woman.

French has four accents. The cedilla makes **Ç** sound like "s" *(façade).* The circumflex makes Ê sound like "eh" *(crêpe),* but has no effect on Â, Î, Ô, or Û. The grave accent stifles **È** into "eh" *(crème),* but doesn't change the stubborn **À** *(à la carte).* The acute accent opens **É** into "ay" *(café).*

French is tricky because the spelling and pronunciation seem to have little to do with each other. ***Qu'est-ce que c'est?*** (What is that?) is pronounced: kehs kuh say.

The final letters of many French words are silent, so **Paris** sounds like pah-ree. The French tend to stress every syllable evenly: pah-ree. In contrast, Americans say **Par**-is, emphasizing the first syllable.

In French, if a word that ends in a consonant is followed by a word that starts with a vowel, the consonant is frequently linked with the vowel. **Mes amis** (my friends) is pronounced: mayz-ah-mee. Some words are linked with an apostrophe. **Ce est** (It is) becomes **C'est**, as in **C'est la vie** (That's life). **Le** and **la** (the masculine and feminine "the") are intimately connected to words starting with a vowel. **La orange** becomes **l'orange.**

French has a few sounds that are unusual in English: the French **u** and the nasal vowels. To say the French **u**, round your lips to say "oh," but say "ee." Vowels combined with either **n** or **m** are often nasal vowels. As you nasalize a vowel, let the sound come through your nose as well as your mouth. The vowel is the important thing. The **n** or **m**, represented in this book by n for nasal, is not pronounced.

There are a total of four nasal sounds, all contained in the phrase **un bon vin blanc** (a good white wine).

Nasal vowels	Phonetics	To make the sound
un	uhn	nasalize the U in lung
bon	bohn	nasalize the O in bone
vin	van	nasalize the A in sack
blanc	blahn	nasalize the A in want

If you practice saying **un bon vin blanc,** you'll learn how to say the nasal vowels...and order a fine white wine.

Here's a guide to the rest of the phonetics in this book:

ah	like A in father
ay	like AY in play
eh	like E in let
ee	like EE in seed
ehr / air	sounds like "air" (in merci and extraordinaire)
ew	pucker your lips and say "ee"
g	like G in go
ī	like I in light

oh	like O in note
oo	like OO in too
s	like S in sun
uh	like U in but
ur	like UR in purr
zh	like S in treasure

FRENCH BASICS

Be creative! You can combine the phrases in this chapter to say "Two, please," or "No, thank you," or "Open tomorrow?" or "Please, where can I buy a ticket?" "Please" is a magic word in any language, especially in French. If you know the word for what you want, such as the bill, simply say *L'addition, s'il vous plaît* (The bill, please).

HELLOS AND GOODBYES

Pleasantries

Hello.	Bonjour. bohn-zhoor
Do you speak English?	Parlez-vous anglais? par-lay-voo ahn-glay
Yes. / No.	Oui. / Non. wee / nohn
I don't speak French.	Je ne parle pas français. zhuh nuh parl pah frahn-say
I'm sorry.	Désolé. day-zoh-lay
Please.	S'il vous plaît. see voo play
Thank you (very much).	Merci (beaucoup). mehr-see (boh-koo)
Excuse me. (to get attention)	Excusez-moi. ehk-skew-zay-mwah
Excuse me. (to pass)	Pardon. par-dohn
OK?	Ça va? sah vah
OK. (two ways to say it)	Ça va. / D'accord. sah vah / dah-kor
Good.	Bien. bee-an
Very good.	Très bien. treh bee-an
Excellent.	Excellent. ehk-seh-lahn
You are very kind.	Vous êtes très gentil. vooz eht treh zhahn-tee
It doesn't matter.	Ça m'est égal. sah meht ay-gahl
No problem.	Pas de problème. pah duh proh-blehm

| You're welcome. | De rien. duh ree-a<u>n</u> |
| Goodbye. | Au revoir. oh ruh-vwahr |

Pardon and *Excusez-moi* aren't interchangeable. Say *Pardon* to get past someone; use *Excusez-moi* to get someone's attention.

Meeting and Greeting

The French begin every interaction with *Bonjour, Monsieur* (to a man) or *Bonjour, Madame* (to a woman). It's impossible to overstate the importance of this courtesy. To the French, a proper greeting respectfully acknowledges the recipient as a person first, and secondly as a professional. Taking the time to say a polite hello marks you as a conscientious visitor and guarantees a warmer welcome.

Good day.	Bonjour. boh<u>n</u>-zhoor
Good morning.	Bonjour. boh<u>n</u>-zhoor
Good evening.	Bonsoir. boh<u>n</u>-swahr
Good night.	Bonne soirée. buhn swah-ray
Hi / Bye. (informal)	Salut. sah-lew
Welcome!	Bienvenue! bee-a<u>n</u>-vuh-new
Mr.	Monsieur muhs-yuh
Mrs.	Madame mah-dahm
Miss	Mademoiselle mahd-mwah-zehl
Good day, gentlemen and ladies.	Bonjour, Messieurs et Madames. boh<u>n</u>-zhoor mays-yuh ay mah-dahm
My name is _____.	Je m'appelle _____. zhuh mah-pehl _____
What's your name?	Quel est votre nom? kehl ay voh-truh noh<u>n</u>
Pleased to meet you.	Enchanté. ah<u>n</u>-shah<u>n</u>-tay
How are you?	Comment allez-vous? koh-mah<u>n</u>t ah-lay-voo
Very well, thank you.	Très bien, merci. treh bee-a<u>n</u> mehr-see

Fine.	Bien. bee-a<u>n</u>
And you?	Et vous? ay voo
Where are you from?	D'où êtes-vous? doo eht-voo
I am from _____.	Je suis de _____. zhuh swee duh _____
I am / We are...	Je suis / Nous sommes... zhuh swee / noo suhm
Are you...?	Êtes-vous...? eht-voo
...on vacation	...en vacances ah<u>n</u> vah-kah<u>n</u>s
...on business	...en voyage d'affaires ah<u>n</u> vwah-yahzh dah-fair

The greeting **Bonjour** (Good day) turns to **Bonsoir** (Good evening) at dinnertime. If the French see someone they've just greeted recently, they may say **Rebonjour**.

You might hear locals use the breezy **Bonjour, Messieurs / Dames** or even **Bonjour, tout le monde** (Hello, everybody) if both men and women are present. But to proper French people, this is too rushed and sloppy. Take the time to say **Bonjour, Messieurs et Madames** (Hello, gentlemen and ladies).

Moving On

I'm going to _____.	Je vais à _____. zhuh vay ah _____
How do I go to _____?	Comment aller à _____? koh-mah<u>n</u>t ah-lay ah _____
Let's go.	Allons-y. ah-loh<u>n</u>-zee
See you later.	À bientôt. ah bee-a<u>n</u>-toh
See you tomorrow!	À demain! ah duh-ma<u>n</u>
So long! (informal)	Salut! sah-lew
Goodbye.	Au revoir. oh ruh-vwahr
Good luck!	Bonne chance! buhn shah<u>n</u>s
Happy travels!	Bon voyage! boh<u>n</u> vwah-yahzh

STRUGGLING WITH FRENCH

Who Speaks What?

French	français frah<u>n</u>-say
English	anglais ah<u>n</u>-glay
Do you speak English?	Parlez-vous anglais? par-lay-voo ah<u>n</u>-glay
A teeny weeny bit?	Un tout petit peu? uh<u>n</u> too puh-tee puh
Please speak English.	Parlez anglais, s'il vous plaît. par-lay ah<u>n</u>-glay see voo play
Slowly.	Lentement. lah<u>n</u>t-mah<u>n</u>
Repeat?	Répétez? ray-pay-tay
I understand.	Je comprends. zhuh koh<u>n</u>-prah<u>n</u>
I don't understand.	Je ne comprends pas. zhuh nuh koh<u>n</u>-prah<u>n</u> pah
Do you understand?	Vous comprenez? voo koh<u>n</u>-pruh-nay
You speak English well.	Vous parlez bien l'anglais. voo par-lay bee-a<u>n</u> lah<u>n</u>-glay
Does somebody nearby speak English?	Quelqu'un près d'ici parle anglais? kehl-kuh<u>n</u> preh dee-see parl ah<u>n</u>-glay
I don't speak French.	Je ne parle pas français. zhuh nuh parl pah frah<u>n</u>-say
I speak a little French.	Je parle un petit peu français. zhuh parl uh<u>n</u> puh-tee puh frah<u>n</u>-say
What does this mean?	Qu'est-ce que ça veut dire? kehs kuh sah vuh deer
How do you say this in French?	Comment dit-on en français? koh-mah<u>n</u> dee-toh<u>n</u> ah<u>n</u> frah<u>n</u>-say
Write it down?	Ecrivez? ay-kree-vay

A French person who is asked "Do you speak English?" assumes you mean "Do you speak English fluently?" and will likely answer no. But if you just keep on struggling in French, you'll bring out the English in most any French person.

Quintessentially French Expressions

Bon appétit!
bohn ah-pay-tee
Enjoy your meal!

Ça va?
sah vah
How are you? (informal)

Ça va. (response to Ça va?)
sah vah
I'm fine.

Sympa. / Pas sympa.
san-pah / pah san-pah
Nice. / Not nice.

C'est chouette. ("That's a female owl.")
say shweht
That's cool.

Ce n'est pas vrai!
suh nay pah vray
It's not true!

C'est comme ça.
say kohm sah
That's the way it is.

Comme ci, comme ça.
kohm see kohm sah
So so.

D'accord.
dah-kor
OK.

Formidable!
for-mee-dah-bluh
Great!

Mon Dieu!
mohn dee-uh
My God!

Tout de suite.
tood sweet
Right away.

Bonne journée.
bohn zhoor-nay
Have a good day.

Voilà.
vwah-lah
Here it is.

Oh la la!
oo lah lah
Wow!

REQUESTS

The Essentials

Can you help me?	Vous pouvez m'aider? voo poo-vay meh-day
Do you have ___?	Avez-vous ___? ah-vay-voo ___
I'd like...	Je voudrais... zhuh voo-dray
We'd like...	Nous voudrions... noo voo-dree-ohn
...this / that.	...ceci / cela. suh-see / suh-lah
How much does it cost, please?	Combien, s'il vous plaît? kohn-bee-an see voo play
Is it free?	C'est gratuit? say grah-twee
Included?	Inclus? an-klew
Is it possible?	C'est possible? say poh-see-bluh
Yes or no?	Oui ou non? wee oo nohn
Where are the toilets?	Où sont les toilettes? oo sohn lay twah-leht
men	hommes ohm
women	dames dahm

To prompt a simple answer, ask *Oui ou non*? (Yes or no?). To turn a word or sentence into a question, ask it in a questioning tone. *C'est bon* (It's good) becomes *C'est bon?* (Is it good?). An easy way to say "Where is the toilet?" is to ask *Toilette, s'il vous plaît?*

Where?

Where?	Où? oo
Where is...?	Où est...? oo ay
...the tourist information office	...l'office de tourisme loh-fees duh too-reez-muh
...a cash machine	...un distributeur uhn dee-stree-bew-tur
...the train station	...la gare lah gar

| Where can I buy _____? | Où puis-je acheter _____? oo pweezh ah-shuh-tay _____ |
| Where can I find _____? | Où puis-je trouver _____? oo pweezh troo-vay _____ |

French makes it easy if you're looking for a *pharmacie, hôtel,* or *restaurant.*

How Much?

How much does it cost, please?	Combien, s'il vous plaît? kohn-bee-an see voo play
Write it down?	Ecrivez? ay-kree-vay
I'd like...	Je voudrais... zhuh voo-dray
...a ticket.	...un billet. uhn bee-yay
...the bill.	...l'addition. lah-dee-see-ohn
This much. (gesturing)	Comme ça. kohm sah
More. / Less.	Plus. / Moins. plew / mwan
Too much.	Beaucoup trop. boh-koo troh

When?

When?	Quand? kahn
What time is it?	Quelle heure est-il? kehl ur ay-teel
At what time?	À quelle heure? ah kehl ur
_____ o'clock	_____ heures _____ ur
opening times	horaires d'ouverture oh-rair doo-vehr-tewr
open / closed	ouvert / fermé oo-vehr / fehr-may
What time does this open / close?	À quelle heure c'est ouvert / fermé? ah kehl ur say oo-vehr / fehr-may
Is this open daily?	C'est ouvert tous les jours? say oo-vehr too lay zhoor

What day is this closed?	C'est fermé quel jour? say fehr-may kehl zhoor
On time?	A l'heure? ah lur
Late?	En retard? ahn ruh-tar
Just a moment.	Un moment. uhn moh-mahn
now / soon / later	maintenant / bientôt / plus tard man-tuh-nahn / bee-an-toh / plew tar
today / tomorrow	aujourd'hui / demain oh-zhoor-dwee / duh-man

For tips on telling time, see "Time and Dates" on page 34.

How Long?

How long does it take?	Ça prend combien de temps? sah prahn kohn-bee-an duh tahn
How many minutes / hours?	Combien de minutes / d'heures? kohn-bee-an duh mee-newt / dur
How far?	C'est loin? say lwan

Just Ask

Why?	Pourquoi? poor-kwah
Why not?	Pourquoi pas? poor-kwah pah
Is it necessary?	C'est nécessaire? say nay-suh-sair
Can I...?	Je peux...? zhuh puh
Can we...?	Nous pouvons...? noo poo-vohn
...borrow that for a moment	...emprunter ça pour un moment ahn-pruhn-tay sah poor uhn moh-mahn
...use the toilet	...utiliser les toilettes ew-tee-lee-zay lay twah-leht
Next? (in line)	Le prochain? luh proh-shan

The last? (in line)	Le dernier? luh dehrn-yay
What? (didn't hear)	Comment? koh-mahn
What is this?	Qu'est-ce que c'est? kehs kuh say
What's going on?	Qu'est-ce qui se passe? kehs kee suh pahs

SIMPLY IMPORTANT WORDS

Numbers

0	zéro zay-roh
1	un uhn
2	deux duh
3	trois trwah
4	quatre kah-truh
5	cinq sank
6	six sees
7	sept seht
8	huit weet
9	neuf nuhf
10	dix dees
11	onze ohnz
12	douze dooz
13	treize trehz
14	quatorze kah-torz
15	quinze kanz
16	seize sehz
17	dix-sept dee-seht
18	dix-huit deez-weet
19	dix-neuf deez-nuhf
20	vingt van

You'll find more to count on in the "Numbers" section (page 26).

The Alphabet

If you're spelling your name over the phone, you can use the nouns in the third column to help make yourself understood. I'd say my name as: **R...Raoul, I...Irma, C...Célestin, K...Kléber.**

A	ah	Anatole	ahn-ah-tohl
B	bay	Berthe	behrt
C	say	Célestin	say-luh-stan
D	day	Désiré	day-zee-ray
E	uh	Emile	eh-meel
F	"f"	François	frahn-swah
G	zhay	Gaston	gah-stohn
H	ahsh	Henri	ahn-ree
I	ee	Irma	eer-mah
J	zhee	Joseph	zhoh-zuhf
K	kah	Kléber	klay-behr
L	"l"	Louis	loo-ee
M	"m"	Marcel	mar-sehl
N	"n"	Nicolas	nee-koh-lahs
O	"o"	Oscar	ohs-kar
P	pay	Pierre	pee-yehr
Q	kew	Quintal	kween-tahl
R	ehr	Raoul	rah-ool
S	"s"	Suzanne	sew-zahn
T	tay	Thérèse	tay-rehs
U	ew	Ursule	ewr-sewl
V	vay	Victor	veek-tor
W	doo-bluh-vay	William	weel-yahm
X	"x"	Xavier	zhahv-yehr
Y	ee-grehk	Yvonne	ee-vohn
Z	zehd	Zoé	zoh-ay

Days and Months

Sunday	dimanche dee-mah<u>n</u>sh
Monday	lundi luh<u>n</u>-dee
Tuesday	mardi mar-dee
Wednesday	mercredi mehr-kruh-dee
Thursday	jeudi zhuh-dee
Friday	vendredi vah<u>n</u>-druh-dee
Saturday	samedi sahm-dee
January	janvier zhah<u>n</u>-vee-yay
February	février fay-vree-yay
March	mars mars
April	avril ahv-reel
May	mai may
June	juin zhwa<u>n</u>
July	juillet zhwee-yay
August	août oot
September	septembre sehp-tah<u>n</u>-bruh
October	octobre ohk-toh-bruh
November	novembre noh-vah<u>n</u>-bruh
December	décembre day-sah<u>n</u>-bruh

Big Little Words

I	je zhuh
you (for formal use or a group)	vous voo
you (informal)	tu tew
we	nous noo
he	il eel
she	elle ehl
it (m / f; varies by gender of noun)	le / la luh / lah

they (m / f)	ils / elles eel / ehl
and	et ay
at	à ah
because	parce que pars kuh
but	mais may
by (train, car, etc.)	par par
for	pour poor
from	de duh
here	ici ee-see
if	si see
in	en ahn
not	pas pah
now	maintenant man-tuh-nahn
of	de / du duh / dew
only	seulement suhl-mahn
or	ou oo
out	dehors / à l'extérieur duh-or / ah lehk-stay-ree-ur
this	ceci suh-see
that	cela suh-lah
to	à ah
too	aussi oh-see
very	très treh

Opposites

good / bad	bon / mauvais bohn / moh-vay
best / worst	le meilleur / le pire luh meh-yur / luh peer
a little / lots	un peu / beaucoup uhn puh / boh-koo
more / less	plus / moins plew / mwan

Simply Important Words

cheap / expensive	bon marché / cher bohn mar-shay / shehr
big / small	grand / petit grah<u>n</u> / puh-tee
hot / cold	chaud / froid shoh / frwah
warm / cool	tiède / frais tee-ehd / fray
cool (nice) / not cool	sympa / pas sympa sa<u>n</u>-pah / pah sa<u>n</u>-pah
open / closed	ouvert / fermé oo-vehr / fehr-may
entrance / exit	entrée / sortie ah<u>n</u>-tray / sor-tee
push / pull	pousser / tirer poo-say / tee-ray
arrive / depart	arriver / partir ah-ree-vay / par-teer
early / late	tôt / tard toh / tar
soon / later	bientôt / plus tard bee-a<u>n</u>-toh / plew tar
fast / slow	vite / lent veet / lah<u>n</u>
here / there	ici / là-bas ee-see / lah-bah
near / far	près / loin preh / lwa<u>n</u>
inside / outside	l'intérieur / dehors la<u>n</u>-tay-ree-ur / duh-or
mine / yours	le mien / le vôtre luh mee-a<u>n</u> / luh voh-truh
this / that	ceci / cela suh-see / suh-lah
easy / difficult	facile / difficile fah-seel / dee-fee-seel
left / right	à gauche / à droite ah gohsh / ah drwaht
up / down	en haut / en bas ah<u>n</u> oh / ah<u>n</u> bah
above / below	au-dessus / en-dessous oh-duh-sew / ah<u>n</u>-duh-soo
young / old	jeune / vieux zhuh<u>n</u> / vee-uh
new / old	neuf / vieux nuhf / vee-uh
heavy / light	lourd / léger loor / lay-zhay
dark / light	sombre / clair soh<u>n</u>-bruh / klair
happy / sad	content / triste koh<u>n</u>-tah<u>n</u> / treest

beautiful / ugly	beau / laid boh / lay
nice / mean	gentil / méchant
zhahn-tee / may-shahn
intelligent / stupid	intelligent / stupide
an-teh-lee-zhahn / stew-peed
vacant / occupied	libre / occupé lee-bruh / oh-kew-pay
with / without	avec / sans ah-vehk / sahn

SIGN LANGUAGE

Here are some signs you may see in your travels.

À disposition ici	Available here
À louer	For rent or for hire
À ne pas utiliser en cas d'urgence	Do not use in case of emergency
À vendre	For sale
À vos risques et périls	At your own risk
Accès réservé au personnel	Authorized personnel only
Alarme incendie	Fire alarm
Appel d'urgence	Emergency call
Appuyer sur l'interrupteur svp	Please press button (to change light)
Arrivées	Arrivals
Attendez	Wait
Attention	Caution
Attention à la marche	Watch your step
Caisse	Cashier
Carte Bancaire (CB) à partir de €_____	Credit cards accepted for purchases over €_____
Centre-ville	Town center
Chambre libre	Vacancy
Chien méchant	Mean dog
Complet	No vacancy
Compostage de billets	Validate tickets here

Composter avant de voyager	Validate tickets before traveling
Compostez ici	Validate tickets here
Dames	Women
Danger	Danger
Défense de fumer	No smoking
Défense de toucher	Do not touch
Défense d'entrer	Keep out
Départs	Departures
Eau non potable	Undrinkable water
Eau potable	Drinking water
En cas d'urgence	In case of emergency
En panne	Out of service
Entrée	Entrance
Entrée interdite	No entry
Entrée libre	Free admission
Étage	Floor
Faites l'appoint	Exact change only
Femmes ("F" on bathroom door)	Women
Fermé	Closed
Fermé pour restauration	Closed for restoration
Fermeture annuelle	Closed for vacation
Guichet	Ticket window
Hommes ("H" on bathroom door)	Men
Horaire	Timetable
Horaires d'ouverture	Opening times
Hors service	Out of service
Interdit	Forbidden
La file commence par la gauche / droite	The line begins at the left / right
Midi / Heure du déjeuner	Midday / Lunch break
Ne pas déranger	Do not disturb
Niveau	Level (of a building)
Nous avons...	We have...

Nous n'acceptons pas les paiements par cartes bancaires (CB)	We do not accept credit cards
Occupé	Occupied
Office de tourisme	Tourist information office
Ouvert	Open
Ouvert de _____ à _____	Open from _____ to _____
Pas de monnaie	No change given
Passage interdit	Do not enter
Passage piéton	Crosswalk / School crossing
Pelouse interdite	Keep off the grass
Poussez	Push
Poussez ici	Push here
Prenez un ticket	Take a ticket
Prudence	Be careful
Réduction	Special offer
Réservé	Reserved
Réservé aux piétons	Pedestrians only
Sens de la file	Direction of the line
Sens de la visite	Direction of the tour
Sens unique	One-way street
Solde	Sale
Sortie	Exit
Sortie de secours	Emergency exit
Stationnement interdit	No parking
Tirez	Pull
Toilettes	Toilets
Veuillez attendre ici	Please wait here
Veuillez prendre un numéro	Please take a number
Voie piétonne	Pedestrian zone
WC	Toilet
Zone piétonne	Pedestrian zone

NUMBERS, MONEY & TIME

Y ou can count on this chapter to cover French numbers, currency, credit and debit cards, time, dates, and major holidays and celebrations.

NUMBERS

0	zéro zay-roh
1	un uhn
2	deux duh
3	trois trwah
4	quatre kah-truh
5	cinq sank
6	six sees
7	sept seht
8	huit weet
9	neuf nuhf
10	dix dees
11	onze ohnz
12	douze dooz
13	treize trehz
14	quatorze kah-torz
15	quinze kanz
16	seize sehz
17	dix-sept dee-seht
18	dix-huit deez-weet
19	dix-neuf deez-nuhf
20	vingt van
21	vingt et un vant ay uhn
22	vingt-deux vant-duh
23	vingt-trois vant-trwah
30	trente trahnt
31	trente et un trahnt ay uhn
40	quarante kah-rahnt

41	quarante et un kah-rah<u>nt</u> ay uh<u>n</u>
50	cinquante sa<u>n</u>-kah<u>nt</u>
51	cinquante et un sa<u>n</u>-kah<u>nt</u> ay uh<u>n</u>
60	soixante swah-sah<u>nt</u>
61	soixante et un swah-sah<u>nt</u> ay uh<u>n</u>
70	soixante-dix swah-sah<u>nt</u>-dees
71	soixante et onze swah-sah<u>nt</u> ay oh<u>n</u>z
72	soixante-douze swah-sah<u>nt</u>-dooz
73	soixante-treize swah-sah<u>nt</u>-trehz
74	soixante-quatorze swah-sah<u>nt</u>-kah-torz
75	soixante-quinze swah-sah<u>nt</u>-kanz
76	soixante-seize swah-sah<u>nt</u>-sehz
77	soixante-dix-sept swah-sah<u>nt</u>-dee-seht
78	soixante-dix-huit swah-sah<u>nt</u>-deez-weet
79	soixante-dix-neuf swah-sah<u>nt</u>-deez-nuhf
80	quatre-vingts kah-truh-va<u>n</u>
81	quatre-vingt-un kah-truh-va<u>n</u>-uh<u>n</u>
82	quatre-vingt-deux kah-truh-va<u>n</u>-duh
83	quatre-vingt-trois kah-truh-va<u>n</u>-trwah
84	quatre-vingt-quatre kah-truh-va<u>n</u>-kah-truh
85	quatre-vingt-cinq kah-truh-va<u>n</u>-sank
86	quatre-vingt-six kah-truh-va<u>n</u>-sees
87	quatre-vingt-sept kah-truh-va<u>n</u>-seht
88	quatre-vingt-huit kah-truh-va<u>n</u>-weet
89	quatre-vingt-neuf kah-truh-va<u>n</u>-nuhf
90	quatre-vingt-dix kah-truh-va<u>n</u>-dees
91	quatre-vingt-onze kah-truh-va<u>n</u>-oh<u>n</u>z
92	quatre-vingt-douze kah-truh-va<u>n</u>-dooz
93	quatre-vingt-treize kah-truh-va<u>n</u>-trehz
94	quatre-vingt-quatorze kah-truh-va<u>n</u>-kah-torz
95	quatre-vingt-quinze kah-truh-va<u>n</u>-kanz
96	quatre-vingt-seize kah-truh-va<u>n</u>-sehz

97	quatre-vingt-dix-sept	kah-truh-van-dee-seht
98	quatre-vingt-dix-huit	kah-truh-van-deez-weet
99	quatre-vingt-dix-neuf	kah-truh-van-deez-nuhf
100	cent	sahn
101	cent un	sahnt uhn
102	cent deux	sahn duh
200	deux cents	duh sahn
300	trois cents	trwah sahn
400	quatre cents	kah-truh sahn
500	cinq cents	sank sahn
600	six cents	sees sahn
700	sept cents	seht sahn
800	huit cents	weet sahn
900	neuf cents	nuhf sahn
1000	mille	meel
2000	deux mille	duh meel
2019	deux mille dix-neuf	duh meel deez-nuhf
2020	deux mille vingt	duh meel van
2021	deux mille vingt et un	duh meel vant ay uhn
2022	deux mille vingt-deux	duh meel vant-duh
2023	deux mille vingt-trois	duh meel vant-trwah
2024	deux mille vingt-quatre	duh meel vant-kah-truh
2025	deux mille vingt-cinq	duh meel vant-sank
2026	deux mille vingt-six	duh meel vant-sees
2027	deux mille vingt-sept	duh meel vant-seht
2028	deux mille vingt-huit	duh meel vant-weet
2029	deux mille vingt-neuf	duh meel vant-nuhf
2030	deux mille trente	duh meel trahnt
million	million	meel-yohn
billion	milliard	meel-yar
number one	numéro un	new-may-roh uhn
first	premier	pruhm-yay

second	deuxième duhz-yehm
third	troisième trwahz-yehm
once	une fois ewn fwah
twice	deux fois duh fwah
a quarter	un quart uhn kar
a third	un tiers uhn tee-ehr
half	demi duh-mee
this much	comme ça kohm sah
a dozen	une douzaine ewn doo-zehn
a handful	une poignée ewn pwahn-yay
enough	suffisament sew-fee-zah-mahn
not enough	pas assez pah ah-say
too much	trop troh
more	plus plew
less	moins mwan
50%	cinquante pour cent san-kahnt poor sahn
100%	cent pour cent sahn poor sahn

French numbers are a little quirky from the seventies through the nineties. Let's pretend momentarily that the French speak English. Instead of saying 70, 71, 72, up to 79, the French say "sixty ten," "sixty eleven," "sixty twelve" up to "sixty nineteen." Instead of saying 80, the French say "four twenties." The numbers 81 and 82 are literally "four twenty one" and "four twenty two." It gets stranger. The number 90 is "four twenty ten." To say 91, 92, up to 99, the French say "four twenty eleven," "four twenty twelve" on up to "four twenty nineteen." But take heart. If little French children can learn these numbers, so can you. Besides, didn't Abe Lincoln say "Four score and seven..."?

Learning how to say your hotel room number is a good way to practice French numbers. You'll likely be asked for the number frequently (at breakfast, or to claim your key when you return to the room).

MONEY

France uses the euro currency. One *euro* (€, uh-roh) is divided into 100 cents (*centimes,* sah<u>n</u>-teem), so "two euros and fifty cents" is *deux euros et cinquante centimes,* or simply *deux-cinquante.*

Use your common cents—cents are like pennies, and the currency has coins like nickels, dimes, and half-dollars. There are also €1 and €2 coins.

Cash Machines (ATMs)

To get cash, ATMs are the way to go. At French banks, you may encounter a security door that allows one person to enter at a time. Push the *entrez* (enter) button, then *attendez* (wait), and *voilà!,* the door opens. Every *distributeur* (cash machine; also called a *point d'argent*) is multilingual, but if you'd like to learn French under pressure, look for these buttons: *annuler* or *annulation* (cancel), *modifier* or *correction* (change), *valider* or *validation* (confirm). Your PIN code is a *code.*

money	argent ar-zhah<u>n</u>
cash	liquide lee-keed
card	carte kart
PIN code	code "code"
Where is a...?	Oú est...? oo ay
...cash machine	...un distributeur uh<u>n</u> dee-stree-bew-tur
...bank	...une banque ewn bah<u>n</u>k
My debit card has been...	Ma carte de débit a été... mah kart duh day-bee ah ay-tay
...demagnetized.	...démagnétisée. day-mah<u>g</u>-nay-tee-zay
...stolen.	...volée. voh-lay
...eaten by the machine.	...avalée par la machine. ah-vah-lay par lah mah-sheen
My card doesn't work.	Ma carte ne marche pas. mah kart nuh marsh pah

Key Phrases: Money

euro(s) (€)	euro(s) uh-roh
cent(s)	centime(s) sahn-teem
cash	liquide lee-keed
Where is a...?	Oú est...? oo ay
...cash machine	...un distributeur uhn dee-stree-bew-tur
...bank	...une banque ewn bahnk
credit card	carte de crédit kart duh kray-dee
debit card	carte de débit kart duh day-bee
Do you accept credit cards?	Vous prenez les cartes de crédit? voo pruh-nay lay kart duh kray-dee

Credit and Debit Cards

Credit cards are widely accepted at larger businesses, though some smaller shops, restaurants, and guest houses might prefer cash. Even if they accept credit cards, some hotels might cut you a discount for paying cash. In France, they often say **Carte Blue**—the name of the most widely used credit card—as a generic term for any credit card. The abbreviation **CB** written on signs usually stands for **carte bancaire** (credit card).

credit card	carte de crédit / carte bancaire kart duh kray-dee / kart bahn-kair
debit card	carte de débit kart duh day-bee
receipt	reçu ruh-sew
sign	signer seen-yay
pay	payer pay-yay
cashier	caisse kehs
cash advance	crédit de caisse kray-dee duh kehs

Do you accept credit cards?	Vous prenez les cartes de crédit? voo pruh-nay lay kart duh kray-dee
Is it cheaper if I pay cash?	C'est moins cher si je paye en espèces? say mwan shehr see zhuh pay ahn ehs-pehs
I do not have a PIN.	Je n'ai pas de code PIN. zhuh nay pah duh "code" peen
Can I sign a receipt instead?	Je peux signer un reçu à la place? zhuh puh seen-yay uhn ruh-sew ah lah plahs
Print a receipt?	Imprimer un reçu? an-pree-may uhn ruh-sew
I have another card.	J'ai une autre carte. zhay ewn oh-truh kart

Credit and debit cards have chips that authenticate and secure transactions. Some European card readers will generate a receipt for you to sign; others may prompt you to enter a PIN (make sure you know it for all cards). If your card won't work (sometimes possible at ticket machines, toll booths, gas pumps, or parking lots), look for a cashier who can process your card manually—or pay in cash.

Paying with a Credit Card

If calling to reserve tickets or a hotel room, you may need to convey your credit-card information over the phone. Prepare in advance: To fill in the blanks, use the numbers, alphabet, and months on pages 16-18 and the years on page 28.

The name on the card is ____.	Le nom sur la carte est ____. luh nohn sewr lah kart ay ____
The credit card number is ____.	Le numéro de carte de crédit est ____. luh new-may-roh duh kart duh kray-dee ay ____
The expiration date is ____.	La date d'expiration est ____. lah daht dehk-spee-rah-see-ohn ay ____

The secret code (on the back) is _____.	Le cryptogramme c'est _____. luh kreep-toh-grahm say _____

Exchanging Money

exchange	bureau de change bew-roh duh shah<u>n</u>zh
change money	changer de l'argent shah<u>n</u>-zhay duh lar-zhah<u>n</u>
exchange rate	taux de change toh duh shah<u>n</u>zh
dollars	dollars doh-lar
buy / sell	acheter / vendre ah-shuh-tay / vah<u>n</u>-druh
commission	commission koh-mee-see-oh<u>n</u>
Any extra fee?	Il y a d'autre frais? eel yah doh-truh fray
I would like...	Je voudrais... zhuh voo-dray
...small bills.	...des petits billets. day puh-tee bee-yay
...large bills.	...des gros billets. day groh bee-yay
...a mix of small and large bills.	...un assortiment de petits et gros billets. uh<u>n</u> ah-sor-tee-mah<u>n</u> duh puh-teet ay groh bee-yay
...coins.	...des pieces. day pee-ehs
Can you break this? (large into small bills)	Vous pouvez casser ça? voo poo-vay kah-say sah
Is this a mistake?	C'est une erreur? sayt ewn ehr-ur
This is incorrect.	C'est incorrect. say a<u>n</u>-koh-rehkt
Where is the nearest casino?	Oú se trouve le casino le plus proche? oo suh troov luh kah-see-noh luh plew prohsh

French banks don't change currency; you'll need to use a *bureau de change.*

TIME AND DATES

Telling Time

In France, the 24-hour clock (military time) is used for setting formal appointments (for instance, arrival times at a hotel), for the opening and closing hours of museums and shops, and for train, bus, and ferry schedules. Informally, Europeans use the 24-hour clock and our 12-hour clock interchangeably—**17:00** is also **5:00 de l'après-midi** (in the afternoon).

What time is it?	Quelle heure est-il? kehl ur ay-teel
_____ o'clock	_____ heures _____ ur
in the morning	dans le matin dah<u>n</u> luh mah-ta<u>n</u>
in the afternoon	dans l'après-midi dah<u>n</u> lah-preh-mee-dee
in the evening	dans le soir dah<u>n</u> luh swahr
at night	la nuit lah nwee
half	la demi lah duh-mee
quarter	le quart luh kar
minute	minute mee-newt
hour	heure ur
It's... / At...	Il est... / À... eel ay / ah
...8:00 in the morning.	...huit heures du matin. weet ur dew mah-ta<u>n</u>
...16:00.	...seize heures. sehz ur
...4:00 in the afternoon.	...quatre heures de l'après-midi. kah-truh ur duh lah-preh-mee-dee
...10:30 in the evening.	...dix heures et demi du soir. deez ur ay duh-mee dew swahr
...a quarter past nine.	...neuf heures et quart. nuhv ur ay kar
...a quarter to eleven.	...onze heures moins le quart. oh<u>n</u>z ur mwa<u>n</u> luh kar

Key Phrases: Time and Dates

What time is it?	Quelle heure est-il? kehl ur ay-teel
_____ o'clock	_____ heures _____ ur
minute	minute mee-newt
hour	heure ur
It's...	Il est... eel ay
...7:00 in the morning.	...sept heures du matin. seht ur dew mah-tan
...2:00 in the afternoon.	...deux heures de l'après-midi. duhz ur duh lah-preh-mee-dee
At what time does this open / close?	À quelle heuere c'est ouvert / fermé? ah kehl ur say oo-vehr / fehr-may
day	jour zhoor
today	aujourd'hui oh-zhoor-dwee
tomorrow	demain duh-man
(this) week	(cette) semaine (seht) suh-mehn
August 21	le vingt et un août luh vant ay uhn oot

at 6:00 sharp	à six heures précises ah sees ur pray-seez
from 8:00 to 10:00	de huit heures à dix heures duh weet ur ah dees ur
noon	midi mee-dee
midnight	minuit meen-wee
It's my bedtime.	C'est l'heure où je me couche. say lur oo zhuh muh koosh
I'll return / We'll return at 11:20.	Je reviens / Nous revenons à onze heures vingt. zhuh ruh-vee-an / noo ruh-vuh-nohn ah ohnz ur van

I'll be / We'll be there by 18:00.	Je serai / Nous serons là avant dix-huit heures.
	zhuh suh-ray / noo suh-rohn lah ah-vahn deez-weet ur

The word *heures* (roughly meaning "o'clock") is sometimes abbreviated as *H* in writing. So *18 H* means 18:00, or 6 p.m.

Timely Questions

When?	Quand? kahn
At what time?	À quelle heure? ah kehl ur
opening times	horaires d'ouverture
	oh-rair doo-vehr-tewr
At what time does this open / close?	À quelle heure c'est ouvert / fermé?
	ah kehl ur say oo-vehr / fehr-may
Is the train...?	Le train est...? luh tran ay
Is the bus...?	Le bus est...? luh bews ay
...early	...en avance ...ahn ah-vahns
...late	...en retard ...ahn ruh-tar
...on time	...à l'heure ...ah lur
When is checkout time?	À quelle heure on doit libérer la chambre?
	ah kehl ur ohn dwah lee-bay-ray lah shahn-bruh

It's About Time

now	maintenant man-tuh-nahn
soon	bientôt bee-an-toh
later	plus tard plew tar
in one hour	dans une heure dahnz ewn ur
in half an hour	dans une demi-heure
	dahnz ewn duh-mee-ur

in three hours	dans trois heures dahn trwahz ur
early / late	tôt / tard toh / tar
on time	à l'heure ah lur
anytime	n'importe quand nan-port kahn
immediately	immédiatement ee-may-dee-aht-mahn
every hour	toutes les heures toot layz ur
every day	tous les jours too lay zhoor
daily	quotidien koh-tee-dee-ahn
last	dernier dehrn-yay
this (m / f)	ce / cette suh / seht
next	prochain proh-shan
before	avant ah-vahn
after	après ah-preh
May 15	le quinze mai luh kanz may
in the future	dans l'avenir dahn lah-vuh-neer
in the past	dans le passé dahn luh pah-say

The Day

day	jour zhoor
today	aujourd'hui oh-zhoor-dwee
sunrise	l'aube lohb
this morning	ce matin suh mah-tan
sunset	le coucher de soleil luh koo-shay duh soh-lay
tonight	ce soir suh swahr
yesterday	hier ee-ehr
tomorrow	demain duh-man
tomorrow morning	demain matin duh-man mah-tan
day after tomorrow	après demain ah-preh duh-man

The Week

Sunday	dimanche dee-mahn<u>sh</u>
Monday	lundi luh<u>n</u>-dee
Tuesday	mardi mar-dee
Wednesday	mercredi mehr-kruh-dee
Thursday	jeudi zhuh-dee
Friday	vendredi vah<u>n</u>-druh-dee
Saturday	samedi sahm-dee
week	semaine suh-mehn
last week	la semaine dernière lah suh-mehn dehr<u>n</u>-yehr
this week	cette semaine seht suh-mehn
next week	la semaine prochaine lah suh-mehn proh-shehn
weekend	week-end "week-end"
this weekend	ce week-end suh "week-end"

The Months

month	mois mwah
January	janvier zhah<u>n</u>-vee-yay
February	février fay-vree-yay
March	mars mars
April	avril ahv-reel
May	mai may
June	juin zhwa<u>n</u>
July	juillet zhwee-yay
August	août oot
September	septembre sehp-tah<u>n</u>-bruh
October	octobre ohk-toh-bruh
November	novembre noh-vah<u>n</u>-bruh
December	décembre day-sah<u>n</u>-bruh

For dates, say the number of the day and then the month. June 19 is *le dix-neuf juin*.

The Year

year	année ah-nay
season	saison say-zohn
spring	printemps pran-tahn
summer	été ay-tay
fall	automne oh-tuhn
winter	hiver ee-vehr

For a list of years, see the "Numbers" section at the beginning of this chapter.

Holidays and Happy Days

holiday	jour férié zhoor fay-ree-ay
festival	festival feh-stee-vahl
Is it a holiday today / tomorrow?	C'est un jour férié aujourd'hui / demain? sayt uhn zhoor fay-ree-ay oh-zhoor-dwee / duh-man
Is a holiday coming up soon?	C'est bientôt un jour férié? say bee-an-toh uhn zhoor fay-ree-ay
When?	Quand? kahn
What is the holiday?	C'est quel jour férié? say kehl zhoor fay-ree-ay
Mardi Gras / Carnival	Mardi Gras / Carnaval mar-dee grah / kar-nah-vahl
Holy Week	Semaine Sainte suh-mehn sant
Easter	Pâques pahk
Ascension	Ascension ah-sahn-see-ohn
Labor Day (May 1)	Fête du Travail (le Premier Mai) feht dew trah-vī (luh pruhm-yay may)

VE Day (Victory in Europe, May 8)	Fête de la Victoire (le Huit Mai) feht duh lah veek-twahr (luh weet may)
Pentecost	Pentecôte pahn-tuh-koht
Corpus Christi	Fête-Dieu feht-dee-uh
Bastille Day (July 14)	Fête Nationale (le Quatorze Juillet) feht nahs-yoh-nahl (luh kah-torz zhwee-yay)
Assumption (Aug 15)	Assomption (le Quinze Août) ah-sohm-see-ohn (luh kanz oot)
All Saints' Day (Nov 1)	Toussaint (le Premier Novembre) too-san (luh pruhm-yay noh-vahn-bruh)
Armistice Day (Nov 11)	Armistice 1918 (le Onze Novembre) ahr-mees-tees meel-nuf-sahn-dees-weet (luh ohnz noh-vahn-bruh)
Christmas Eve	Réveillon de Noël ray-vay-ohn duh noh-ehl
Christmas	Noël noh-ehl
Merry Christmas!	Joyeux Noël! zhwah-yuh noh-ehl
New Year's Eve	La Saint-Sylvestre lah san-seel-vehs-truh
New Year's Day	Jour de l'An zhoor duh lahn
Happy New Year!	Bonne année! buhn ah-nay
wedding anniversary	anniversaire de marriage ah-nee-vehr-sair duh mah-ree-ahzh
Happy anniversary!	Bon anniversaire de mariage! bohn ah-nee-vehr-sair duh mah-ree-ahzh
Best wishes!	Meilleurs vœux! may-ur vuh
birthday	anniversaire ah-nee-vehr-sair
Happy birthday!	Joyeux anniversaire! zhwah-yuhz ah-nee-vehr-sair

The French sing "Happy Birthday" to the same tune we do. Here are the words: *Joyeux anniversaire, joyeux anniversaire, joyeux anniversaire* (fill in name), *joyeux anniversaire.*

TRANSPORTATION

Thise chapter will help you buy transit tickets, get around—by train, bus, subway, taxi, rental car, and foot—and generally find your way around.

GETTING AROUND

train	train tran
city bus	bus bews
shuttle bus	navette nah-veht
long-distance bus	car / bus kar / bews
subway	Métro may-troh
taxi	taxi tahk-see
car	voiture vwah-tewr
walk / by foot	marcher / à pied mar-shay / ah pee-ay
Where is the...?	Où est...? oo ay
...train station	...la gare lah gar
...bus station	...la gare routière lah gar root-yehr
...bus stop	...l'arrêt de bus lah-reh duh bews
...subway station	...la station de Métro lah stah-see-ohn duh may-troh
...taxi stand	...la station de taxi lah stah-see-ohn duh tahk-see
I'm going / We're going to _____.	Je vais / Nous allons à _____. zhuh vay / nooz ah-lohn ah _____
What is the cheapest / fastest / easiest way...?	Quel est le moins cher / plus rapide / plus facile...? kehl ay luh mwan shehr / plew rah-peed / plew fah-seel
...to downtown	...au centre-ville oh sahn-truh-veel
...to the train station	...à la gare ah lah gar
...to my / our hotel	...à mon / notre hôtel ah mohn / noh-truh oh-tehl
...to the airport	...à l'aéroport ah lah-ay-roh-por

Getting Tickets

When it comes to buying tickets for the bus, train, or subway, the following phrases will come in handy.

Where can I buy a ticket?	Où puis-je acheter un billet? oo pweezh ah-shuh-tay uhn bee-yay
How much (is a ticket to _____)?	C'est combien (le ticket pour _____)? say kohn-bee-an (luh tee-kay poor _____)
I want to go to _____.	Je veux aller à _____. zhuh vuh ah-lay ah _____
One ticket / Two tickets (to _____).	Un billet / Deux billets (pour _____). uhn bee-yay / duh bee-yay (poor _____)
When is the next train / bus (to _____)?	A quelle heure part le prochain train / bus (pour _____)? ah kehl ur par luh proh-shan tran / bews (poor _____)
What time does it leave?	Il part à quelle heure? eel par ah kehl ur
Is it direct?	C'est direct? say dee-rehkt
Is a reservation required?	Une réservation est obligatoire? ewn ray-zehr-vah-see-ohn ay oh-blee-gah-twahr
I'd like / We'd like to reserve a seat.	Je voudrais / Nous voudrions réserver une place. zhuh voo-dray / noo voo-dree-ohn ray-zehr-vay ewn plahs
Can I buy a ticket on board?	Est-ce que je peux acheter un ticket à bord? ehs kuh zhuh puh ah-shuh-tay uhn tee-kay ah bor
Exact change only?	Montant exact seulement? mohn-tahn ehg-zahkt suhl-mahn

TRAINS

For tips and strategies about rail travel and railpasses in France, see www.ricksteves.com/rail. Note that many of the following train phrases work for bus travel as well.

Ticket Basics

At the train station, you can buy tickets at the *espace de vente* (sales area). Choose between the ticket office or window *(guichet)* and the machines (marked *achat-retrait-échange*). On tickets, *1ère* means first class, and *2ème* means second class.

ticket	billet	bee-yay
reservation	réservation	ray-zehr-vah-see-ohn
ticket office	guichet	gee-shay
ticket machine	guichet automatique	gee-shay oh-toh-mah-teek
validate	composter	kohn-poh-stay
Where can I buy a ticket?	Où puis-je acheter un billet?	oo pweez ah-shuh-tay uhn bee-yay
Is this the line for...?	C'est la file pour...?	say lah feel poor
...tickets	...les billets	lay bee-yay
...reservations	...les réservations	lay ray-zehr-vah-see-ohn
...information	...l'accueil	lah-kuh-ee
One ticket (to ____).	Un billet (pour ____).	uhn bee-yay (poor ____)
Two tickets.	Deux billets.	duh bee-yay
I want to go to ____.	Je veux aller à ____.	zhuh vuh ah-lay ah ____
How much (is a ticket to____)?	C'est combien (le ticket pour ____)?	say kohn-bee-an (luh tee-kay poor____)
one-way	aller simple	ah-lay san-pluh

round-trip	aller retour ah-lay ruh-toor
today / tomorrow	aujourd'hui / demain
	oh-zhoor-dwee / duh-man

Ticket Specifics

As trains and buses can sell out, it's smart to buy your tickets at least a few days in advance, even for short rides. For phrases related to discounts (such as children, families, or seniors), see page 48.

schedule	horaire oh-rair
When is the next train / bus (to ____)?	A quelle heure part le prochain train / bus (pour ____)?
	ah kehl ur par luh proh-shan tran / bews (poor ____)
What time does it leave?	Il part à quelle heure?
	eel par ah kehl ur
I'd like / We'd like to leave...	Je voudrais / Nous voudrions partir...
	zhuh voo-dray / noo voo-dree-ohn par-teer
I'd like / We'd like to arrive...	Je voudrais / Nous voudrions arriver...
	zhuh voo-dray / noo voo-dree-ohn ah-ree-vay
...by ____ o'clock.	...avant ____ heures.
	ah-vahn ____ ur
...at ____ o'clock...	...à ____ heures... ah ____ ur
...in the morning.	...le matin. luh mah-tan
...in the afternoon.	...l'après-midi. lah-preh-mee-dee
...in the evening.	...le soir. luh swahr
Is there a... train / bus?	Il y a un train / bus...?
	eel yah uhn tran / bews
...earlier	...plus tôt plew toh
...later	...plus tard plew tar
...overnight	...de nuit duh nwee

...cheaper	...moins cher mwah<u>n</u> shehr
...express	...rapide rah-peed
...direct	...direct dee-rehkt
Is it direct?	C'est direct? say dee-rehkt
Is a transfer required?	Un transfert est nécessaire? uh<u>n</u> trah<u>n</u>s-fehr ay nay-suh-sair
How many transfers?	Combien de correspondances? koh<u>n</u>-bee-a<u>n</u> duh koh-rehs-poh<u>n</u>-dah<u>n</u>s
When? Where?	À quelle heure? Où? ah kehl ur / oo
first / second class	première / deuxième classe pruhm-yehr / duhz-yehm klahs
How long is this ticket valid?	Ce billet est bon pour combien de temps? suh bee-yay ay boh<u>n</u> poor koh<u>n</u>-bee-a<u>n</u> duh tah<u>n</u>
Can you validate my railpass?	Pouvez-vous valider mon passe Eurail? poo-vay-voo vah-lee-day moh<u>n</u> pahs "eurail"

When buying tickets, you'll either wait in line or take a number (*Prenez un ticket* or *Prenez un numéro*). The number readout screen says *Nous appellons le numéro...* or simply *Numéro* (the number currently being served) and *Guichet* (the numbered or lettered window to report to).

Be sure you go to the correct window: *Départ immédiat* is for trains departing immediately, *Autres départs* is for other trains, *Ventes internationales* is international, and *Toutes ventes* is for any tickets.

Train Reservations

You're required to pay for a *réservation* for any TGV train, for selected other routes, and for couchettes (sleeping berths on night trains). On other trains, reservations aren't required, but are advisable during busy times (e.g., Friday and Sunday afternoons, Saturday mornings, weekday rush hours, and particularly holiday weekends). If you have a railpass, you're still required to reserve a seat for any TGV train (only a limited number of reservations are available for passholders, so book early) and some high-speed international trains as well—look for the Ⓡ symbol in the timetable.

Is a reservation required?	Une réservation est obligatoire? ewn ray-zehr-vah-see-ohn ay oh-blee-gah-twahr
I'd like / We'd like to reserve...	Je voudrais / Nous voudrions réserver... zhuh voo-dray / noo voo-dree-ohn ray-zehr-vay
...a seat.	...une place. ewn plahs
...an aisle seat.	...une place côté couloir. ewn plahs koh-tay kool-wahr
...a window seat.	...une place côté fenêtre. ewn plahs koh-tay fuh-neh-truh
...two seats.	...deux places. duh plahs
...a couchette (sleeping berth).	...une couchette. ewn koo-sheht
...an upper / middle / lower berth.	...une couchette en haut / milieu / en bas. ewn koo-sheht ahn oh / meel-yuh / ahn bah
...two couchettes.	...deux couchettes. duh koo-sheht
...a sleeper (with two beds).	...un compartiment privé (à deux lits). uhn kohn-par-tee-mahn pree-vay (ah duh lee)
...the entire train.	...le train entier. luh tran ahn-tee-ay

Ticket Machines

The ticket machines available at most train stations are great time-savers for short trips when ticket-window lines are long (but be prepared to use euros, in case your American credit card does not work in the machines). Some have English instructions, but for those that don't, you'll see the following prompts. The default is usually what you want;

turn the dial or touch the screen to make your choice, and press **Validez** to agree to each step.

Quelle est votre destination?	What's your destination?
Billet Plein Tarif	Full-fare ticket (yes for most)
1ère ou 2ème	First or second class
Aller simple ou aller retour?	One-way or round-trip?
Prix en Euro	Price in euros

Discounts

Is there a cheaper option?	Il y a un solution moins cher? eel yah uhn soh-lew-see-ohn mwan shehr
discount	réduction ray-dewk-see-ohn
reduced fare	tarif réduit tah-reef ray-dwee
refund	remboursement rahn-boor-suh-mahn
Is there a discount for...?	Il y a une réduction pour les...? eel yah ewn ray-dewk-see-ohn poor lay
...children	...enfants ahn-fahn
...youths	...jeunes zhuhn
...seniors	...personnes âgées pehr-suhn ah-zhay
...families	...familles fah-mee
...groups	...groupes groop
...advance purchase	...achat à l'avance ah-shaht ah lah-vahns
...weekends	...week-ends "week-end"
Are there any deals for this journey?	Il y a des réductions pour ce voyage? eel yah day ray-dewk-see-ohn poor suh vwah-yahzh

At the Train Station

La gare means train station. Big cities can have several. High-speed, long-distance trains use the *gare TGV,* which can be on the outskirts of town; *gare ville* or *gare centre-ville* is near the city center.

Key Phrases: Trains

train station	gare gar
train	train tran
platform	quai kay
track	voie vwah
What track does the train leave from?	Le train part de quelle voie? luh tran par duh kehl vwah
Is this the train to _____?	C'est le train pour _____? say luh tran poor _____
Which train to _____?	Quel train pour _____? kehl tran poor _____
Tell me when to get off?	Dîtes-moi quand je descends? deet-mwah kahn zhuh day-sahn
transfer (n)	correspondance koh-rehs-pohn-dahns
Change here for _____?	Transfère ici pour _____? trahns-fehr ee-see poor _____

Where is...?	Où est...? oo ay
...the train station	...la gare lah gar
train information	accueil / renseignements SNCF ah-kuh-ee / rahn-sehn-yuh-mahn S N say F
customer service	conseiller clientèle kohn-say-yay klee-ahn-tehl
tickets	billets bee-yay
departures	départs day-par
arrivals	arrivées ah-ree-vay
On time?	À l'heure? ah lur
Late?	En retard? ahn ruh-tar
How late?	Combien de retard? kohn-bee-an duh ruh-tar

platform / track	quai / voie kay / vwah
What track does the train leave from?	Le train part de quelle voie? luh tran par duh kehl vwah
waiting room	salle d'attente sahl dah-tahnt
VIP lounge	salon grand voyageur sah-lohn grahn voy-ah-zhur
locker	consigne automatique kohn-seen-yuh oh-toh-mah-teek
baggage-check room	consigne de bagages / espaces bagages kohn-seen-yuh duh bah-gahzh / ehs-pahs bah-gahzh
tourist info office	office du tourisme oh-fees dew too-reez-muh
lost and found office	bureau des objets trouvés bew-roh dayz ohb-zhay troo-vay
toilets	toilettes twah-leht

In French rail stations, look for the *Accueil* office, where you can get information about train schedules without waiting in a long ticket line.

French trains are operated by *SNCF* (pronounced "S N say F"). The country is connected by an ever-growing network of high-speed trains called TGV (tay zhay vay, *train à grande vitesse*—also called "InOui"). There are also regional and suburban lines that go by various names; for example, around Paris you'll see *RER, Transilien, banlieue,* and *trains Ile-de-France.*

For security reasons, all luggage (including day packs) must carry a tag with the traveler's first and last name and current address. Free tags are available at all train stations in France.

Train and Bus Schedules

European timetables use the 24-hour clock. It's like American time until noon. After that, subtract twelve and add p.m. So 13:00 is 1 p.m., 20:00 is 8 p.m., and 24:00 is midnight.

To ask for a schedule at an information window, say **Horaire** (oh-rair) **pour ____, s'il vous plaît** (Schedule for ____ [city], please). French train schedules show blue (quiet), white (normal), and red (peak and holiday) times. You can save money if you get the blues (travel during off-peak hours).

à	to
à l'heure	on time
accès aux quais / trains	to the trains
arrivée	arrival
aussi	also
avant	before
de	from
départ	departure
dernier passage	last trip
desserte	initial departure time
destination (finale)	(final) destination
dimanche	Sunday
direction	goes
en retard	late
en semaine	weekdays
environ ____ minutes de retard	about ____ minutes late
et	and
heure	time / hour
heures	hours
horaire	timetable
intervalle prévu	during this time
jour férié	holiday
jours	days
jusqu'à	until
minutes	minutes
nature	company and / or type of train
numéro / nº	train number
par	via
parcularités	specific details
pas	not
pour	to
premier passage	first trip

provenance	coming from
régime	major stops en route
retard / retardé	late
samedi	Saturday
sauf	except
seulement	only
terminus	final destination
tous	every
tous les jours	daily
train direct	does not make every stop
train omnibus	makes every stop ("milk run")
vacances	holidays
voie	track number
1ère	first class
2ème	second class
1-5	Monday-Friday
6 / 7	Saturday / Sunday

All Aboard

In the station, *accès aux quais* or *accès aux trains* signs direct you to the trains. (A sign reading *voyageurs munis de billets* means that it's an area only for passengers with tickets in hand.) At the track, you are required to *composter* (validate) all train tickets and reservations. Look for the yellow, waist-high boxes marked *compostage de billets*. (Do not *composte* your railpass, but do validate it at a ticket window before the first time you use it.)

platform / track	quai / voie kay / vwah
number	numéro new-may-roh
train	train tran
train car	voiture vwah-tewr
conductor	conducteur kohn-dewk-tur
Is this the train to ____?	C'est le train pour ____? say luh tran poor ____

Which train to ____?	Quel train pour ____?
	kehl tran poor ____
Which train car to ____?	Quelle voiture pour ____?
	kehl vwah-tewr poor ____
Where is...?	Où est...? oo ay
Is this...?	C'est...? say
...my seat	...ma place mah plahs
...first / second class	...la première / deuxième classe
	lah pruhm-yehr / duhz-yehm klahs
...the dining car	...la voiture restaurant
	lah vwah-tewr rehs-toh-rahn
...the sleeper car	...la voiture-lit lah vwah-tewr-lee
...the toilet	...la toilette lah twah-leht
front / middle / back	à l'avant / au milieu / au fond
	ah lah-vahn / oh meel-yuh / oh fohn
reserved / occupied / free	réservé / occupé / libre
	ray-zehr-vay / oh-kew-pay / lee-bruh
aisle / window	couloir / fenêtre
	kool-wahr / fuh-neh-truh
Is this (seat) free?	C'est libre? say lee-bruh
May I / May we...?	Je peux / Nous pouvon...?
	zhuh puh / noo poo-vohn
...sit here	...s'asseoir ici sah-swahr ee-see
...open the window	...ouvrir la fenêtre
	oo-vrer lah fuh-neh-truh
...eat here	...manger ici mahn-zhay ee-see
...eat your meal	...manger votre repas
	mahn-zhay voh-truh ruh-pah
(I think) that's my seat.	(Je pense que) c'est ma place.
	(zhuh pahns kuh) say mah plahs
These are our seats.	Ce sont nos places. suh sohn noh plahs
Save my place?	Garder ma place? gar-day mah plahs
Save our places?	Garder nos places? gar-day noh plahs

Where are you going?	Où allez-vous? oo ah-lay-voo
I'm going / We're going to _____.	Je vais / Nous allons à _____. zhuh vay / nooz ah-lohn ah _____
Does this train stop in _____?	Ce train s'arrête à _____? suh tran sah-reht ah _____
When will it arrive in _____?	Il va arriver à _____ à quelle heure? eel vah ah-ree-vay ah _____ ah kehl ur
Where is a (handsome) conductor?	Où est un (beau) conducteur? oo ay uhn (boh) kohn-dewk-tur
Tell me when to get off?	Dîtes-moi quand je descends? deet-mwah kahn zhuh day-sahn
I'm getting off.	Je descends. zhuh day-sahn
How do I open the door?	Comment puis-je ouvrir la porte? koh-mahn pweezh oo-vreer lah port

To confirm you're boarding the right train, point to the train, and ask a conductor *À* _____ [city]? For example, *À Chartres?* means "To Chartres?" Some longer trains split cars en route; make sure your train car is continuing to your destination by asking *Cette voiture va à Chartres?* (This car goes to Chartres?).

If a non-TGV train seat is reserved, it'll usually be labeled *réservé*, with the cities to and from which it is reserved.

As you approach a station on the train, you will hear an announcement such as: *Mesdames, Messieurs, dans quelques minutes, nous entrons en gare de Paris* (In a few minutes, we will arrive in Paris).

Changing Trains

Change here for _____?	Transfère ici pour _____? trahns-fehr ee-see poor _____
Where does one change for _____?	Où faut-il changer pour _____? oo foh-teel shahn-zhay poor _____
At what time?	À quelle heure? ah kehl ur

From what track does the connecting train leave?	De quelle voie part le train en correspondance?
	duh kehl vwah par luh tran ahn koh-rehs-pohn-dahns
How many minutes in _____ (to change trains)?	Combien de minutes à _____ (pour changer de train)?
	kohn-bee-an duh mee-newt ah _____ (poor shahn-zhay duh tran)

Strikes

If a strike is pending, hoteliers or travel agencies can check for you to see when the strike goes into effect and which trains will continue to run.

strike	grève grehv
Is there a strike?	Il y a une grève? eel yah ewn grehv
Only for today?	Juste pour aujourd'hui?
	zhewst poor oh-zhoor-dwee
Tomorrow, too?	Demain aussi? duh-man oh-see
Are there some trains today?	Il y a quelques trains aujourd'hui?
	eel yah kehl-kuh tran oh-zhoor-dwee
I'm going to _____.	Je voyage à _____.
	zhuh voy-ahzh ah _____

CITY BUSES AND SUBWAYS

Ticket Talk

Most big cities offer deals on transportation, such as one-day tickets, multi-day passes, or cheaper fares for youths and seniors. In Paris, you'll save money by buying a *carnet* (kar-nay, batch of 10 tickets) at virtually any Métro station. The tickets, which are shareable, are valid on the buses, Métro, and RER (suburban railway) within the city limits.

Key Phrases: City Buses and Subways

bus	bus bews
subway	Métro may-troh
tram	tramway trahm-way
How do I get to _____?	Comment je vais à _____? koh-mahn zhuh vay ah _____
Which stop for _____?	Quel arrêt pour _____? kehl ah-reh poor _____
Tell me when to get off?	Dîtes-moi quand je descends? deet-mwah kahn zhuh day-sahn

Where can I buy a ticket?	Où puis-je acheter un ticket? oo pweezh ah-shuh-tay uhn tee-kay
I want to go to _____.	Je veux aller à _____. zhuh vuh ah-lay ah _____
How much (is a ticket to _____)?	C'est combien (le ticket pour _____)? say kohn-bee-an (luh tee-kay poor _____)
single (trip)	aller simple ah-lay san-pluh
batch of 10 tickets	carnet kar-nay
a day pass	un passe à la journée uhn pahs ah lah zhoor-nay
Is this ticket valid (for _____)?	Ce ticket est bon (pour _____)? suh tee-kay ay bohn (poor _____)
Can I buy a ticket on board the bus?	Est-ce que je peux acheter un ticket à bord le bus? ehs kuh zhuh puh ah-shuh-tay uhn tee-kay ah bor luh bews
Exact change only?	Montant exact seulement? mohn-tahn ehg-zahkt suhl-mahn
validate (here)	composter (ici) kohn-poh-stay (ee-see)

Transit Terms

city bus	bus	bews
bus stop	arrêt de bus	ah-reh duh bews
bus map	plan de bus	plah<u>n</u> duh bews
subway	Métro	may-troh
tram	tramway	trahm-way
suburban train (Paris)	RER	ehr-uh-ehr
subway station	station de Métro	stah-see-oh<u>n</u> duh may-troh
subway map	plan du Métro	plah<u>n</u> dew may-troh
subway entrance	l'entrée du Métro	lah<u>n</u>-tray dew may-troh
subway stop	arrêt de Métro	ah-reh duh may-troh
exit	sortie	sor-tee
line (bus / subway)	ligne (de bus / de Métro)	lee<u>n</u>-yuh (duh bews / duh may-troh)
direction	direction	dee-rehk-see-oh<u>n</u>
direct	direct	dee-rehkt
connection	correspondance	koh-rehs-poh<u>n</u>-dah<u>n</u>s
public transit map	plan des lignes	plah<u>n</u> day lee<u>n</u>-yuh
pickpocket	pickpocket / voleur	peek-poh-keht / voh-lur

Before entering the Métro system, be very clear on which line you'll be taking, and what direction you're headed toward (i.e., the name of the final station on that line). At major Métro stations, several lines intersect, creating a labyrinth of underground corridors; following signs for your direction is the only way you'll find the right platform.

Once at your platform, look for the digital information board. See the first column below for examples, with the English explanation:

M-1 (or M-2, etc.)	Métro line number
La Défense (or Balard, etc.)	end station (direction)

1er train	time until arrival of the next train
2e train	time until arrival of the following train
correspondance	connections to another line, listed by direction

Riding Public Transit

How do I get to _____?	Comment je vais à _____? koh-mahn zhuh vay ah _____
How do we get to _____?	Comment nous allons à _____? koh-mahn nooz ah-lohn ah _____
Which bus to _____?	Quel bus pour _____? kehl bews poor _____
Does it stop at _____?	Il s'arrête à _____? eel sah-reht ah _____
Which bus stop for _____?	Quel arrêt pour _____? kehl ah-reh poor _____
Which subway stop for _____?	Quel arrêt de Métro pour _____? kehl ah-reh duh may-troh poor _____
Which direction for _____?	Quelle direction pour _____? kehl dee-rehk-see-ohn poor _____
Is there a transfer?	Il y a une correspondance? eel yah ewn koh-rehs-pohn-dahns
When is the...?	C'est quand le...? say kahn luh
...first / next / last...	...premier / prochain / dernier... pruhm-yay / proh-shan / dehrn-yay
...bus / subway	...bus / Métro bews / may-troh
How often does it run per hour / day?	Combien de fois par heure / jour? kohn-bee-an duh fwah par ur / zhoor
When does the next one leave?	Quand part le prochain? kahn par luh proh-shan
Where does it leave from?	D'où il part? doo eel par

Tell me when to get off?	Dîtes-moi quand je descends? deet-mwah kah_n_ zhuh day-sah_n_
I'm getting off.	Je descends. zhuh day-sah_n_
How do I open the door?	Comment je peux ouvrir la porte? koh-mah_n_ zhuh puh oo-vreer lah port

If you press the button to request a stop on a bus or tram, a sign lights up that says **Arrêt demandé** (Stop requested). Upon arrival, you might have to press a green button or pull a lever to open the door—watch locals and imitate.

Before leaving the Métro through the **sortie** (exit), check the helpful **plan du quartier** (map of the neighborhood) to get your bearings and decide which **sortie** you want—this can save lots of walking.

TAXIS

While Paris and other major cities have slick public transportation, taxis are generally affordable, efficient, and worth considering. Taxis can take up to four people, and larger taxis take more. So you'll know what to expect, ask your hotelier about typical taxi fares. Fares go up at night and on Sundays, and drivers always charge for loading baggage in the trunk. Your fare can nearly double if you're taking a short trip with lots of bags.

If you're having a tough time hailing a taxi, ask for the nearest taxi stand **(station de taxi)** or seek out a big hotel where they're usually waiting for guests. The simplest way to tell a cabbie where you want to go is by stating your destination followed by "please" **(Louvre, s'il vous plaît).** Tipping isn't expected, but it's polite to round up. So if the fare is €19, round up to €20.

Getting a Taxi

Taxi!	Taxi! tahk-see
Can you call a taxi?	Pouvez-vous appeler un taxi? poo-vay-voo ah-puh-lay uh_n_ tahk-see

Key Phrases: Taxis

Taxi!	Taxi! tahk-see
taxi stand	station de taxi stah-see-oh<u>n</u> duh tahk-see
Are you free?	Vous êtes libre? vooz eht lee-bruh
Occupied.	Occupé. oh-kew-pay
To _____, please.	À _____, s'il vous plaît. ah _____ see voo play
The meter, please.	Le compteur, s'il vous plaît. luh koh<u>n</u>-tur see voo play
Stop here.	Arrêtez-vous ici. ah-reh-tay-voo ee-see
My change, please.	La monnaie, s'il vous plaît. lah moh-nay see voo play
Keep the change.	Gardez la monnaie. gar-day lah moh-nay

Where can I get a taxi?	Où puis-je trouver un taxi? oo pweezh troo-vay uh<u>n</u> tahk-see
Where is a taxi stand?	Où est une station de taxi? oo ay ewn stah-see-oh<u>n</u> duh tahk-see
Are you free?	Vous êtes libre? vooz eht lee-bruh
Occupied.	Occupé. oh-kew-pay
To _____, please.	À _____, s'il vous plaît. ah _____ see voo play
To this address.	À cette adresse. ah seht ah-drehs
Approximately how much does it cost to go...?	C'est environ combien pour aller...? say ah<u>n</u>-vee-roh<u>n</u> koh<u>n</u>-bee-a<u>n</u> poor ah-lay
...to _____	...à _____ ah _____
...to the airport	...à l'aéroport ah lah-ay-roh-por

...to the train station	...à la gare ah lah gar
...to this address	...à cette adresse ah seht ah-drehs
Is there an extra supplement?	Il y a un supplément? eel yah uhn sew-play-mahn
It's too much.	C'est trop. say troh
Can you take _____ people?	Pouvez-vous prendre _____ passagers? poo-vay-voo prahn-druh _____ pah-sah-zhay
Any extra fee?	Il y a d'autres frais? eel yah doh-truh fray
Do you have an hourly rate?	Avez-vous un taux par heure? ah-vay-voo uhn toh par ur
How much for a one-hour city tour?	Combien pour une visite d'une heure en ville? kohn-bee-an poor ewn vee-zeet dewn ur ahn veel

Before hopping in a taxi, it's smart to ask roughly how much your trip will cost. Also, Uber works in many European cities.

Cabbie Conversation

The meter, please.	Le compteur, s'il vous plaît. luh kohn-tur see voo play
Where is the meter?	Où est le compteur? oo ay luh kohn-tur
I'm / We're in a hurry.	Je suis / Nous sommes pressé. zhuh swee / noo suhm preh-say
Slow down.	Ralentissez. rah-lahn-tee-say
If you don't slow down, I'll throw up.	Si vous ne ralentissez pas, je vais vomir. see voo nuh rah-lahn-tee-say pah zhuh vay voh-meer
Left.	À gauche. ah gohsh
Right.	À droite. ah drwaht
Straight ahead.	Tout droit. too drwah

Please stop here...	S'il vous plaît arrêtez-vous ici... see voo play ah-reh-tay-voo ee-see
...for a moment.	...un instant uhn an-stahn
...for _____ minutes.	...pour _____ minutes. poor _____ mee-newt
Can you wait?	Pouvez-vous attendre? poo-vay voo ah-tahn-druh
Crazy traffic, isn't it?	C'est fou, cette circulation, non? say foo seht seer-kew-lah-see-ohn nohn
You drive like a madman!	Vous conduisez comme un fou! voo kohn-dwee-zay kohm uhn foo
You drive very well.	Vous conduisez très bien. voo kohn-dwee-zay treh bee-an
I can see it from here.	Je peux le voir d'ici. zhuh puh luh vwahr dee-see
Point it out?	Vous pouvez me le montrer? voo poo-vay muh luh mohn-tray
Stop here.	Arrêtez-vous ici. ah-reh-tay-voo ee-see
Here is fine.	Ici c'est bien. ee-see say bee-an
At this corner.	À ce coin. ah suh kwan
The next corner.	Au prochain coin. oh proh-shan kwan
My change, please.	La monnaie, s'il vous plaît. lah moh-nay see voo play
Keep the change.	Gardez la monnaie. gar-day lah moh-nay
This ride is / was more fun than Disneyland.	Ce trajet est / était plus drôle que Disneyland. suh trah-zhay ay / ay-tay plew drohl kuh "Disneyland"

DRIVING

Renting Wheels

I'd like to rent a...	Je voudrais louer... zhuh voo-dray loo-ay
...car.	...une voiture. ewn vwah-tewr
...station wagon.	...un break. uhn brayk
...van.	...un van. uhn vahn
...convertible.	...une décapotable. ewn day-kah-poh-tah-bluh
...motorcycle.	...un moto. uhn moh-toh
...motor scooter.	...un scooteur. uhn skoo-tur
How much per...?	Combien par...? kohn-bee-an par
...hour	...heure ur
...half-day	...demi-journée duh-mee-zhoor-nay
...day	...jour zhoor
...week	...semaine suh-mehn
car rental agency	agence de location de voiture ah-zhahns duh loh-kah-see-ohn duh vwah-tewr
tax / insurance	taxe / assurance tahx / ah-sewr-rahns
Includes taxes and insurance?	Taxes et assurances comprises? tahx ay ah-sewr-ahns kohn-preez
Any extra fees?	Il y a d'autres frais? eel yah doh-truh fray
Unlimited mileage?	Kilométrage illimité? kee-loh-may-trahzh ee-lee-mee-tay
manual / automatic transmission	boîte manuelle / boîte automatique bwaht mah-new-ehl / bwaht oh-toh-mah-teek
pick up	prendre prahn-druh
drop off	retour / dépose véhicule ruh-toor / day-pohz vay-ee-kewl

Key Phrases: Driving

car	voiture vwah-tewr
gas station	station service stah-see-oh<u>n</u> sehr-vees
parking lot	parking par-keeng
Where can I park?	Où puis-je me garer? oo pweezh muh gah-ray
downtown	centre-ville sah<u>n</u>-truh-veel
straight ahead	tout droit too drwah
left	à gauche ah gohsh
right	à droite ah drwaht
I'm lost.	Je suis perdu. zhuh swee pehr-dew
How do I get to _____?	Comment je vais à _____? koh-mah<u>n</u> zhuh vay ah _____

Is there a...?	Est-ce qu'il y a...? ehs keel yah
...discount	...une réduction ewn ray-dewk-see-oh<u>n</u>
...deposit	...une caution ewn koh-see-oh<u>n</u>
...helmet	...un casque uh<u>n</u> kahsk
When must I bring it back?	Je dois le ramener à quelle heure? zhuh dwah luh rah-muh-nay ah kehl ur
Can I drop it off in another city / in _____?	Est-ce que je peux déposer le véhicule dans une autre ville / dans _____? ehs kuh zhuh puh day-poh-zay luh vay- ee-kewl dah<u>n</u>z ewn oh-truh veel / dah<u>n</u> _____
How do I get to the expressway / to _____?	Comment puis-je rejoindre l'autoroute / en direction de _____? koh-mah<u>n</u> pweezh ray-zhwa<u>n</u>-druh loh-toh- root / ah<u>n</u> dee-rehk-see-oh<u>n</u> duh _____

Before leaving the car-rental office, get directions to your next destination—or at least to the *autoroute* (expressway).

For all the details on the dizzying variety of insurance options, see www.ricksteves.com/cdw.

Getting to Know Your Rental Car

Before driving off, familiarize yourself with your rental car. Examine it to be sure that all damage is already noted on the rental agreement so you won't be held responsible for it later.

It's damaged here.	Il est endommagée ici. eel ay ahn-doh-mah-zhay ee-see
Please add it to the rental agreement.	Veuillez l'ajouter au contrat de location. vuh-yay lah-zhoo-tay oh kohn-trah duh loh-kah-see-ohn
That scratch / dent was already here.	Cette éraflure / bosse était déjà présente ici. seht ay-rah-flewr / bohs ay-tay day-zhah pray-zahnt ee-cee
What kind of fuel does it take?	Quel type de carburant doit-on utiliser? kehl teep duh kar-bewr-ahn dwah-tohn ew-tee-lee-zay
gas	essence eh-sahns
diesel	gazole / gasoil gah-zohl / gah-zwahl
How do I open the gas cap?	Comment puis-je ouvrir le réservoir? koh-mahn pweezh oo-vreer luh ray-zehr-vwahr
How does this work?	Comment ça fonctionne? koh-mahn sah fohnk-see-ohn
key	clé / clef klay / kleh
headlights	phares far
radio	radio rahd-yoh
windshield wipers	essuies-glace ehs-wee-glahs

alarm / security system	alarme / système de sécurité ah-larm / see-stehm duh say-kew-ree-tay
How do I turn off the security system?	Comment puis-je déconnecter le système de sécurité? koh-mahn pweezh day-koh-nehk-tay luh see-stehm duh say-kew-ree-tay
GPS	GPS zhay pay ehs
How do I change the language to English?	Comment peut-on basculer sur l'anglais? koh-mahn puh-tohn bah-skew-lay sewr lahn-glay

Sometimes you can rent a GPS device with your car. The language for the menus and instructions can be changed to English.

Traffic Troubles

traffic	circulation seer-kew-lah-see-ohn
traffic jam	bouchon boo-shohn
rush hour	heure de pointe ur duh pwant
delay	délai / retard / ralentissement day-lay / ruh-tar / rah-lahn-tees-mahn
construction	travaux trah-voh
accident	accident ahk-see-dahn
detour	déviation day-vee-ah-see-ohn
How long is the delay?	Combien de temps dure le ralentissement? kohn-bee-an duh tahn dewr luh rah-lahn-tees-mahn
Is there another way to go (to _____)?	Il y a un autre itinéraire pour aller (à_____)? eel yah uhn oh-truh ee-tee-nay-rair poor ah-lay (ah _____)

Along the *autoroute,* electronic signs flash messages to let you know what's ahead: *bouchon* (traffic jam), *circulation* (traffic), and *fluide* (no traffic). For more navigational words, see "Finding Your Way," on page 72.

Tolls

The shortest distance between any two points in France is the *autoroute,* but the tolls add up. (You'll travel cheaper, but slower, on a *route nationale.*) You'll usually take a ticket when entering an *autoroute* and pay when you leave (plan to pay with cash, since some US credit and debit cards may not work in the machines). Shorter *autoroute* sections have periodic toll booths, where you can pay by dropping coins into a basket.

toll road	autoroute oh-toh-root
toll	péage pay-ahzh
tollbooth	poste de péage pohst duh pay-ahzh
toll ticket	ticket de péage tee-kay duh pay-ahzh
cash	espèces / monnaie ehs-pehs / moh-nay
card	carte kart
pay	payer pay-ay

At the Gas Station

Unleaded is *sans plomb* (which can be *normale* or *super*), and diesel is *gazole* or *gasoil*. The cheapest gas in France is sold in *hypermarché* (supermarket) parking lots. Prices are listed per liter; there are about four liters in a gallon.

gas station	station service stah-see-ohn sehr-vees
The nearest gas station?	La plus proche station service? lah plew prohsh stah-see-ohn sehr-vees
Self-service?	Libre service? lee-bruh sehr-vees
Fill it up.	Faites le plein. feht luh plan
I need...	Il me faut... eel muh foh
...gas.	...de l'essence. duh leh-sahns

...unleaded.	...sans plomb. sahn plohn
...regular.	...normale. nor-mahl
...super.	...du super. dew sew-pehr
...diesel.	...gazole / gasoil. gah-zohl / gah-zwahl

Parking

parking lot	parking par-keeng
parking garage	garage de stationnement gah-rahzh duh stah-see-ohn-mahn
parking space	place de parking plahs duh par-keeng
ticket-vending machine	horodateur or-oh-dah-tur
parking meter	parcomètre par-koh-meh-truh
available / full	libre / complet lee-bruh / kohn-play
Where can I park?	Où puis-je me garer? oo pweezh muh gah-ray
Is parking nearby?	Il y a un parking près d'ici? eel yah uhn par-keeng preh dee-see
Can I park here?	Je peux me garer ici? zhuh puh muh gah-ray ee-see
Is it safe?	C'est prudent? say prew-dahn
How long can I park here?	Je peux me garer ici pour combien de temps? zhuh puh muh gah-ray ee-see poor kohn- bee-an duh tahn
Is it free?	C'est gratuit? say grah-twee
Where do I pay?	Je paie où? zhuh pay oo
How much per hour / day?	Combien par heure / jour? kohn-bee-an par ur / zhoor

Get safe parking tips from your hotelier, and leave nothing of value in your car.

Many cities use remote meters for curbside parking. After you park, find the ticket-vending machine *(horodateur)* or parking meter *(parcomètre)*. Insert coins to reach the desired amount of time, press the button to print out a ticket, and put it on your dashboard. Instructions on the machine or meter may list times you have to pay; for example, all days *sauf* (except) *dimanches et jours feries* (Sundays and holidays). Keep an eye on the *durée maximale* (maximum stay time).

Garages are more expensive than street parking but are safe, save time, and help you avoid the stress of parking tickets. After parking, take your ticket with you and pay before returning to your car. As you enter a big city, signs may direct you to various garages and indicate the number of available parking spaces (for example, *129 places libres*).

Car Trouble and Parts

accident	accident ahk-see-dahn
fender-bender	accrochage ah-kroh-shahzh
breakdown	en panne ahn pahn
dealership / repair shop	Atelier de réparation automobile ah-tuh-lee-ay duh reh-pah-rah-see-ohn aw-tuh-moh-beel
strange noise	bruit curieux brwee kew-ree-uh
electrical problem	problème d'électricité proh-blehm day-lehk-tree-see-tay
warning light	feux de détresse fuh duh day-trehs
smoke	fumée few-may
My car won't start.	Ma voiture ne démarre pas. mah vwah-tewr nuh day-mar pah
My car is broken.	Ma voiture ne marche pas. mah vwah-tewr nuh marsh pah
This doesn't work.	Ça ne marche pas. sah nuh marsh pah
Please check this.	Merci de bien vouloir verifier ceci. mehr-see duh bee-an vool-wahr vehr-ee-fee-ay suh-see
oil	l'huile lweel

tire (flat)	pneu (crevé) pnuh (kruh-vay)
air in the tires	pression dans les pneus preh-see-ohn dahn lay pnuh
radiator	radiateur rahd-yah-tur
battery (dead)	batterie (à plat) bah-tuh-ree (ah plah)
sparkplugs	bougies boo-zhee
fuses	fusibles few-zee-bluh
headlights	phares far
taillights	feux arrières fuh ah-ree-ehr
turn signal	clignotant kleen-yoh-tahn
brakes	freins fran
window	fenêtre fuh-neh-truh
windshield	pare-brise par-breez
windshield wipers	essuie-glaces ehs-wee-glahs
engine	moteur moh-tur
fan belt	courroie du ventilateur koor-wah dew vahn-tee-lah-tur
starter	starter star-tehr
transmission	transmission trahns-mee-see-ohn
transmission (fluid)	(liquide de) transmission (lee-keed duh) trahns-mee-see-ohn
radio	radio rahd-yoh
key	clé / clef klay / kleh
alarm	alarme ah-larm
It's overheating.	Le moteur surchauffe. luh moh-tur sewr-shohf
It's a lemon ("rattletrap").	C'est un tas de féraille. sayt uhn tah duh fay-rī
I need...	J'ai besoin... zhay buh-zwan
...a tow truck.	...d'un dépanneur. duhn day-pah-nur
...a mechanic.	...d'un mécanicien. duhn may-kah-nee-see-an

| ...a stiff drink. | ...d'un bon coup à boire.
duhn bohn koo ah bwahr |

In France, people with car problems go to the dealership. If you're renting a troubled Renault, your rental agency may direct you to the nearest concessionaire Renault. For help with repair, see "Repairs" on page 282.

The Police

In any country, the flashing lights of a patrol car are a sure sign that someone's in trouble. If it's you, try this handy phrase: *Pardon, je suis un touriste* (Sorry, I'm a tourist). Or, for the adventurous: *Si vous n'aimez pas ma conduite, vous n'avez que descendre du trottoir.* (If you don't like how I drive, get off the sidewalk.) If you're in serious need of assistance, turn to the Help! chapter.

police officer	agent de police ah-zhahn duh poh-lees
driver's license	permis de conduire pehr-mee duh kohn-dweer
What seems to be the problem?	Quel est le problème? kehl ay luh proh-blehm
restricted zone	zone interdite / accès restreint zohn an-tehr-deet / ahk-seh rehs-tran
pedestrian-only	zone piétonne zohn pee-ay-tohn
speeding	dépasser la vitesse autorisée day-pah-say lah vee-tehs oh-toh-ree-zay
I didn't know the speed limit.	Je ne savais pas qu'elle était la limitation de vitesse. zhuh nuh sah-vay pah kehl ay-tay lah lee-mee-tah-see-ohn duh vee-tehs
parking ticket	une amende ewn ah-mahnd
I didn't know where to park.	Je ne savais pas où me garer. zhuh nuh sah-vay pah oo muh gah-ray
I'm very sorry.	Je suis vraiment désolé. zhuh swee vray-mahn day-zoh-lay

| Can I buy your hat? | Je peux acheter votre chapeau?
zhuh puh ah-shuh-tay voh-truh shah-poh |

FINDING YOUR WAY

Whether you're driving, walking, or biking, these phrases will help you get around.

Route-Finding Phrases

I'm going / We're going to _____.	Je vais / Nous allons à _____. zhuh vay / nooz ah-lohn ah _____
Do you have a...?	Avez-vous...? ah-vay-vooz
...city map	...un plan de la ville uhn plahn duh lah veel
...road map	...une carte routière ewn kart root-yehr
How many minutes...?	Combien de minutes...? kohn-bee-an duh mee-newt
...on foot	...à pied ah pee-yay
...by bicycle	...à bicyclette ah bee-see-kleht
...by car	...en voiture ahn vwah-tewr
How many kilometers to _____?	Combien de kilomètres à _____? kohn-bee-an duh kee-loh-meh-truh ah _____
What's the... route to Paris?	Quelle est la... route pour Paris? kehl ay lah... root poor pah-ree
...most scenic	...plus belle plew behl
...fastest	...plus directe plew dee-rehkt
...easiest	...plus facile plew fah-seel
...most interesting	...plus intéressante plewz an-tay-reh-sahnt
Point it out?	Montrez-moi? mohn-tray mwah

Where is this address?	Où se trouve cette adresse? oo suh troov seht ah-drehs

Directions

Following signs to *centre-ville* will land you in the heart of things.

downtown	centre-ville sahn-truh-veel
straight ahead	tout droit too drwah
to the left	à gauche ah gohsh
to the right	à droite ah drwaht
first	premier pruhm-yay
next	prochain proh-shan
intersection	carrefour kar-foor
corner	au coin oh kwan
block	paté de maisons pah-tay duh may-zohn
roundabout	rond-point rohn-pwan
stoplight	feu fuh
(main) square	place (principale) plahs (pran-see-pahl)
street	rue rew
avenue	avenue ah-vuh-new
boulevard	boulevard bool-var
curve	virage vee-rahzh
bridge	pont pohn
tunnel	tunnel tew-nehl
road	route root
ring road	périphérique pay-ree-fay-reek
expressway	autoroute oh-toh-root
north	nord nor
south	sud sewd
east	est ehst
west	ouest wehst

shortcut	raccourci rah-koor-see
traffic jam	bouchon boo-shoh<u>n</u>

Lost Your Way

I'm lost.	Je suis perdu. zhuh swee pehr-dew
We're lost.	Nous sommes perdus. noo suhm pehr-dew
Can you help me?	Vous pouvez m'aider? voo poo-vay meh-day
Where am I?	Où suis-je? oo sweezh
Where is ____?	Où est ____? oo ay ____
How do I get to ____?	Comment est-ce que j'arrive à ____? koh-mah<u>n</u> ehs kuh zhah-reev ah ____
Can you show me the way?	Vous pouvez me montrer le chemin? voo poo-vay muh moh<u>n</u>-tray luh shuh-ma<u>n</u>

Reading Road Signs

Aire	Rest stop on expressway
Allumez vos feux	Turn on your lights
Attention	Caution
Attention travaux	Workers ahead
Autres directions (follow when leaving a town)	Other directions
Bouchon	Traffic jam ahead
Céder le passage	Yield
Centre-ville	Center of town
Centre commercial	Grouping of large, suburban stores (not city center)
Déviation	Detour
Doublage interdit	No passing
Entrée	Entrance
Feu	Traffic signal

Fluide	No traffic ahead
Horadateur	Parking meter
Interdit	Not allowed
Par temps de pluie	When raining (modified speed limit signs)
Parc de stationnement	Parking lot
Parking interdit	No parking
Péage	Toll
Priorité	Right-of-way
Priorité à droite	Right-of-way is for cars coming from the right
Prochaine sortie	Next exit
Ralentir	Slow down
Rappel	Remember to obey the sign
Réservé aux piétons	Pedestrians only
Route barrée	Road blocked
Rue piétonne	Pedestrian-only street
Sans issue	Dead end
Sauf riverains	Local access only
Sens unique	One-way street
Sortie	Exit
Sortie des camions	Work truck exit
Stationnement interdit	No parking
Stop	Stop
Télépéage	Automated toll booths
Toutes directions (follow when leaving a town)	All directions
Travaux	Construction
Virages	Curves
Voie piétonne	Pedestrian zone
Vous n'avez pas la priorité	You don't have the right of way (when merging)

For a list of other signs you might see, turn to page 21 in the French Basics chapter.

AND LEARN THESE ROAD SIGNS

Speed Limit
(km/hr)

Speed Limit
No Longer
Applies

No
Passing

End of
No Passing
Zone

One Way

Intersection

Main
Road

Expressway

Danger

No Entry

Cars
Prohibited

All Vehicles
Prohibited

No Through
Road

Restrictions
No Longer
Apply

Yield to
Oncoming
Traffic

No
Stopping

Parking

No Parking

Customs

Yield

Going Places

On your travels through France, you're likely to see these place names. If French clerks at train stations and train conductors don't understand your pronunciation, write the town name on a piece of paper.

Alsace	ahl-sahs
Amboise	ahm-bwahz
Annecy	ahn-see
Antibes	ahn-teeb
Arles	arl
Arromanches	ah-roh-mahnsh
Avignon	ah-veen-yohn
Bayeux	bah-yuh
Beaune	bohn
Beynac	bay-nak
Bordeaux	bor-doh
Calais	kah-lay
Carcassonne	kar-kah-suhn
Chambord	shahn-bor
Chamonix	shah-moh-nee
Chartres	shar-truh
Chenonceau	shuh-nohn-soh
Cherbourg	shehr-boor
Chinon	shee-nohn
Collioure	kohl-yoor
Colmar	kohl-mar
Côte d'Azur	koht dah-zewr
Dijon	dee-zhohn
Dordogne	dor-dohn-yuh
Giverny	zhee-vehr-nee
Grenoble	gruh-noh-bluh
Honfleur	ohn-flur
Le Havre	luh hah-vruh
Loire	lwahr
Lyon	lee-ohn
Marseille	mar-say
Mont Blanc	mohn blahn
Mont St-Michel	mohn san-mee-shehl

Nantes	nah<u>n</u>t
Nice	nees
Normandy	nor-mah<u>n</u>-dee
Paris	pah-ree
Provence	proh-vah<u>n</u>s
Reims	ra<u>n</u>s
Rouen	roo-ah<u>n</u>
Roussillon	roo-see-yoh<u>n</u>
Sarlat	sar-lah
Strasbourg	strahs-boorg
Verdun	vehr-duh<u>n</u>
Versailles	vehr-sī
Villefranche	veel-frah<u>n</u>sh

SLEEPING

This chapter covers making reservations, hotel stays (including checking in, making requests, and dealing with difficulties), specific concerns (such as families and mobility issues), and hostels.

RESERVATIONS

Making a Reservation

reservation	réservation ray-zehr-vah-see-ohn
Do you have...?	Avez-vous...? ah-vay-voo
I'd like to reserve...	Je voudrais réserver... zhuh voo-dray ray-zehr-vay
...a room...	...une chambre... ewn shahn-bruh
...for one person / two people	...pour une personne / deux personnes poor ewn pehr-suhn / duh pehr-suhn
...for today / tomorrow	...pour aujourd'hui / demain poor oh-zhoor-dwee / duh-man
...for one night	...pour une nuit poor ewn nwee
two / three nights	deux / trois nuits duh / trwah nwee

Key Phrases: Sleeping

Do you have a room?	Avez-vous une chambre? ah-vay-voo ewn shahn-bruh
for one person / two people	pour une personne / deux personnes poor ewn pehr-suhn / duh pehr-suhn
today / tomorrow	aujourd'hui / demain oh-zhoor-dwee / duh-man
How much is it?	C'est combien? say kohn-bee-an
hotel	hôtel oh-tehl
inexpensive hotel	pension pahn-see-ohn
vacancy / no vacancy	chambre libre / complet shahn-bruh lee-bruh / kohn-play

June 21	le vingt et un juin luh vant ay uhn zhwan
How much is it?	C'est combien? say kohn-bee-an
Anything cheaper?	Rien de moins cher? ree-an duh mwan shehr
I'll take it.	Je la prends. zhuh lah prahn
My name is _____.	Je m'appelle _____. zhuh mah-pehl _____
Do you need a deposit?	Avez-vous besoin d'un acompte? ah-vay-voo buh-zwan duhn ah-kohnt
Do you accept credit cards?	Vous prenez les cartes de crédit? voo pruh-nay lay kart duh kray-dee
Can I reserve with a credit card and pay in cash?	Je peux faire une réservation avec une carte de crédit et payer plus tard en liquide? zhuh puh fair ewn ray-zehr-vah-see-ohn ah-vehk ewn kart duh kray-dee ay pay-ay plew tar ahn lee-keed

French hotels are rated from one to five stars (check the blue-and-white plaque by the front door). For budget travelers, one or two stars is the best value. Prices vary widely under one roof. You'll save money if you get a room with a double bed (**grand lit**) instead of twin beds (**deux petits lits**), and a bathroom with a shower (**salle d'eau**) instead of a bathroom with a bathtub (**salle de bains**). You'll pay less for a room with just a toilet and sink (**cabinet de toilette**, or **C. de T.**), and even less for a room with only a sink (**lavabo seulement**).

Many people stay at a **hôtel,** but you have other choices:

Hôtel-château (oh-tehl-shah-toh): Castle hotel
Auberge (oh-behrzh): Small hotel with restaurant
Pension (pahn-see-ohn): Small hotel
Chambre d'hôte (shahn-bruh doht): B&B or room in a private home; a table d'hôte is a chambre d'hôte that offers an optional, reasonably priced home-cooked dinner.
Gîte (zheet): Country home rental
Auberge de jeunesse (oh-behrzh duh zhuh-nehs): Hostel

Getting Specific

I'd like a...	Je voudrais une... zhuh voo-dray ewn
...single room.	...chambre simple. shahn-bruh san-pluh
...double room.	...chambre double. shahn-bruh doo-bluh
...triple room.	...chambre triple. shahn-bruh tree-pluh
...room for _____ people.	...chambre pour _____ personnes. shahn-bruh poor _____ pehr-suhn
with / without / and	avec / sans / et ah-vehk / sahn / ay
king-size bed	king size keeng "size"
queen-size bed	lit de cent-soixante lee duh sahn-swah-sahnt
double bed	grand lit grahn lee
twin beds...	deux petits lits / deux lits jumeaux... duh puh-tee lee / duh lee zhew-moh
...together / separate	....ensemble / séparés ahn-sahn-bluh / say-pah-ray
single bed	petit lit / lit jumeau puh-tee lee / lee zhew-moh
without footboard	sans pied de lit sahn pee-ay duh lee
private bathroom	salle de bain privée sahl duh ban pree-vay
toilet	WC vay say
shower	douche doosh
bathtub	baignoire behn-wahr
with only a sink	avec lavabo seulement ah-vehk lah-vah-boh suhl-mahn
shower outside the room	une douche sur le palier ewn doosh sewr luh pahl-yay
balcony	balcon bahl-kohn
view	vue vew
cheap	pas cher / bon marché pah shehr / bohn mar-shay

quiet	tranquille trah<u>n</u>-keel
romantic	romantique roh-mah<u>n</u>-teek
on the ground floor	au rez-de-chaussée oh ray-duh-shoh-say
Do you have...?	Avez-vous...? ah-vay-voo
...an elevator	...un ascenseur uh<u>n</u> ah-sah<u>n</u>-sur
...air-conditioning	...climatisation klee-mah-tee-zah-see-oh<u>n</u>
...Wi-Fi (in the room)	...Wi-Fi (dans la chambre) wee-fee (dah<u>n</u> lah shah<u>n</u>-bruh)
...parking	...un parking uh<u>n</u> par-keeng
...a garage	...un parking couvert uh<u>n</u> par-keeng koo-vehr
What is your...?	Quel est votre...? kehl ay voh-truh
...email address	...adresse email ah-drehs "email"
...cancellation policy	...conditions d'annulation koh<u>n</u>-dees-yoh<u>n</u> dah-new-lah-see-oh<u>n</u>

In France, a room with one double bed is generally smaller than a room with two twin beds *(deux petits lits)*. An American-size double bed (55 inches wide) is called *un grand lit*. A queen-size bed is *un lit de cent-soixante*—literally a 160-centimeter bed (63 inches wide). And *le king size* is usually two twin beds pushed together and sheeted as one big bed. You may find any of these in a French "double room." If you'll take either twins or a double, ask generically for *une chambre pour deux* (a room for two) to avoid being needlessly turned away. Taller guests may want to request a bed *sans pied de lit* (without footboard).

Nailing Down the Price

price	prix / tarif pree / tah-reef
How much is...?	Combien...? koh<u>n</u>-bee-a<u>n</u>
...a room for ____ people	...une chambre pour ____ personnes ewn shah<u>n</u>-bruh poor ____ pehr-suhn

What Your Hotelier Wants to Know

If you'd like to reserve by email, your hotelier needs to know the following information: number and type of rooms (i.e., single or double); number of nights; date of arrival (written day/month/year); date of departure; and any special needs (bathroom in the room, cheapest room, twin beds vs. one big bed, crib, air-conditioning, quiet, view, ground floor, no stairs, and so on). Here's a sample email I'd send to make a reservation.

From:	rick@ricksteves.com
Sent:	Today
To:	info@hotelcentral.com
Subject:	Reservation request for 19-22 July

Dear Hotel Central,

I would like to stay at your hotel. Please let me know if you have a room available and the price for:
• 2 people
• Double bed and en suite bathroom in a quiet room
• Arriving 19 July, departing 22 July (3 nights)

Thank you!
Rick Steves

The hotel will reply with its room availability and rates for your dates. This is not a confirmation—you must email back to say that you want the room at the given rate, and you'll likely be asked for your credit card number for a deposit.

...your cheapest room	...la chambre la moins chère lah shahn-bruh lah mwan shehr
Is breakfast included?	Le petit déjeuner est compris? luh puh-tee day-zhuh-nay ay kohn-pree
Complete price?	Tout compris? too kohn-pree
Is it cheaper if...?	C'est moins cher si je...? say mwan shehr see zhuh
...I stay three nights	...vais rester trois nuits vay rehs-tay trwah nwee
...I pay in cash	...paie en liquide pay ahn lee-keed

Some hotels may offer a lower price if you stay for longer periods and/ or pay in cash. Rates can vary by season: High season (*haute saison*) is more expensive than low season (*basse saison*). In resort towns, some hotels offer half-pension (*demi-pension*), which includes two meals per day served at the hotel: breakfast and your choice of lunch or dinner. The price for half-pension is often listed per person rather than per room. Hotels that offer half-pension often require it in summer. The meals are usually good, but if you want more freedom, look for hotels that don't push half-pension.

Arrival and Departure

arrival	arrivée ah-ree-vay
arrival date	la date d'arrivée lah daht dah-ree-vay
departure date	la date de départ lah daht duh day-par
I'll arrive / We'll arrive...	J'arrive / Nous arrivons... zhah-reev / nooz ah-ree-vohn
I'll depart / We'll depart...	Je pars / Nous partons...... zhuh par / noo par-tohn
...June 16.	...le seize juin. luh sehz zhwan

...in the morning / afternoon / evening.	...dans la matinée / l'après-midi / la soirée. dahn lah mah-tee-nay / lah-preh-mee-dee / lah swah-ray
...Friday before 6 p.m.	...vendredi avant six heures du soir. vahn-druh-dee ah-vahn seez ur dew swahr
I'll stay...	Je reste... zhuh rehst
We'll stay...	Nous restons... noo rehs-tohn
...two nights.	...deux nuits. duh nwee
We arrive Monday, depart Wednesday.	Nous arrivons lundi, et partons mercredi. nooz ah-ree-vohn luhn-dee ay par-tohn mehr-kruh-dee

For help with saying dates in French, see "Time and Dates," starting on page 34.

Confirm, Change, or Cancel

It's smart to call a day or two in advance to confirm your reservation.

I have a reservation.	J'ai une réservation. zhay ewn ray-zehr-vah-see-ohn
My name is _____.	Je m'appelle _____. zhuh mah-pehl _____
I'd like to... my reservation.	Je voudrais... ma réservation. zhuh voo-dray... mah ray-zehr-vah-see-ohn
...confirm	...confirmer kohn-feer-may
...change	...modifier moh-dee-fee-ay
...cancel	...annuler ah-new-lay
The reservation is for...	La réservation est pour... lah ray-zehr-vah-see-ohn ay poor
...today / tomorrow.	...aujourd'hui / demain. oh-zhoor-dwee / duh-man
...August 13.	...le treize août. luh trehz oot

Did you find the reservation?	Avez-vous trouvé la réservation? ah-vay-voo troo-vay lah ray-zehr-vah-see-ohn
Is everything OK?	Ça va marcher? sah vah mar-shay
See you then.	À bientôt. ah bee-an-toh
I'm sorry, but I need to cancel.	Je suis désolé, mais j'ai besoin d'annuler. zhuh swee day-zoh-lay may zhay buh-zwan dah-new-lay
Are there cancellation fees?	Il y a des frais d'annulation? eel yah day fray dah-new-lah-see-ohn

Depending on how far ahead you cancel a reservation—and on the hotel's cancellation policy—you might pay a penalty. Most likely your credit card will be billed for one night.

AT THE HOTEL

Checking In

My name is _____.	Je m'appelle _____. zhuh mah-pehl
I have a reservation.	J'ai une réservation. zhay ewn ray-zehr-vah-see-ohn
one night	une nuit ewn nwee
two / three nights	deux / trois nuits duh / trwah nwee
Where is....?	Où est....? oo ay
...my room	...ma chambre mah shahn-bruh
...the elevator	...l'ascenseur lah-sahn-sur
...the breakfast room	...la salle du petit déjeuner lah sahl dew puh-tee day-zhuh-nay
Is breakfast included?	Le petit déjeuner est compris? luh puh-tee day-zhuh-nay ay kohn-pree
When does breakfast start and end?	Le petit déjeuner commence et termine à quelle heure? luh puh-tee day-zhuh-nay koh-mahns ay tehr-meen ah kehl ur

key	clé klay
Two keys, please.	Deux clés, s'il vous plaît. duh klay see voo play

Choosing a Room

Can I see...?	Je peux voir...? zhuh puh vwahr
...a room	...une chambre ewn shah<u>n</u>-bruh
...a different room	...une chambre différente ewn shah<u>n</u>-bruh dee-fay-rah<u>n</u>t
Do you have something...?	Avez-vous quelque chose de...? ah-vay-voo kehl-kuh shohz duh
...larger / smaller	...plus grand / moins grand plew grah<u>n</u> / mwa<u>n</u> grah<u>n</u>
...better / cheaper	...meilleur / moins cher meh-yur / mwa<u>n</u> shehr
...brighter	...plus clair plew klair
...quieter	...plus tranquille plew trah<u>n</u>-keel
...in the back	...derrière dehr-yehr
...with a view	...avec une vue ah-vehk ewn vew
...on a lower / higher floor	...sur un étage plus bas / plus haut sewr uh<u>n</u> ay-tahzh plew bah / plew oh
No, thank you.	Non, merci. noh<u>n</u> mehr-see
What a charming room!	Quelle chambre charmante! kehl shah<u>n</u>-bruh shar-mah<u>n</u>t
I'll take it.	Je la prends. zhuh lah prah<u>n</u>

Be aware that a room *avec une vue* (with a view) can also come with more noise. If a *tranquille* room is important to you, say so.

Hotel Words

cancellation policy	conditions d'annulation kohn-dees-yohn dah-new-lah-see-ohn
check-in time	heure d'enrégistrement ur dahn-ray-zhee-struh-mahn
check-out time	heure limite d'occupation ur lee-meet doh-kew-pah-see-ohn
elevator	ascenseur ah-sahn-sur
emergency exit	issue / sortie de secours ee-sew / sor-tee duh suh-koor
fire escape	escalier d'incendie ehs-kahl-yay dan-sahn-dee
floor...	étage... ay-tahzh
...lower / higher	...plus bas / plus haut plew bah / plew oh
ground floor	rez-de-chaussée ray-duh-shoh-say
laundry	linge / lessive lanzh / luh-seev
parking	parking / garage par-keeng / gah-rahzh
price list	liste des tarifs leest day tah-reef
reservation	réservation ray-zehr-vah-see-ohn
a room...	une chambre... ewn shahn-bruh
...single	...single san-guhl
...double	...double doo-bluh
...triple	...triple tree-pluh
family room	une grande chambre / une suite ewn grahnd shahn-bruh / ewn sweet
stairs	escalier ehs-kahl-yay
suite	suite sweet
swimming pool	piscine pee-seen
view	vue vew
Wi-Fi	Wi-Fi wee-fee

In Your Room

air-conditioner	climatisation klee-mah-tee-zah-see-ohn
alarm clock	réveil ray-vay
baggage	bagages bah-gahzh
balcony	balcon bahl-kohn
bathroom	salle de bains sahl duh ban
bathtub	baignoire behn-wahr
bed	lit lee
bedspread	couvre-lit koo-vruh-lee
blanket	couverture koo-vehr-tewr
blinds	stores stor
city map	plan de la ville plahn duh lah veel
chair	chaise shehz
closet	placard plah-kar
corkscrew	tire-bouchon teer-boo-shohn
crib	berceau behr-soh
curtains	rideaux ree-doh
door	porte port
double bed	grand lit grahn lee
drain	descente d'eau day-sahnt doh
electrical adapter	adaptateur électrique ah-dahp-tah-tur ay-lehk-treek
electrical outlet	prise preez
faucet	robinet roh-bee-nay
hair dryer	sèche-cheveux sehsh-shuh-vuh
hanger	porte-manteau port-mahn-toh
key	clé klay
kitchenette	kitchenette keet-cheh-neht
lamp	lampe lahmp
lightbulb	ampoule ahn-pool
lock	serrure suh-rewr
mirror	miroir meer-wahr

pillow	oreiller oh-ray-yay
radio	radio rahd-yoh
remote control...	télécommande... tay-lay-koh-mah<u>nd</u>
...for TV	...pour la télé poor lah tay-lay
...for air-conditioner	...pour la climatisation poor lah klee-mah-tee-zah-see-oh<u>n</u>
safe (n)	coffre-fort koh-fruh-for
scissors	ciseaux see-zoh
shampoo	shampooing shah<u>n</u>-pwan
sheets	draps drah
shower	douche doosh
shutters	volets voh-lay
single bed	petit lit / lit jumeau puh-tee lee / lee zhew-moh
sink	lavabo lah-vah-boh
sink stopper	bouchon pour le lavabo boo-shoh<u>n</u> poor luh lah-vah-boh
soap	savon sah-voh<u>n</u>
telephone	téléphone tay-lay-fohn
television	télévision tay-lay-vee-zee-oh<u>n</u>
toilet	toilette twah-leht
toilet paper	papier toilette pahp-yay twah-leht
towel (hand)	petite serviette puh-teet sehrv-yeht
towel (bath)	serviette de bain sehrv-yeht duh ban
twin beds	deux petits lits / deux lits jumeaux duh puh-tee lee / duh lee zhew-moh
wake-up call	réveil téléphoné ray-vay tay-lay-foh-nay
washcloth	gant de toilette gah<u>n</u> duh twah-leht
water (hot / cold)	eau (chaude / froide) oh (shohd / frwahd)
window	fenêtre fuh-neh-truh
window screen	moustiquaire moos-tee-kair

If you don't see remote controls in the room (for the TV or air-conditioner), ask for them at the front desk. A comfortable setting for the air-conditioner is about 20 degrees Celsius. On French faucets, a **C** stands for *chaud* (hot)—the opposite of cold.

If you'd rather not struggle all night with a log-style French pillow, check in the closet to see if there's a fluffier American-style pillow, or ask for a *coussin* (koo-sa<u>n</u>).

Hotel Hassles

Combine these phrases with the words in the previous table to make simple and clear statements such as: *La toilette ne marche pas*. (The toilet doesn't work.)

I have a problem in the room.	J'ai un problème dans la chambre. zhay uh<u>n</u> proh-blehm dah<u>n</u> lah shah<u>n</u>-bruh
Come with me.	Venez avec moi. vuh-nay ah-vehk mwah
The room is...	La chambre est... lah shah<u>n</u>-bruh ay
It's...	C'est... say
...dirty.	...sale. sahl
...moldy.	...moisie. mwah-zee
...smoky.	...enfumée. ah<u>n</u>-few-may
...stinky.	...puante. pew-ah<u>n</u>t
It's noisy.	C'est bruyante. say brew-yah<u>n</u>t
The room is too hot / too cold.	La chambre est trop chaude / trop froide. lah shah<u>n</u>-bruh ay troh shohd / troh frwahd
How can I make the room cooler / warmer?	Comment je peux rendre la chambre plus fraîche / chaude? koh-mah<u>n</u> zhuh puh rah<u>n</u>-druh lah shah<u>n</u>-bruh plew frehsh / shohd
There's no (hot) water.	Il n'y a pas d'eau (chaude). eel nee ah pah doh (shohd)

I can't open / shut / lock...	Je ne peux pas ouvrir / fermer / fermer à clé... zhuh nuh puh pah oo-vreer / fehr-may / fehr-may ah klay
...the door / the window.	...la porte / la fenêtre. lah port / lah fuh-neh-truh
How does this work?	Comment ça marche? koh-mahn sah marsh
This doesn't work.	Ça ne marche pas. sah nuh marsh pah
When will it be fixed?	Quand est-ce qu'il sera réparé? kahn ehs keel suh-rah ray-pah-ray
The bed is too soft / hard.	Le lit est trop mou / dur. luh lee ay troh moo / dewr
I can't sleep.	Je ne peux pas dormir. zhuh nuh puh pah dor-meer
ants	fourmis foor-mee
bedbugs	punaises pew-nehz
cockroaches	cafards kah-far
mice	souris soo-ree
mosquitoes	moustiques moos-teek
I'm covered with bug bites.	Je suis couvert de piqures d'insectes. zhuh swee koo-vehr duh pee-kewr dan-sehkt
My... was stolen.	On m'a volé... ohn mah voh-lay
...money	...l'argent. lar-zhahn
...computer	...l'ordinateur. lor-dee-nah-tur
...camera	...l'appareil-photo. lah-pah-ray-foh-toh
I need to speak to the manager.	J'ai besoin de parler au gérant / directeur. zhay buh-zwan duh par-lay oh zhay-rahn / dee-rehk-tur
I want to make a complaint.	Je veux faire une réclamation. zhuh vuh fair ewn ray-klah-mah-see-ohn
The visitors' book, please.	Le livre d'or, s'il vous plaît. luh lee-vruh dor see voo play

Keep your valuables with you, out of sight in your room, or in a room safe (if available). For help on dealing with theft or loss, including a list of items, see page 272.

Most reputable hotels have a visitors' book in which guests can write their comments, good or bad, about their stay and the service. Asking to see the *livre d'or* (literally "golden book") can inspire the hotelier to find a solution for your problem.

Hotel Help

Use the "In Your Room" words (on page 90) to fill in the blanks.

I'd like...	Je voudrais... zhuh voo-dray
Do you have...?	Avez-vous...? ah-vay-voo
a / another	un / un autre uhn / uhn oh-truh
extra	supplémentaire sew-play-mahn-tair
different	différent dee-fay-rahn
Please change...	Changez, s'il vous plaît... shahn-zhay see voo play
Please don't change...	Ne changez pas, s'il vous plaît... nuh shahn-zhay pah see voo play
...the towels / the sheets.	...les serviettes / les draps. lay sehrv-yeht / lay drah
What is the charge to...?	Ça coûte combien pour...? sah koot kohn-bee-an poor
...use the telephone	...utiliser le téléphone ew-tee-lee-zay luh tay-lay-fohn
...use the Internet	...utiliser l'internet ew-tee-lee-zay lan-tehr-neht
Do you have Wi-Fi...?	Avez-vous le Wi-Fi...? ah-vay-voo luh wee-fee
...in the room / in the lobby	...dans les chambres / à la réception dahn lay shahn-bruh / ah lah ray-sehp-see-ohn

What is the network name / the password?	Quel est le nom du réseau / le mot de passe? *kehl ay luh nohn dew ray-zoh / luh moh duh pahs*
Where is a nearby...?	Où se trouve le... le plus proche? *oo suh troov luh... luh plew prohsh*
...full-service laundry	...blanchisserie service complet *blahn-shee-suh-ree sehr-vees kohn-play*
...self-service laundry	...laverie automatique *lah-vuh-ree oh-toh-mah-teek*
...pharmacy	...pharmacie *far-mah-see*
...grocery store	...supermarché / épicerie *sew-pehr-mar-shay / ay-pee-suh-ree*
...restaurant	...restaurant *rehs-toh-rahn*
Where do you go for lunch / dinner / coffee?	Vous allez où pour déjeuner / dîner / un café? *vooz ah-lay oo poor day-zhuh-nay / dee-nay / uhn kah-fay*
Will you call a taxi for me?	Pourriez-vous appeler un taxi pour moi? *poor-yay-voo ah-puh-lay uhn tahk-see poor mwah*
Where can I park?	Je peux me garer où? *zhuh puh muh gah-ray oo*
What time do you lock up?	Vous fermez à quelle heure? *voo fehr-may ah kehl ur*
Please wake me at 7:00.	Réveillez-moi à sept heures, s'il vous plaît. *ray-vay-ay-mwah ah seht ur see voo play*
I'd like to stay another night.	Je voudrais rester encore une nuit. *zhuh voo-dray rehs-tay ahn-kor ewn nwee*

Will you call my next hotel...?	Pourriez-vous appeler mon prochain hotel...? poor-yay-voo ah-puh-lay mohn proh-shan oh-tehl
...for tonight	...pour ce soir poor suh swahr
...to make / to confirm a reservation	...pour faire / confirmer une réservation poor fair / kohn-feer-may ewn ray-zehr-vah-see-ohn
Will you call another hotel for me? (if hotel is booked)	Vous pourriez contacter un autre hôtel pour moi? voo poor-yay kohn-tahk-tay uhn oh-truh oh-tehl poor mwah
I will pay for the call.	Je paierai l'appel. zhuh pay-uh-ray lah-pehl

Checking Out

When is check-out time?	A quelle heure on doit libérer la chambre? ah kehl ur ohn dwah lee-bay-ray lah shahn-bruh
Can I check out later?	Je peux libérer la chambre plus tard? zhuh puh lee-bay-ray lah shahn-bruh plew tar
I'll leave...	Je pars... zhuh par
We'll leave...	Nous partons... noo par-tohn
...today / tomorrow.	...aujourd'hui / demain. oh-zhoor-dwee / duh-man
...very early.	...très tôt. treh toh
Can I pay now?	Je peux régler la note maintenant? zhuh puh ray-glay lah noht man-tuh-nahn

The bill, please.	La note, s'il vous plaît. lah noht see voo play
I think this is too high.	Je pense que c'est trop. zhuh pahns kuh say troh
Can you explain / itemize the bill?	Vous pouvez expliquer / détailler cette note? voo poo-vay ehk-splee-kay / day-tī-yay seht noht
Do you accept credit cards?	Vous prenez les cartes de crédit? voo pruh-nay lay kart duh kray-dee
Is it cheaper if I pay in cash?	C'est moins cher si je paie en liquide? say mwan shehr see zhuh pay ahn lee-keed
Everything was great.	C'était super. say-tay sew-pehr
I slept like a baby.	J'ai dormi comme un enfant. zhay dor-mee kohm uhn ahn-fahn
Can I / Can we...?	Je peux / Nous pouvons...? zhuh puh / noo poo-vohn
...leave baggage here until _____ o'clock	...laisser les baggages ici jusqu'à _____ heure leh-say lay bah-gahzh ee-see zhews-kah _____ ur
A tip for you.	Un pourboire pour vous. uhn poor-bwahr poor voo

Your bill will include a small *taxe du séjour,* the daily hotel tax.

SPECIAL CONCERNS

Families

Do you have...?	Vous avez...? vooz ah-vay
...a family room	...une grande chambre / une suite ewn grahnd shahn-bruh / ewn sweet
...a family rate	...un tarif famille uhn tah-reef fah-mee

...a discount for children	...un tarif réduit pour enfants uhn tah-reef ray-dwee poor ahn-fahn
I have / We have...	J'ai / Nous avons... zhay / nooz ah-vohn
...one child.	...un enfant. uhn ahn-fahn
...two children.	...deux enfants. duhz ahn-fahn
_____ months old	de _____ mois duh _____ mwah
_____ years old	de _____ ans duh _____ ahn
Do you accept children?	Vous recevez des enfants? voo ruh-suh-vay dayz ahn-fahn
age limit	limite d'âge lee-meet dahzh
I'd like / We'd like...	Je voudrais / Nous voudrions... zhuh voo-dray / noo voo-dree-ohn
...a crib.	...un berceau. uhn behr-soh
...an extra bed.	...un lit supplémentaire. uhn lee sew-play-mahn-tair
...bunk beds.	...lits superposés. lee sew-pehr-poh-zay
babysitting service	service de babysitting sehr-vees duh "babysitting"
Is... nearby?	Il y a... près d'ici? eel yah... preh dee-see
...a park	...un parc uhn park
...a playground	...une aire de jeux ewn air duh juh
...a swimming pool	...une piscine ewn pee-seen

Mobility Issues

For related phrases, see page 310 in the Personal Care and Health chapter.

Do you have...?	Vous avez...? vooz ah-vay
...an elevator	...un ascenseur uhn ah-sahn-sur

...a ground floor room	...une chambre au rez-de-chaussée ewn shahn-bruh oh ray-duh-shoh-say
...a wheelchair-accessible room	...une chambre accessible à un fauteuil roulant ewn shahn-bruh ahk-suh-see-bluh ah uhn foh-tuh-ee roo-lahn

AT THE HOSTEL

Europe's cheapest beds are in hostels, open to travelers of any age. Official hostels (affiliated with Hostelling International) are usually big and institutional. Independent hostels are more casual, with fewer rules.

hostel	auberge de jeunesse oh-behrzh duh zhuh-nehs
dorm bed	lit dortoir lee dor-twahr
How many beds per room?	Il y a combien de lits par chambre? eel yah kohn-bee-an duh lee par shahn-bruh
dorm for women only	dortoir uniquement pour les femmes dor-twahr ew-neek-mahn poor lay fahm
co-ed dorm	dortoir mixte dor-twahr meekst
double room	chambre double shahn-bruh doo-bluh
family room	salle de séjour sahl duh say-zhoor
Is breakfast included?	Le petit déjeuner est compris? luh puh-tee day-zhuh-nay ay kohn-pree
curfew	couvre-feu koov-ruh-fuh
lockout	portes fermées port fehr-may
membership card	carte de membre kart duh mahn-bruh

EATING

Dig into this chapter's phrases for dining at restaurants, special concerns (including dietary restrictions, children, and being in a hurry), types of food and drink, and shopping for your picnic. The next chapter is a Menu Decoder.

French restaurants normally serve from noon to 2 p.m. and from 7 p.m. until about 10 p.m. Brasseries and some cafés serve throughout the day. The menu is posted right on the front door or window, and "window shopping" for your meal is a fun, important part of the experience. While the slick self-service restaurants are easy to use, you'll often eat better for the same money in a good little family bistro. The inside seating in all French restaurants is now non-smoking.

RESTAURANTS

Diners around the world recognize French food as a work of art. French cuisine is sightseeing for your taste buds.

Styles of cooking include **haute cuisine** (classic, elaborately prepared, multi-course meals), **cuisine bourgeoise** (the finest-quality home cooking), **cuisine des provinces** (traditional dishes of specific regions), and **nouvelle cuisine** (a focus on smaller portions and closer attention to the texture and color of the ingredients).

Types of Restaurants

Restaurant: Generally elegant, expensive eatery serving haute cuisine

Café / Brasserie: Informal eateries offering quick, simple food and drink; brasseries often serve meals throughout the day

Bistro: Small, usually casual neighborhood restaurant offering straightforward, traditional food

Auberge / Hostellerie / Relais: Country inn serving high-quality traditional food

Crêperie: Street stand or café specializing in crêpes (thin pancakes, usually served with sweet fillings)

Salon de thé: Tea and coffee house offering pastries, desserts, and sometimes light meals

Buffet-express / Snack bar: Cafeteria, usually near a train or bus station

Key Phrases: Restaurants

Where's a good restaurant nearby?	Où se trouve un bon restaurant près d'ici?
	oo suh troov uhn bohn rehs-toh-rahn preh dee-see
I'd like...	Je voudrais... zhuh voo-dray
We'd like...	Nous voudrions... noo voo-dree-ohn
...a table for one / two.	...une table pour un / deux.
	ewn tah-bluh poor uhn / duh
Is this table free?	Cette table est libre?
	seht tah-bluh ay lee-bruh
How long is the wait?	Combien de temps faut-il attendre?
	kohn-bee-an duh tahn foh-teel ah-tahn-druh
The menu (in English), please.	La carte (en anglais), s'il vous plaît.
	lah kart (ahn ahn-glay) see voo play
The bill, please.	L'addition, s'il vous plaît.
	lah-dee-see-ohn see voo play
Credit card OK?	Carte de crédit OK?
	kart duh kray-dee "OK"

Traiteur ("caterer"): Like a delicatessen, selling prepared hot foods to go

Comptoir ("counter"): Generally a snack bar-type place, serving basic food

Cabaret: Supper club featuring entertainment

Cave à manger: Wine shop that also sells wine by the glass and snacks

Routier: Truck stop dishing up basic, decent food

Finding a Restaurant

Where's a good... restaurant nearby?	Où se trouve un bon restaurant... près d'ici? oo suh troov uhn bohn rehs-toh-rahn... preh dee-see
...cheap	...bon marché bohn mar-shay
...local-style	...cuisine régionale kwee-zeen ray-zhee-oh-nahl
...untouristy	...pas touristique pah too-ree-steek
...romantic	...romantique roh-mahn-teek
...vegetarian	...végétarien vay-zhay-tah-ree-an
...fast	...fast-food fahst food
...self-service buffet	...buffet de libre service bew-fay duh lee-bruh sehr-vees
...Asian	...asiatique ah-zee-ah-teek
popular with locals	fréquenté par les gens du coin fray-kahn-tay par lay zhahn dew kwan
moderate price	prix modéré pree moh-day-ray
splurge	faire une folie fair ewn foh-lee
Is it better than McDonald's?	C'est mieux que Mac Do? say mee-uh kuh mahk doh

This is the sequence of a typical restaurant experience: To get the waiter's attention, simply ask *S'il vous plaît?* The waiter will give you a menu *(carte)* and then ask what you'd like to drink *(Vous voulez quelques choses à boire?)*, if you're ready to order *(Vous êtes prêts à commander?)*, or what you'd like to eat *(Qu'est-ce que je vous sers?)*. Later the server will ask if everything is OK *(Tout va bien?)*, if you'd like dessert *(Vous voulez un dessert?)*, and if you're finished *(Vous avez terminé?)*. When you're ready, ask for the bill *(L'addition, s'il vous plaît)*.

Getting a Table

I'd like...	Je voudrais... zhuh voo-dray
We'd like...	Nous voudrions... noo voo-dree-ohn

...a table...	...une table... ewn tah-bluh
...for one / two.	...pour un / deux. poor uhn / duh
...inside / outside.	...à l'intérieur / dehors. ah lan-tay-ree-ur / duh-or
...by the window.	...à côté de la fenêtre. ah koh-tay duh lah fuh-neh-truh
...with a view.	...avec une vue. ah-vehk ewn vew
quiet	tranquille trahn-keel
Is this table free?	Cette table est libre? seht tah-bluh ay lee-bruh
Can I sit here?	Je peux m'asseoir ici? zhuh puh mah-swahr ee-see
Can we sit here?	Nous pouvons nous asseoir ici? noo poo-vohn nooz ah-swahr ee-see
How long is the wait?	Combien de temps faut-il attendre? kohn-bee-an duh tahn foh-teel ah-tahn-druh
How many minutes?	Combien de minutes? kohn-bee-an duh mee-newt
Where are the toilets?	Où sont les toilettes? oo sohn lay twah-leht

At a *café* or a *brasserie*, if the table is not set, it's fine to seat yourself and just have a drink. However, if it's set with a placemat and cutlery, you should wait to be seated and plan to order a meal. If you're unsure, ask the server *Je peux m'asseoir ici?* (Can I sit here?) before taking a seat.

Reservations

reservation	réservation ray-zehr-vah-see-ohn
Are reservations recommended?	Les réservations sont conseillées? lay ray-zehr-vah-see-ohn sohn kohn-seh-yay

I'd like to make a reservation...	Je voudrais faire une réservation... zhuh voo-dray fair ewn ray-zehr-vah-see-ohn
...for one person / for myself.	...pour moi-même. poor mwah-mehm
...for two people.	...pour deux personnes. poor duh pehr-suhn
...for today / tomorrow.	...pour aujourd'hui / demain. poor oh-zhoor-dwee / duh-man
...for lunch / dinner.	...pour le déjeuner / le dîner. poor luh day-zhuh-nay / luh dee-nay
...at _____ o'clock.	...à _____ heures. ah _____ uhr
My name is _____.	Je m'appelle _____. zhuh mah-pehl _____
I have a reservation for _____ people.	J'ai une réservation pour _____ personnes. zhay ewn ray-zehr-vah-see-ohn poor _____ pehr-suhn

The Menu

Here are a few food categories and other restaurant lingo you might see on the menu.

menu	carte kart
The menu (in English), please.	La carte (en anglais), s'il vous plaît. lah kart (ahn ahn-glay) see voo play
fixed-price meal	menu / prix fixe muh-new / pree feeks
special of the day	plat du jour plah dew zhoor
specialty of the house	spécialité de la maison spay-see-ah-lee-tay duh lah may-zohn
fast service special	formule rapide for-mewl rah-peed
tourist menu (fixed-price meal)	menu touristique muh-new too-ree-steek

A Sample Menu of the Day

Choose a first course, second course, dessert, and beverage.

Restaurant La Mer
18, rue de la Gare, Marseille

MENU TOURISTIQUE €22

Entrée au choix (FIRST COURSE CHOICES)

- SOUPE DE POISSONS (FISH SOUP)
- 12 ESCARGOTS EN COQUILLE (SNAILS IN SHELL)
- SALADE NIÇOISE
- SUGGESTION DU CHEF

Plat au choix (SECOND COURSE CHOICES)

- PLATEAU FRUITS DU MER (PLATTER OF MIXED COLD SEAFOOD)
- POISSON DU MARCHE (FISH FROM THE MARKET)
- POULET BASQUAISE (CHICKEN BASQUE STYLE)
- STEAK-FRITES, SAUCE A L'ECHALOTE (STEAK W/FRIES + SHALLOT SAUCE)

Dessert au choix (DESSERT CHOICES)

- FROMAGE (CHEESE)
- PATISSERIE DU JOUR (PASTRY OF THE DAY)
- GLACE OU SORBET (ICE CREAM OR SHERBET)
- CREME BRULEE

~SERVICE COMPRIS~ (SERVICE INCLUDED)

Merci et Bon Appetit!

children's plate	assiette d'enfant	ahs-yeht dah<u>n</u>-fah<u>n</u>
seniors' menu	une carte de seniors	
	ewn kart duh seen-yor	
breakfast	petit déjeuner	puh-tee day-zhuh-nay
lunch	déjeuner	day-zhuh-nay
dinner	dîner	dee-nay
dishes (prepared dishes)	des plats	
	day plah	
warm / cold plates	plats chauds / froids	plah shoh / frwah
appetizers	hors d'oeuvres	or duh-vruh
sandwiches	sandwichs	sah<u>n</u>d-weech
bread	pain	pa<u>n</u>
cheese	fromage	froh-mahzh
soup	soupe	soop
salad	salade	sah-lahd
first course	entrée	ah<u>n</u>-tray
main course	plat principal	plah pra<u>n</u>-see-pahl
fish	poisson	pwah-soh<u>n</u>
poultry	volaille	voh-lī
meat	viande	vee-ah<u>n</u>d
seafood	fruits de mer	frwee duh mehr
egg dishes	plats d'oeufs	plah duhf
side dishes	plats d'accompagnement	
	plah dah-koh<u>n</u>-pah<u>n</u>-yuh-mah<u>n</u>	
vegetables	légumes	lay-gewm
fruit	fruit	frwee
dessert	dessert	day-sehr
drink menu	carte des consommations	
	kart day koh<u>n</u>-soh-mah-see-oh<u>n</u>	
beverages	boissons	bwah-soh<u>n</u>
beer	bière	bee-ehr
wine	vin	va<u>n</u>

service included	service compris sehr-vees koh<u>n</u>-pree
service not included	service non compris sehr-vees noh<u>n</u> koh<u>n</u>-pree
hot / cold	chaud / froid shoh / frwah
comes with	servi avec sehr-vee ah-vehk
choice of	le choix de luh shwah duh

In French restaurants, you can order off the menu, which is called a *carte*, or you can order a multi-course, fixed-price meal, which, confusingly, is called a *menu* (so if you ask for a *menu* instead of the *carte*, you'll get a fixed-price meal). Most restaurants also have a few special dishes of the day, called *plat du jour*, or simply *plat*.

Menus, which usually include three courses, are generally a good value and will help you pace your meal like the locals: You'll get your choice of soup, appetizer, or salad; your choice of three or four main courses with vegetables; plus a cheese course and/or a choice of desserts. Wine and other drinks are generally extra. Certain premium items add a few euros to the price, clearly noted on the menu (*supplément* or *sup.*). Many restaurants offer less expensive, abbreviated versions of their *menu* at lunchtime, allowing you to select two courses rather than three or four. These pared-down *menus* are sometimes called *formules* and feature an *entrée et plat* (first course and main dish) or *plat et dessert* (main dish and dessert).

If you order *à la carte* (from what we would call the "menu"), you'll have a wider selection of food. It's traditional to order an *entrée* (which—again, confusingly—is a starter rather than a main dish) and a *plat principal* (main course). The *plats* are generally more meat-based, while the *entrées* are where you can get your veggies. (The *menu*, while time-consuming if you're in a rush, creates the appropriate balance of veggies to meat.) Elaborate meals may also have *entremets*—tiny dishes served between courses.

Service compris (s.c.) means that the tip is included.

Ordering

To get a waiter's attention, simply ask *S'il vous plaît?* (Please?). If you have allergies or dietary restrictions, see page 117.

waiter	Monsieur muhs-yuh
waitress	Mademoiselle / Madame mahd-mwah-zehl / mah-dahm
I'm / We're ready to order.	Je suis / Nous sommes prêt à commander. zhuh swee / noo suhm preh ah koh-mahn-day
I need / We need more time.	J'ai besoin de / Nous avons besoin de plus de temps. zhay buh-zwan duh / nooz ah-vohn buh-zwan duh plew duh tahn
I'd like / We'd like...	Je voudrais / Nous voudrions... zhuh voo-dray / noo voo-dree-ohn
...just a drink.	...une consommation seulement. ewn kohn-soh-mah-see-ohn suhl-mahn
...to see the menu.	...voir la carte. vwahr lah kart
Do you have...?	Avez-vous...? ah-vay-voo
...an English menu	...une carte en anglais ewn kart ahn ahn-glay
...a lunch special	...un plat du jour uhn plah dew zhoor
...half-portions	...des demi-portions day duh-mee-por-see-ohn
What do you recommend?	Qu'est-ce que vous recommandez? kehs kuh voo ruh-koh-mahn-day
What's your favorite dish?	Quel est votre plat favori? kehl eh voh-truh plah fah-voh-ree
What is better? (point to menu items)	Qu'est-ce qui vaut mieux? kehs kee voh mee-uh
What is...?	Qu'est-ce qui est...? kehs kee ay
Is it...?	C'est...? say
...good	...bon bohn

...affordable	...abordable ah-bor-dah-bluh
...expensive	...cher shehr
...local	...de la région / du pays duh lah ray-zhee-ohn / dew pay-ee
...fresh	...frais fray
...fast (already prepared)	...déjà préparé day-zhah pray-pah-ray
...spicy (hot)	...piquant pee-kahn
Is it filling?	C'est copieux? say koh-pee-uh
Make me happy.	Rendez-moi content. rahn-day-mwah kohn-tahn
Around _____ euros.	Environ _____ euros. ahn-vee-rohn _____ uh-roh
What is that? (pointing)	C'est quoi ça? say kwah sah
How much is it?	C'est combien? say kohn-bee-an
Nothing with eyeballs.	Rien avec des yeux. ree-an ah-vehk dayz yuh
Can I substitute (something) for _____?	Je peux substituer (quelque chose) pour _____? zhuh puh sewb-stee-tew-ay (kehl-kuh shohz) poor _____
Can I / Can we get it "to go"?	Je peux / Nous pouvons prendre ça "à emporter"? zhuh puh / noo poo-vohn prahn-druh sah ah ahn-por-tay

Once you're seated, the table is yours for the entire lunch or dinner period. The waiter or waitress is there to serve you, but only when you're ready. When going to a good restaurant with an approachable staff, I like to say, "Make me happy," and set a price limit.

Some eateries will let you split a dish; others won't. If you are splitting a main dish, it's polite to get one or two *entrées* (starters) as well. In most cases, it's fine for a person to get only a *plat* (main dish). You can never split a multi-course *menu*.

If you want just a simple meal—like soup, a salad, a sandwich, or an omelet—go to a *café* or *brasserie* instead of a *restaurant*.

There's always one more question at the end of any sales encounter (whether finishing a meal or buying cheese at a *fromagerie*): Will there be anything else? The French have a staggering number of ways to say this, including: *Ça sera tout?* (Will that be all?), *Et avec ça?* (And with this?), *Vous-avez terminé?* (Have you finished?), *Désirez-vous autre chose?* (Would you like anything else?), *Ça vous a plû?* (Have you enjoyed it?), and so on. Your response can be a simple *Ça va, merci.* (Everything is fine, thanks.)

Tableware and Condiments

I need / We need a...	J'ai besoin / Nous avons besoin... zhay buh-zwan / nooz ah-vohn buh-zwan
...napkin.	...d'une serviette. dewn sehrv-yeht
...knife.	...d'un couteau. duhn koo-toh
...fork.	...d'une fourchette. dewn foor-sheht
...spoon.	...d'une cuillère. dewn kwee-yehr
...cup.	...d'une tasse. dewn tahs
...glass.	...d'un verre. duhn vehr
...carafe.	...d'une carafe. dewn kah-rahf
Please...	S'il vous plaît... see voo play
...another table setting.	...d'un autre couvert. duhn oh-truh koo-vehr
...another plate.	...d'une autre assiette. dewn oh-truh ahs-yeht
silverware	des couverts day koo-vehr
water	d'eau doh
bread	de pain duh pan
butter	de beurre duh bur
margarine	de margarine duh mar-gah-reen
salt / pepper	de sel / de poivre duh sehl / duh pwah-vruh

sugar	de sucre duh sew-kruh
artificial sweetener	de faux-sucre duh foh-sew-kruh
honey	de miel duh mee-ehl
mustard	de moutarde duh moo-tard
ketchup	de ketchup duh "ketchup"
mayonnaise	de mayonnaise duh mah-yoh-nehz
toothpick	d'un cure-dents duhn kewr-dahn

The Food Arrives

Your meal might begin with an *amuse-bouche*—literally, "palate amusement" (included with your meal). After bringing your food, your server might wish you a cheery *"Bon appétit!"*

Looks delicious!	Ça a l'air délicieux! sah ah lair day-lee-see-uh
Is it included with the meal?	C'est inclus avec le repas? say an-klew ah-vehk luh ruh-pah
I did not order this.	Je n'ai pas commandé ça. zhuh nay pah koh-mahn-day sah
We did not order this.	Nous n'avons pas commandé ça. noo nah-vohn pah koh-mahn-day sah
Can you heat this up?	Vous pouvez réchauffer ça? voo poo-vay ray-shoh-fay sah
A little.	Un peu. uhn puh
More. / Another.	Plus. / Un autre. plew / uhn oh-truh
One more, please.	Encore un, s'il vous plaît. ahn-kor uhn see voo play
The same.	La même chose. lah mehm shohz
Enough.	Assez. ah-say
Finished.	Terminé. tehr-mee-nay
Thank you.	Merci. mehr-see

Complaints

This is...	C'est... say
...dirty.	...sale. sahl
...greasy.	...graisseux. gray-suh
...salty.	...salé. sah-lay
...undercooked.	...pas assez cuit. pah ah-say kwee
...overcooked.	...trop cuit. troh kwee
...inedible.	...immangeable. an-mahn-zhah-bluh
...cold.	...froid. frwah
...disgusting.	...dégoûtant. day-goo-tahn
Do any of your customers return?	Avez-vous des clients qui reviennent? ah-vay-voo day klee-ahn kee ruh-vee-ehn
Yuck!	Berk! behrk

Compliments to the Chef

Yummy!	Miam-miam! myahm-myahm
Delicious!	Délicieux! day-lee-see-uh
Magnificent!	Magnifique! mahn-yee-feek
Very tasty!	Très bon! treh bohn
I love French food.	J'aime la cuisine française. zhehm lah kwee-zeen frahn-sehz
My compliments to the chef!	Félicitations au chef! fay-lee-see-tah-see-ohn oh shehf

If you've really enjoyed the meal, learn and use this phrase liberally: *Félicitations au chef!* (My compliments to the chef!). French chefs take their work seriously and appreciate knowing you were satisfied.

Paying

bill	addition ah-dee-see-ohn
The bill, please.	L'addition, s'il vous plaît. lah-dee-see-ohn see voo play
Together.	Ensemble. ahn-sahn-bluh
Separate checks.	Notes séparées. noht say-pah-ray
Credit card OK?	Carte de crédit OK? kart duh kray-dee "OK"
This is not correct.	Ce n'est pas exact. suh nay pah ehg-zahkt
Can you explain this?	Vous pouvez expliquez ça? voo poo-vay ehk-splee-kay sah
Can you itemize the bill?	Vous pouvez détailler cette note? voo poo-vay day-tī-yay seht noht
What if I wash the dishes?	Et si je lave la vaisselle? ay see zhuh lahv lah vay-sehl
May I have a receipt, please?	Je peux avoir une facture, s'il vous plaît? zhuh puh ah-vwahr ewn fahk-tewr see voo play
Thank you very much.	Merci beaucoup. mehr-see boh-koo

In France, slow service is good service (fast service would rush the diners). Out of courtesy, your waiter will not bring your bill until you ask for it. Here's a good strategy: When you're done with your dessert, your waiter will ask if you'd like some coffee (which is typically taken after, rather than with, the dessert). This gives you the perfect opening to ask for the bill.

If you're paying with your credit card in cafés and restaurants, the waiter will come by your table with a little machine that the French jokingly call the "game boy." This device will print a receipt for you to sign. If splitting the bill, tell your server the amount you want to charge to each card. If you want to leave a tip, do it in cash (see next section).

It's extremely rare for the French to request separate checks; usually they just split the bill evenly or take turns treating each other.

Tipping

Because a service charge is already included in the bill, an additional tip is not required, but appreciated. My French friends, who understand that it bothers Americans to "undertip," suggest this: Imagine that the bill already includes a 15 percent tip, then add whatever you feel is appropriate—maybe 5 percent for good service, or up to 10 percent for exceptional service. It's often most convenient to simply round up the bill (for example, for an €18.80 check, round up to €20)—hand your payment to the waiter and say *C'est bon* (say bohn), meaning "It's good—keep the change." If you order your food at a counter, don't tip.

tip	pourboire poor-bwahr
service included	service compris sehr-vees kohn-pree
service not included	service non compris sehr-vees nohn kohn-pree
Is tipping expected?	Je dois laisser un pourboire? zhuh dwah lay-say uhn poor-bwahr
What percent?	Quel pourcentage? kehl poor-sahn-tahzh
Keep the change.	Gardez la monnaie. gar-day lah moh-nay
Change, please.	La monnaie, s'il vous plaît. lah moh-nay see voo play
This is for you.	C'est pour vous. say poor voo

SPECIAL CONCERNS

In a Hurry

Europeans take their time at meals, so don't expect speedy service. However, if you're in a rush, be proactive and let your server know in advance, or seek out a *brasserie* or restaurant that offers *service rapide* (fast food).

I'm / We're in a hurry.	Je suis / Nous sommes pressé. zhuh swee / noo suhm preh-say
I'm sorry.	Désolé. day-zoh-lay
I need / We need...	J'ai besoin / Nous avons besoin... zhay buh-zwan / nooz ah-vohn buh-zwan
...to be served quickly.	...d'être servi vite. deh-truh sehr-vee veet
I must / We must...	Je dois / Nous devons... zhuh dwah / noo duh-vohn
...leave in 30 minutes / one hour.	...partir dans trente minutes / une heure. par-teer dahn trahnt mee-newt / ewn ur
Will the food be ready soon?	Ce sera prêt bientôt? suh suh-rah preh bee-an-toh
The bill, please.	L'addition, s'il vous plaît. lah-dee-see-ohn see voo play

Allergies and Other Dietary Restrictions

Think of your meal (as the French do) as if it's a finely crafted creation by a trained artist. The chef knows what goes well together, and substitutions are considered an insult to his training. Picky eaters should just take it or leave it. However, French restaurants are willing to accommodate genuine dietary restrictions and other special concerns (or at least point you to an appropriate choice on the menu). These phrases might help. If the food you're unable to eat doesn't appear in this list, look for it in the Menu Decoder (next chapter). You'll find vegetarian phrases in the next section.

I'm allergic to...	Je suis allergique à... zhuh sweez ah-lehr-zheek ah
I cannot eat...	Je ne peux pas manger de... zhuh nuh puh pah mahn-zhay duh
He / She cannot eat...	Il / Elle ne peut pas manger de... eel / ehl nuh puh pah mahn-zhay duh

He / She has a life-threatening allergy to...	Il / Elle a une allergie très grave à... eel / ehl ah ewn ah-lehr-zhee treh grahv ah
No...	Non... nohn
...dairy products.	...aux produits laitiers. oh proh-dwee layt-yay
...any kind of nut.	...aux toutes sortes de noix. oh toot sort duh nwah
...peanuts.	...aux cacahuètes. oh kah-kah-weht
...walnuts.	...aux noix. oh nwah
...wheat / gluten.	...au blé / au gluten. oh blay / oh glew-tehn
...shellfish.	...crustacés. krew-stah-say
...salt / sugar.	...sel / sucre. sehl / sew-kruh
I'm a diabetic.	Je suis diabétique. zhuh swee dee-ah-bay-teek
He / She is lactose intolerant.	Il / Elle est intolérant au lactose. eel / ehl ay an-toh-lay-rahnt oh lahk-tohz
I'd like / We'd like a meal that's...	Je voudrais / Nous voudrions un repas qui est... zhuh voo-dray / noo voo-dree-ohn uhn ruh-pah kee ay
...kosher.	...kasher. kah-shehr
...halal.	...halal. ah-lahl
...low-fat.	...allege en matières grasses. ah-lehzh ahn mah-tee-yehr grahs
Low cholesterol.	Allégé. ah-lay-zhay
No caffeine.	Décaféiné. day-kah-fay-nay
No alcohol.	Sans alcool. sahnz ahl-kohl
Organic.	Biologique. bee-oh-loh-zheek
I eat only insects.	Je ne mange que les insectes. zhuh nuh mahnzh kuh layz an-sehkt

Vegetarian Phrases

Many French people think "vegetarian" means "no red meat" or "not much meat." If you're a strict vegetarian, be very specific: Tell your server what you don't eat—and it can be helpful to clarify what you do eat. Write it out on a card and keep it handy.

I'm a...	Je suis... zhuh swee
...vegetarian. (male)	...végétarien. vay-zhay-tah-ree-an
...vegetarian. (female)	...végétarienne. vay-zhay-tah-ree-ehn
...strict vegetarian.	...strict végétarien. streekt vay-zhay-tah-ree-an
...vegan. (m / f)	...végétalien / végétalienne. vay-zhay-tah-lee-an / vay-zhay-tah-lee-ehn
Is any animal product used in this?	Il y a des produits d'origine animale dedans? eel yah day proh-dwee doh-ree-zheen ah-nee-mahl duh-dahn
What is vegetarian? (pointing to menu)	Qu'est-ce qu'il y a de végétarien? kehs keel yah duh vay-zhay-tah-ree-an
I don't eat...	Je ne mange pas... zhuh nuh mahnzh pah
I'd like this without...	Je voudrais cela sans... zhuh voo-dray suh-lah sahn
...meat.	...viande. vee-ahnd
...eggs.	...oeufs. uhf
...animal products.	...produits d'origine animale. proh-dwee doh-ree-zheen ah-nee-mahl
I eat...	Je mange... zhuh mahnzh
Do you have...?	Avez-vous...? ah-vay-voo
...anything with tofu	...quelque chose avec du tofu kehl-kuh shohz ah-vehk dew toh-few
...a veggie burger	...un hamburger végétarien uhn ahn-bur-gehr vay-zhay-tah-ree-an

Children

Do you have a...?	Vous avez...? vooz ah-vay
...children's menu	...une carte d'enfants ewn kart dah<u>n</u>-fah<u>n</u>
...children's portion	...une assiette enfant ewn ahs-yeht ah<u>n</u>-fah<u>n</u>
...half-portion	...une demi-portion ewn duh-mee-por-see-oh<u>n</u>
...high chair	...une chaise haute ewn shehz oht
...booster seat	...un réhausseur uh<u>n</u> ray-oh-sur
noodles / rice	pâtes / riz paht / ree
with butter	avec beurre ah-vehk bur
without sauce	pas de sauce pah duh sohs
sauce or dressing on the side	sauce à part sohs ah par
pizza	pizza "pizza"
...cheese only	...juste fromage zhewst froh-mahzh
...pepperoni	...chorizo shoh-ree-zoh
grilled ham and cheese sandwich	croque monsieur krohk muhs-yuh
hot dog and fries	saucisse-frites soh-sees-freet
hamburger	hamburger ah<u>n</u>-bur-gehr
cheeseburger	cheeseburger sheez-bur-gehr
French fries	frites freet
ketchup	ketchup "ketchup"
milk	lait lay
straw	paille pī-yuh
More napkins, please.	Des serviettes, s'il vous plaît. day sehrv-yeht see voo play

EATING

Special Concerns

WHAT'S COOKING?

Breakfast

French hotel breakfasts are small, expensive, and often optional. The basic continental breakfast has three parts: (1) *boisson chaude*—a hot drink, such as *café au lait* (coffee with milk), *thé* (tea), or *chocolat chaud* (hot chocolate); (2) *viennoiserie*—your choice of sweet rolls, including *croissants*; and (3) *une tartine*—a fancy word for a *baguette* with *beurre* (butter) and *confiture* (jam). You may also get some *jus de fruit* (fruit juice, usually orange), but it likely costs extra. Many hotels now provide breakfast buffets with fruit, cereal, yogurt, and cheese (usually for a few extra euros and well worth it).

You can save money by breakfasting at a *bar* or *café*, where it's usually acceptable to bring in a *croissant* from the neighboring *boulangerie* (bakery). Or just order *une tartine* with your *café au lait*. French people almost never eat eggs for breakfast, but if you're desperate, you can get an *omelette* almost any time of day at a café.

I'd like / We'd like...	Je voudrais / Nous voudrions... zhuh voo-dray / noo voo-dree-ohn
breakfast	petit déjeuner puh-tee day-zhuh-nay
bread	pain pan
roll	petit pain puh-tee pan
little loaf of bread	baguette bah-gheht
toast	toast "toast"
butter	beurre bur
jam	confiture kohn-fee-tewr
honey	miel mee-ehl
fruit cup	salade de fruits sah-lahd duh frwee
pastry	pâtisserie pah-tee-suh-ree
croissant	croissant krwah-sahn
cheese	fromage froh-mahzh
yogurt	yaourt yah-oort
cereal	céréale say-ray-ahl

Key Phrases: What's Cooking?

food	nourriture noo-ree-tewr
breakfast	petit déjeuner puh-tee day-zhuh-nay
lunch	déjeuner day-zhuh-nay
dinner	dîner dee-nay
bread	pain pan
cheese	fromage froh-mahzh
soup	soupe soop
salad	salade sah-lahd
fish	poisson pwah-sohn
chicken	poulet poo-lay
meat	viande vee-ahnd
vegetables	légumes lay-gewm
fruit	fruit frwee
dessert	dessert day-sehr

milk	lait lay
coffee / tea	café / thé kah-fay / tay
fruit juice	jus de fruit zhew duh frwee
orange juice (fresh)	jus d'orange (pressé) zhew doh-rahnzh (preh-say)
hot chocolate	chocolat chaud shoh-koh-lah shoh

Pastries

Baked goods are divided into two general categories: a **boulangerie** specializes in breads and yeasty sweet rolls (such as **croissants** or **brioche**, collectively called **viennoiserie**). A **pâtisserie** deals with cakes and other treats. It's said that a baker cannot be both good at bread and good at pastry. That's not always the case, though at cooking school, they major in one or the other. In general, people eat *viennoiserie* earlier in the day and *pâtisserie* later in the day. Here are a few examples of *viennoiserie*, which break into general categories.

These *viennoiserie* are made with puff pastry *(pâte feuilletée)*—buttery, crispy, and flaky:

croissant krwah-sah<u>n</u>
classic French crescent roll

pain au chocolat pa<u>n</u> oh shoh-koh-lah
buttery, flaky pastry filled with chocolate (sometimes called "chocolate croissant")

palmier pahlm-yay
"palm"-shaped, light and delicate buttery pastry

chausson aux pommes shoh-soh<u>n</u> oh pohm
"slipper" filled with apples (like an apple turnover)

grillé pommes gree-yay pohm
apple-filled pastry with "grill" pattern

anglaise ahn-glehz
"English" apple pastry with large vents cut into the top

oranais oh-rah<u>n</u>-ay
apricot danish

jesuit zhehz-weet
pastry filled with almond crème, shaped like a Jesuit's triangular hat

mille-feuille meel-fuh-ee
light pastry with a "thousand sheets" of delicate dough and layers of cream; a.k.a. Napoleon

pithivier pee-teev-yay
spiral pie made of puff pastry, usually filled with almond paste

vol-au-vent vohl-oh-vah<u>n</u>
hollow, cylindrical pastry that's so light it's called "windblown"; generally cherry-filled, but sometimes savory

jambon-mornay zhah<u>n</u>-boh<u>n</u>-mor-nay
savory puff pastry with ham and cheese

Pastries (cont.)

These are puffier and more bread-like:

brioche bree-ohsh
big, puffy roll made with eggs

cramique krah-meek
brioche bread with raisins ("ceramic")

pain aux raisins / escargot raisins
pan oh ray-zan / ehs-kar-goh ray-zan
spiral, "snail"-shaped, glazed pastry with raisins

pain au lait pan oh lay
"milk bread"; small, flaky roll

tresse trehs
"braid"-shaped brioche

cannelé kah-nuh-lay
small, "fluted" pastry with caramelized crust and custard filling

These are heavier, using an eggy dough with lots of butter and no yeast
(called **pâte à choux**):

beignet behn-yay
deep-fried dough triangle sprinkled with powdered sugar

profiterole proh-fee-tuh-rohl
cream puff

chouquette shoo-keht
dense little baked doughnut speckled with sugar

éclair ay-klair oblong, iced sweet roll filled with custard

religieuse ruh-lee-zhee-uhz round éclair shaped like a nun

Other goodies are prepared in a variety of ways:

macaron mah-kah-rohn
cookie with a puffy but hard crust sandwiching a thin layer of cream

madeleine mah-duh-lehn
bite-size buttery sponge cake with a shell-like shape

mignardise   meen-yar-deez
miniature petit four (see next)

petit four   puh-tee foor
bite-sized, frosted cake served at parties

roulé aux noix   roo-lay oh nwah
"walnut roll" with a layer of nutty paste

tarte   tart
miniature pie, generally filled with fruit

For other types of desserts—as well as handy phrases for fillings in many of the above items—see page 156.

What's Probably Not for Breakfast

You likely won't see any of these items at a traditional French breakfast table, but you may see them at international hotels or cafés catering to foreigners.

omelet	omelette	oh-muh-leht
eggs	des oeufs	dayz uhf
fried eggs	oeufs au plat	uhf oh plah
scrambled eggs	oeufs brouillés	uhf broo-yay
boiled egg...	oeuf à la coque...	uhf ah lah kohk
...soft / hard	...mollet / dur	moh-lay / dewr
poached egg	oeuf poché	uhf poh-shay
ham	jambon	zhahn-bohn

Snacks and Quick Lunches

omelet	omelette	oh-muh-leht
quiche...	quiche...	keesh
...with cheese	...au fromage	oh froh-mahzh
...with ham	...au jambon	oh zhahn-bohn
...with onions	...aux oignons	ohz ohn-yohn

EATING

What's Cooking?

...with leeks	...aux poireaux	oh pwah-roh
...with mushrooms	...aux champignons oh shahn-peen-yohn	
...with bacon, cheese, and onions	...lorraine lor-rehn	
...with tuna	...au thon	oh tohn
...with salmon	...au saumon	oh soh-mohn
paté	pâté	pah-tay
onion tart	tarte à l'oignon	tart ah lohn-yohn
cheese tart	tarte au fromage	tart oh froh-mahzh

Light meals are quick and easy at *cafés, brasseries,* and *bars* throughout France. (These are about the same, except that *brasseries* serve food all day, whereas some *cafés* close their kitchens between lunch and dinner—around 4 p.m. to 6 p.m.—but stay open to serve snacks and drinks.) These places generally have more limited menus than restaurants, but they offer more budget options.

A *salade, crêpe* (see next), *quiche,* or *omelette* is a fairly cheap way to fill up, even in Paris. Each can be made with various extras like ham, cheese, mushrooms, and so on.

Crêpes

The quintessentially French thin pancake called a *crêpe* (rhymes with "step," not "grape") is a good budget standby: It's filling, usually inexpensive, and generally quick. A place that sells them is a *crêperie* (krehp-eh-ree).

Crêpes generally come in two types: *sucrée* (sweet) and *salée* (savory). Technically, a savory *crêpe* should be made with a heartier buckwheat batter, and is called a *galette* (gah-leht). However, many cheap and lazy *crêperies* use the same sweet batter *(de froment)* for both their sweet and savory *crêpes.*

For savory *crêpes,* the standard toppings include *fromage* (cheese, usually Swiss-style Gruyère or Emmental), *jambon* (ham), *oeuf* (an egg that's cracked and scrambled right on the hot plate), and *champignons* (mushrooms).

For sweet *crêpes*, common toppings are *chocolat* (chocolate syrup), Nutella (the delicious milk chocolate-hazelnut spread), jam or jelly, and powdered sugar.

savory crêpe	crêpe salée krehp sah-lay
buckwheat crêpe	galette gah-leht
with...	au... oh
...cheese	...fromage froh-mahzh
...ham	...jambon zhah<u>n</u>-boh<u>n</u>
...eggs	...oeufs uhf
...mushrooms	...champignons shah<u>n</u>-peen-yoh<u>n</u>
sweet crêpe	crêpe sucrée krehp sew-kray
with...	au... oh
...sugar	...sucre sew-kruh
...chocolate	...chocolat shoh-koh-lah
...Nutella	...Nutella new-teh-lah
...jam	...confiture koh<u>n</u>-fee-tewr
...whipped cream	...chantilly shah<u>n</u>-tee-yee
...apple jam	...compote de pommes koh<u>n</u>-poht duh pohm
...chestnut cream	...crème de marrons krehm duh mah-roh<u>n</u>
...orange liqueur	...Grand Marnier grah<u>n</u> marn-yay
chickpea crêpe	socca soh-kah

During slow times, the *crêperie* chef might make several *crêpes* to be stacked up, then reheated later. Don't be surprised if he doesn't make a fresh one for you.

EATING What's Cooking?

Sandwiches

I'd like a sandwich.	Je voudrais un sandwich. zhuh voo-dray uh<u>n</u> sah<u>n</u>d-weech
toasted	grillé gree-yay
cheese	fromage froh-mahzh
tuna	thon toh<u>n</u>
fish	poisson pwah-soh<u>n</u>
chicken	poulet poo-lay
turkey	dinde da<u>n</u>d
ham	jambon zhah<u>n</u>-boh<u>n</u>
salami	salami sah-lah-mee
boiled egg	oeuf dur uhf dewr
garnished with veggies	crudités krew-dee-tay
lettuce	salade sah-lahd
tomato	tomate toh-maht
onions	oignons ohn-yoh<u>n</u>
mustard	moutarde moo-tard
mayonnaise	mayonnaise mah-yoh-nehz
without mayonnaise	sans mayonnaise sah<u>n</u> mah-yoh-nehz
peanut butter	beurre de cacahuètes bur duh kah-kah-weht
jam / jelly	confiture koh<u>n</u>-fee-tewr
pork sandwich	sandwich au porc sah<u>n</u>d-weech oh por
grilled / heated	grillé / réchauffé gree-yay / ray-shoh-fay
Does this come cold or warm?	C'est servi froid ou chaud? say sehr-vee frwah oo shoh

Sandwiches, as well as small quiches, often come ready-made at **bou-langeries** (bakeries). When buying a sandwich, you might see signs for **emporté** (to go) or **sur place** (to eat here).

Types of Sandwiches

Here are a few basic sandwich options you're likely to see.

canapé kah-nah-pay
small, open-faced sandwich

croque madame krohk mah-dahm
grilled ham and cheese sandwich topped with a fried egg

croque monsieur krohk muhs-yuh
grilled ham and cheese sandwich

jambon beurre zhah<u>n</u>-boh<u>n</u> bur
ham and butter (boring for most)

jambon crudités zhah<u>n</u>-boh<u>n</u> krew-dee-tay
ham with tomatoes, lettuce, cucumbers, and mayonnaise

pain salé pa<u>n</u> sah-lay
bread rolled up with salty bits of bacon, cheese, or olives

pan bagnat pah<u>n</u> bahn-yah
tuna salad (salade niçoise) stuffed into a hollowed-out soft roll

poulet crudités poo-lay krew-dee-tay
chicken with tomatoes, lettuce, maybe cucumbers, and mayonnaise

saucisson beurre soh-see-soh<u>n</u> bur
thinly sliced sausage and butter

tartine tar-teen
slice of bread with toppings (like an open-faced sandwich)

thon crudités toh<u>n</u> krew-dee-tay
tuna with tomatoes, lettuce, maybe cucumbers, and mayonnaise

à la provençale ah lah proh-vah<u>n</u>-sahl
with marinated peppers, tomatoes, and eggplant

à la italienne ah lah ee-tahl-yehn
grilled panini

A slice of bread topped with just about anything is called a *tartine.* These all-purpose, open-faced sandwiches are so beloved that French youth use the word *tartine* as a slang term meaning "cool."

Crunchy, grilled *croque* sandwiches (literally "crunch")—such as the *croque madame* or the *croque monsieur*—are a French café staple.

Other variations include *croque provençal* (with tomato), *croque norvégien* (with smoked salmon), *croque tartiflette* (with potatoes), *croque sucré* (a sweet variation with powdered sugar), and even *croque hawaiian* (with pineapple).

If You Knead Bread

A good baker *(boulanger)* is a highly valued commodity within his or her community; it's said that "good bread makes a happy village." Here are a few of the many types of bread you'll find in French *boulangeries*.

pain pan
bread

baguette bah-geht
big ol' "stick" of white bread

baguette de tradition bah-geht duh trah-dee-see-yohn
traditional baguette, made according to government specifications

flûte flewt
"flute," slightly slimmer than a baguette

bâtard bah-tar
"bastard," larger version of a baguette

ficelle fee-sehl
"string," super-thin baguette

couronne koo-ruhn
"crown," ring-shaped baguette that can be broken into individual rolls

gros pain groh pan
"fat" baguette

miche meesh
large round loaf

boule bool
round loaf (like a squashed "ball")

pain de campagne pan duh kahn-pahn-yuh
"country bread" with various grains and a thicker crust (often a large circular loaf)

pain complet pan kohn-play
wholemeal bread

multicéréales mewl-tee-say-ray-ahl
multigrain

pain au froment pan oh froh-mahn
wheat bread

pain de seigle pan duh seh-gluh
rye bread

pain au levain pan oh luh-van
sourdough ("yeast") bread

pain bis pan bees
dark-grain bread

pain pavé pan pah-vay
"cobblestone"-shaped bread, often rye

pain de mie pan duh mee
American-style sandwich bread

pain viennois pan vee-ehn-wah
soft, shiny, slightly sweeter baguette

pain doré / pain perdu pan doh-ray / pan pehr-dew
French toast ("golden bread" / "lost bread")

pain d'épices pan day-pees
gingerbread ("spice bread")

petit pain puh-tee pan
roll

Poilâne pwah-lahn
big, round loaf of rustic bread with floured crust

tartine tar-teen
baguette slice slathered with toppings, often butter and / or jam

brioche bree-ohsh
sweet, soft bun (for more pastries, see page 122)

fougasse foo-gahs
spindly, lace-like bread sometimes flavored with nuts, herbs,
olives, or ham

If You Knead Bread *(cont.)*

pain brié pa<u>n</u> bree-ay
dense, crusty, football-shaped bread with ridges

pissaladière pee-sah-lahd-yehr
bread dough topped with onions, olives, and anchovies

croûte au fromage kroot oh froh-mahzh
cheese pastry

gougères goo-zhehr
savory cream puffs made with cheese

Other terms you might see at a *boulangerie* include *quotidien* (every-day), *ordinaire* (ordinary), *de ménage* or *fait maison* (homemade), *paysanne* (peasant), *à l'ancienne* (old-fashioned), and *de fantasie* (fancy; sometimes means sold by the piece). *Gana* and *Banette* are specific brands of baguettes.

Say Cheese

Like fine wines, French cheeses come in a staggering variety—each one with its own subtle features. Cheeses range from very fresh (aged one day) to aged for weeks. The older the cheese, the more dried and shrunken. Cheeses come in many shapes (round, logs, pyramids) and various sizes (from single-bite mouthfuls to wheels that will feed you for several meals). Some are sprinkled with herbs or spices; others are speckled with edible mold; and still others are more adorned, such as those rolled in ash *(à la cendre)* or wrapped in leaves *(banon)*.

Broadly speaking, French cheeses are divided into a few categories:

cheese	fromage froh-mahzh
goat	chèvre sheh-vruh
cow	vache vahsh
sheep / ewe	brebis bruh-bee
blue	bleu bluh
gooey cheese with edible rind (like brie)	à pâte molle ah paht mohl

Specific Qualities of Cheese

Once you've settled on the type of cheese, you can hone in on the characteristics you'd like.

I like cheese that is...	J'aime le fromage qui est... zhehm luh froh-mahzh kee ay
young (smooth)	ferme fehrm
aged (mature, stronger flavor)	bien fait bee-an fay
mild or soft	doux doo
sharp	fort for
hard / soft / semi-soft	dur / mou / plutôt mou dewr / moo / plew-toh moo
nutty	le goût de noisettes luh goo duh nwah-zeht
pungent	relevé ruh-luh-vay
with herbs	aux herbes ohz ehrb
with spices	aux épices ohz ay-pees
rolled in ashes	aux cendres oh san-druh
creamy	à la crème ah lah krehm
of the region	de la région duh lah ray-zhee-ohn
rind	croûte kroot
bloomy / washed / natural	fleurie / lavée / naturelle fluh-ree / lah-vay / nah-tew-rehl
interior part of cheese	pâte paht

When it comes to soft, like brie, there are two types of rinds: A "bloomy" rind (*croûte fleurie*) is mild and lighter-colored (white or off-white), while a washed rind (*croûte lavée*) is orange or reddish and more pungent. Harder cheeses usually have a natural rind (*croûte naturelle*)—hard and inedible.

In the Cheese Shop

Visit a *fromagerie* or a *crémerie* (cheese shop) and experiment, using the terms in the previous table. Consider simply putting yourself in the *fromagerie* clerk's capable hands—ask her to choose for you. She might appreciate the chance to help you select a few that complement each other and show off her craft. Don't expect to be offered a taste.

Some cheeses come in hockey-puck-sized disks called *crottin* (kroh-tan). You can't just buy part of a *crottin*—you must get the whole thing. Other cheeses come in larger wheels that can be sliced. When cutting you a *tranche* (trah<u>n</u>sh; slice), the *fromagerie* clerk will want to know how much you want: *Comme ça?* (Like this?) *Plus?* (More?) *Moins?* (Less?). And especially for the little *crottins* of soft cheeses, plan to eat them the same day—they don't keep.

cheese shop	fromagerie / crémerie froh-mah-zhuh-ree / kray-muh-ree
cheese platter	plâteau de fromages plah-toh duh froh-mahzh
I would like three types of cheese for a picnic.	Je voudrais trois sortes de fromage pour une pique-nique. zhuh voo-dray trwah sort duh froh-mahzh poor ewn peek-neek
I like a cheese that is _____ and _____. (use phrases in previous table)	J'aime un fromage qui est _____ et _____. zhehm uh<u>n</u> froh-mahzh kee ay _____ ay _____
Choose for me, please.	Choisissez pour moi, s'il vous plaît. shwah-zee-say poor mwah see voo play
What type?	Quel sorte? kehl sort
Like this. (showing size)	Comme ça. kohm sah

Cheese Specialties

There are over 500 different French cheeses to try; here's a selection of my favorites.

Auvergne oh-vehrn-yuh
broad category of cow cheese, sold in big wheels

Aisy Cendré ay-zee sahn-druh
soft, Époisses-like cow cheese coated in ash

Banon de Banon / Banon à la feuille
bah-nohn duh bah-nohn / bah-nohn ah lah fuh-ee
goat cheese soaked in *eau-de-vie* (the highly alcoholic "water of life"), then wrapped in chestnut leaves

Beaufort boh-for
hard, sharp, strong cow cheese aged for two years; like "Swiss cheese" but with no holes

Bleu d'Auvergne bluh doh-vehrn-yuh
pungent blue cow cheese

Boursin boor-san
soft, creamy cow cheese with herbs

Brie (de Meaux) bree (duh moh)
mild, flowery, creamy, soft (almost runny) cow cheese with an edible white rind, sold in large wedges

Brillat-Savarin bree-yah-sah-vah-ran
buttery, slightly sour Brie variant

Brocciu broh-choo
sweet, fresh Corsican goat or ewe cheese

Brousse du Rove broos dew rohv
fresh, creamy goat cheese, often served with cream and sugar

Cabécou kah-bay-koo
silver-dollar-size, pungent, nutty-flavored goat cheese

Camembert kah-mahn-behr
pungent, semi-creamy cow cheese sold in round wooden containers

Cantal kahn-tahl
aged, semi-hard cow cheese, sold in big wheels

Cheese Specialties *(cont.)*

Cendré de Champagne sahn-druh duh shahn-pahn-yuh
similar to Brie but the size of a large Camembert, with a thin, edible
ash covering

Comté kohn-tay
Gruyère-like "Swiss cheese" from cow's milk

Coulommiers koo-lohm-yay
soft, rich, creamy, Brie-like cow cheese

Crottin de Chavignol kroh-tan duh shah-veen-yohl
small flattened ball of goat cheese; turns blue and becomes
crumbly with age

Echourgnac eh-shoorn-yahk
Trappist monk-made cow cheese with brown rind

Emmentaler eh-mahn-tah-lay
classic "Swiss cheese," with holes

Époisses (de Bourgogne) ay-pwahs (duh boor-gohn-yuh)
gooey, pungent, rich cow cheese with orange rind sold in small,
round wooden containers

Fourme d'Ambert foorm dahn-behr
pungent, semi-hard blue cow cheese

Gruyère grew-yehr
"Swiss cheese" from the French Swiss town of the same name

Langres lahn-gruh
soft cow cheese similar to Époisses but less flavorful

Livarot lee-vah-roh
pungent, "barnyard"-scented cow cheese with a rich, creamy taste

Montrachet mohn-trah-shay
soft, tangy goat cheese, often covered in ash

Morbier mor-bee-yay
semi-soft cow cheese with a charcoal streak down the middle

Munster mewn-stehr
stinky, soft, aged cow cheese

Ossau-Iraty oh-soh-ee-rah-tee
smooth, firm, buttery ewe's cheese

Pavé d'Auge pah-vay dohzh
spicy, tangy, square-shaped cow cheese

Pélardon pay-lar-doh<u>n</u>
nutty, round goat cheese

Picodon pee-koh-doh<u>n</u>
spicy goat cheese

Pont l'Evêque poh<u>n</u> lay-vehk
flavorful, smooth, square-shaped cow cheese with an earthy flavor

Port Salut por sah-lew
semi-soft, sweet cow cheese served in a wedge

Pur Brebis pewr bruh-bee
"pure sheep" cheese from the Pyrenees

Reblochon ruh-bloh-shoh<u>n</u>
soft, gooey, mild, creamy, Brie-like cow cheese

Roquefort rohk-for
powerful, blue-veined, tangy sheep cheese

Selles-sur-Cher sehl-sewr-shehr
mild goat cheese

Saint-Marcellin sa<u>n</u>-mar-suh-la<u>n</u>
soft cow cheese with white edible rind

Sainte-Maure sa<u>n</u>t-mor
soft, creamy goat cheese in a cylindrical shape (Loire)

Saint-Nectaire sa<u>n</u>-nehk-tair
semi-soft, nutty cow cheese sold in big rounds

Tomme (de Savoie) tohm (duh sah-vwah)
mild, semi-soft cow cheese

Valençay vah-lah<u>n</u>-say
firm, nutty, ash- and mold-covered goat cheese shaped like a flat-topped pyramid

Soups and Stews

soup (of the day)	soupe (du jour)	soop (dew zhoor)
broth...	bouillon...	boo-yoh<u>n</u>
...chicken	...de poulet	duh poo-lay
...beef	...de boeuf	duh buhf
...with noodles	...aux nouilles	oh noo-ee
...with rice	...au riz	oh ree
thick vegetable soup	potage de légumes	poh-tahzh duh lay-gewm
Provençal vegetable soup	soupe au pistou	soop oh pee-stoo
onion soup	soupe à l'oignon	soop ah lohn-yoh<u>n</u>
cream of asparagus soup	crème d'asperges	krehm dah-spehrzh
potato and leek soup	vichyssoise	vee-shee-swahz
garlic soup	soupe à l'ail / tourin	soop ah lī / too-ra<u>n</u>
shellfish chowder	bisque	beesk
seafood stew	bouillabaisse	boo-yah-behs
meat and vegetable stew	pot au feu	poht oh fuh
meat stew	ragoût	rah-goo

Salads

Salads are usually served with a vinaigrette dressing and often eaten after the main course (to aid digestion).

salad...	salade...	sah-lahd
...green / mixed	...verte / mixte	vehrt / meekst
...with goat cheese	...au chèvre chaud	oh sheh-vruh shoh
...chef's	...composée	koh<u>n</u>-poh-zay
...seafood	...océane	oh-say-ahn
...tuna	...de thon	duh toh<u>n</u>

...veggie	...crudités krew-dee-tay
...with ham / cheese / egg	...avec jambon / fromage / oeuf ah-vehk zhahn-bohn / froh-mahzh / uhf
lettuce	laitue / salade lay-tew / sah-lahd
tomatoes	tomates toh-maht
onions	oignons ohn-yohn
cucumber	concombre kohn-kohn-bruh
oil / vinegar	huile / vinaigre weel / vee-nay-gruh
dressing on the side	sauce à part sohs ah par
What is in this salad?	Qu'est-ce qu'il ya dans cette salade? kehs keel yah dahn seht sah-lahd

Salad Specialties

Here are a few salads you'll see on café menus. They're typically large— one is perfect for lunch or a light dinner.

salade niçoise sah-lahd nee-swahz
green salad topped with green beans, tomatoes, anchovies, olives, hard-boiled eggs, and tuna

salade au chèvre chaud sah-lahd oh sheh-vruh shoh
green salad topped with warm goat cheese on toasted bread croutons

salade composée sah-lahd kohn-poh-zay
"composed" of multiple ingredients, which can include bacon, Comté or Roquefort cheese, egg, walnuts, and ham

salade paysanne sah-lahd pī-sahn
usually comes with potatoes, walnuts, tomatoes, ham, and egg

salade aux gésiers sah-lahd oh gay-zee-ay
salad with chicken gizzards (and often slices of duck)

salade lyonnaise sah-lahd lee-oh-nehz
croutons, fried bits of ham, and a poached egg on a bed of lettuce

First Courses and Appetizers

These smaller dishes are typically served at the start of the meal. See also "Soups and Stews" and "Salads" on page 138.

artichauts à la vinaigrette   ar-tee-shoh ah lah vee-nay-greht
artichokes in a vinaigrette dressing

bouchée à la reine   boo-shay ah lah rehn
pastry shell filled with creamed veal brains and mushrooms

crudités   krew-dee-tay
raw and lightly cooked fresh vegetables with vinaigrette

escargots   ehs-kar-goh
snails baked in the shell with garlic butter

(pâté de) foie gras   (pah-tay duh) fwah grah
rich, expensive goose- or duck-liver spread

huîtres   wee-truh
oysters (usually served on the half shell)

oeuf mayo   uhf mah-yoh
hard-boiled egg topped with mayonnaise

oeufs en meurette   uhf ah<u>n</u> muh-reht
poached eggs in a red wine sauce, often served on a large crouton

pâté   pah-tay
smooth, highly seasoned ground meat (usually pork, sometimes game, poultry liver, or rabbit) that's served in slices with mustard and cornichons (little pickles)

pommes de terre duchesse   pohm duh tehr dew-shehs
"duchess potatoes"–mashed potatoes that are baked

quenelles   keh-nehl
dumplings with meat or fish in white sauce

soufflé   soo-flay
fluffy eggs baked with savory fillings (cheese, meat, and vegetables)

tapenade   tah-puh-nahd
paste made from olives, anchovies, lemon, and olive oil

terrine   tehr-een
chunkier form of pâté (see above) served in a deep pan

Seafood

seafood	fruits de mer frwee duh mehr
assorted seafood	assiette de fruits de mer ahs-yeht duh frwee duh mehr
fish	poisson pwah-sohn
shellfish	crustacés / coquillages krew-stah-say / koh-kee-ahzh
anchovies	anchois ahn-shwah
clams	palourdes pah-loord
cod	cabillaud kah-bee-yoh
crab	crabe krahb
halibut	flétan flay-tahn
herring	hareng ah-rahn
lobster	homard oh-mar
mussels	moules mool
oysters	huîtres wee-truh
prawns	scampi skahn-pee
salmon	saumon soh-mohn
salty cod	morue moh-rew
sardines	sardines sar-deen
scallops	coquilles Saint-Jacques koh-keel san-zhahk
shrimp	crevettes kruh-veht
squid	calamar kah-lah-mar
trout	truite trweet
tuna	thon tohn
How much for a portion?	C'est combien la portion? say kohn-bee-an lah por-see-ohn
What's fresh today?	Qu'est-ce que c'est frais aujourd'hui? kehs kuh say fray oh-joord-wee
How do you eat this?	Comment est-ce que ça se mange? koh-mahn ehs kuh sah suh mahnzh

| Do you eat this part? | Ça se mange? sah suh mahnzh |
| Just the head, please. | Seulement la tête, s'il vous plaît. suhl-mahn lah teht see voo play |

Poultry

poultry	volaille voh-lī
chicken	poulet poo-lay
duck	canard kah-nar
goose	oie wah
turkey	dinde dand
breast	le blanc / le filet luh blahn / luh fee-lay
thigh	la cuisse lah kwees
drumstick	le pilon luh pee-lohn
white meat	viande blanche vee-ahnd blahnsh
eggs	des oeufs dayz uhf
free-range	élevé en liberté / élevé en plein air ay-luh-vay ahn lee-behr-tay / ay-luh-vay ahn plehn air
How long has this been dead?	Il est mort depuis longtemps? eel ay mor duh-pwee lohn-tahn

Meat

meat	viande vee-ahnd
meat cured with salt / smoked meat	viandes salées / viandes fumées vee-ahnd sah-lay / vee-ahnd few-may
beef	boeuf buhf
boar	sanglier sahn-glee-ay
cold cuts	assiette de charcuterie ahs-yeht duh shar-kew-tuh-ree
cutlet	côtelette koh-tuh-leht

Avoiding Mis-Steaks

By American standards, the French undercook meats. In France, rare (*saignant,* literally "bloody") is nearly raw, medium (*à point*) is rare, and well done (*bien cuit*) is medium. These shorter cooking times help the meat from getting overcooked, since French steak is usually thinner and tougher than American steak. Also for this reason, French steak is always served with sauces (*au poivre* is a pepper sauce; *une sauce roquefort* is a blue-cheese sauce).

alive	vivant	vee-vahn
raw	cru	krew
very rare	bleu	bluh
rare	saignant	sehn-yahn
medium	à point	ah pwan
well-done	bien cuit	bee-an kwee
very well-done	très bien cuit	treh bee-an kwee
almost burnt	presque carbonisé	prehs-kuh kar-boh-nee-zay
thick hunk of prime steak	pavé	pah-vay
flank steak	bavette	bah-veht
hanger steak	onglet	ohn-glay
sirloin	faux-filet	foh-fee-lay
rib-eye steak	entrecôte	ahn-truh-koht
tenderloin	médaillon	may-dī-yohn
T-bone	côte de boeuf	koht duh buhf
fillet	filet	fee-lay
tenderloin of T-bone	tournedos	toor-nuh-doh

frog legs	cuisses de grenouilles
	kwees duh greh-noo-ee
ham	jambon zhahn-bohn
lamb	agneau ahn-yoh
mixed grill	grillades gree-yahd
mutton	mouton moo-tohn
organs	organes or-gahn
oxtail	queue de boeuf kuh duh buhf
pork	porc por
rabbit	lapin lah-pan
roast beef	rosbif rohs-beef
sausage	saucisse soh-sees
blood sausage	boudin noir boo-dan nwahr
snails	escargots ehs-kar-goh
steak	bifteck beef-tehk
veal	veau voh
venison	viande de chevreuil
	vee-ahnd duh shuh-vruh-ee
Is this cooked?	C'est cuit? say kwee

Meat, but...

These are the cheapest items on a menu for good reason.

brains	cervelle sehr-vehl
calf pancreas	ris de veau ree duh voh
calf liver	foie de veau fwah duh voh
calf kidneys	rognons de veau rohn-yohn duh voh
calf head	tête de veau teht duh voh
horse meat	viande de cheval
	vee-ahnd duh shuh-vahl
sausage made of intestines	andouillette
	ahn-doo-yeht

liver	foie fwah
tongue	langue lah<u>ng</u>
tripe	tripes / tablier de sapeur treep / tah-blee-ay duh sah-pur
dish of sheep's feet and tripe	pieds et paquets pee-ay ay pah-kay

Main Course Specialties

The "French Regional Specialties" sidebar (on pages 148-149) lists some unique dishes you'll find in certain areas of France, but the following (some of which started as regional dishes) have become standard menu items nationwide.

boeuf bourguignon buhf boor-geen-yoh<u>n</u>
beef stew slowly cooked in red wine and served with onions, bacon, potatoes, and mushrooms (Burgundy)

boudin blanc boo-da<u>n</u> blah<u>n</u>
bratwurst-like sausage

confit de canard koh<u>n</u>-fee duh kah-nar
duck that has been preserved in its own fat, then cooked in its fat, and often served with potatoes in the same fat (Dordogne)

coq au vin kohk oh va<u>n</u>
chicken braised ever so slowly in red wine, cooked until it melts in your mouth (Burgundy)

daube dohb
long and slowly simmered dish (usually with beef, sometimes with lamb), typically paired with noodles or other pasta

escalope normande ehs-kah-lohp nor-mah<u>n</u>d
turkey or veal in a cream sauce (Normandy)

gigot d'agneau zhee-goh dahn-yoh
leg of lamb often grilled and served with white beans; the best lamb, *pré salé*, has been raised in salt-marsh lands (Provence)

Main Course Specialties *(cont.)*

magret de canard   mah-gray duh kah-nar
sliced duck breast

poulet rôti   poo-lay roh-tee
roasted chicken on the bone—French comfort food

ratatouille   rah-tah-too-ee
mix of vegetables (often eggplant, zucchini, onions, and peppers) in
a thick, herb-flavored tomato sauce (Provence)

saumon   soh-moh<u>n</u>
salmon usually from the North Sea and served with sauce, most
commonly a sorrel *(oseille)* sauce; *saumon tartare* is raw salmon

steak haché (à cheval)   stehk ah-shay (ah shuh-vahl)
lean, gourmet hamburger patty served sans bun (with an egg on top)

steak tartare   stehk tar-tar
very lean, raw hamburger served with savory seasonings (usually
Tabasco, capers, raw onions, salt, and pepper on the side) and
topped with a raw egg yolk

How Food Is Prepared

aged	vieilli	vee-ay-ee
assorted	assiette / variés	ahs-yeht / vah-ree-ay
baked	cuit au four	kweet oh foor
boiled	bouilli	boo-yee
braised	braisé	breh-zay
breaded	pané	pah-nay
broiled	grillé	gree-yay
browned	doré	doh-ray
cold	froid	frwah
cooked	cuit	kwee
chopped	haché	ah-shay
crispy	croustillant	kroo-stee-ah<u>n</u>

(side margin) EATING   What's Cooking?

cured	salé / fumé
(salted / smoked)	sah-lay / few-may
deep-fried	frit free
fillet	filet fee-lay
fresh	frais fray
fried	frit free
garnish	garniture gar-nee-tewr
glazed	glacé glah-say
grated	râpé rah-pay
grilled	grillé gree-yay
homemade	fait maison fay may-zoh<u>n</u>
hot	chaud shoh
in cream sauce	en crème ah<u>n</u> krehm
juicy	juteux zhew-tuh
marinated	mariné mah-ree-nay
medium	à point ah pwa<u>n</u>
melted	fondu foh<u>n</u>-dew
microwave	four à micro-ondes foor ah mee-kroh-oh<u>n</u>d
mild	doux doo
minced	haché ah-shay
mixed	mixte meekst
pan-fried	poêlé poh-eh-lay
pickled	au vinaigre oh vee-nay-gruh
poached	poché poh-shay
rare	saignant sehn-yah<u>n</u>
raw	cru krew
roasted	rôti roh-tee
sautéed	sauté soh-tay
smoked	fumé few-may
steamed	à la vapeur ah lah vah-pur
stuffed	farci far-see
well-done	bien cuit bee-a<u>n</u> kwee

EATING What's Cooking?

French Regional Specialties

Alps (Chamonix): Try *raclette* (melted cheese over potatoes and meats), *fondue savoyarde* (cheese fondue), *gratin savoyard* (potatoes with cheese), *tartiflette* (scalloped potatoes with melted cheese), and *croziflette* (like *tartiflette* with buckwheat pasta).

Alsace (Colmar): Flavored by German heritage, Alsace is known for *choucroute garnie* (sauerkraut and sausage), *Rösti* (like hash browns), *Spätzle* (soft egg noodles), *tarte à l'oignon* (onion tart), *tarte flambée* (like a thin-crust pizza with cream, onion, and bacon bits), *Baeckeoffe* (stew of onions, meat, and potatoes), and *poulet/coq au Riesling* (chicken/rooster slow-cooked in white wine).

Basque Country (St-Jean-de-Luz): This region is known for its spicy red peppers called *piments d'Espelette.* Anything *basquaise* ("Basque-style") is cooked with tomato, eggplant, red pepper, and garlic. Dishes include *ttoro* (seafood stew) and *marmitako* (hearty tuna stew). The local dry-cured ham, *jambon de Bayonne,* is famous throughout France. *Gâteau basque* is a buttery cherry-and-almond cake.

Brittany (Dinan): Look for *galettes* (savory buckwheat crêpes), *huîtres* (oysters), and the frothy, fermented milk drink called *lait ribot*. Many dishes are prepared *marinière*, with a white-wine and shallot sauce.

Burgundy (Beaune): This wine region excels in *coq au vin* (chicken with wine sauce), *boeuf bourgignon* (beef stew cooked with wine, bacon, onions, potatoes, and mushrooms), *oeufs en meurette* (eggs poached in red wine), *escargots* (snails in garlic), *jambon persillé* (ham with garlic and parsley preserved in gelatin), *gougères* (eggy cheese puffs), and *moutarde de Dijon* (hot Dijon mustard).

Champagne (Reims): Dishes include *salade de pissenlit* (warm dandelion salad with bacon), *potée champenoise* (rabbit blood pudding), *jambon de Reims* (ham cooked in champagne and wrapped in a pastry shell), and *truite* (trout).

Dordogne/Périgord (Sarlat): The speciality here is *foie gras* (goose-liver pâté). Also try the *confit de canard* (duck cooked in its own fat), *salade périgourdine* (mixed green salad with *foie gras,* gizzards, and various duck parts), *pommes de terre sarladaise* (potatoes fried in duck fat), and anything with *noix* (walnuts).

Languedoc (Carcassonne): Try the hearty *cassoulet* (white bean, duck, and sausage stew), *canard* (duck), *cargolade* (snail, lamb, and sausage stew), and *aligot* (mashed potatoes with cheese).

Loire Valley (Amboise): Savor the fresh *truite* (trout), *veau* (veal), *rillettes* (cold, minced, shredded pork paté), *fromage du chèvre* (goat cheese), *aspèrges* (asparagus), and *champignons* (mushrooms).

Lyon: The culinary capital of France specializes in *salade lyonnaise* (croutons, fried ham, and a poached egg on a bed of lettuce), green lentils *(lentilles)* served on a salad or with sausages, *quenelles de brochet* (fish dumplings in a creamy sauce), and *filet de sandre* (whitefish).

Normandy (Bayeux): Munch some *moules* (mussels) and *escalope Normande* (veal in cream sauce). Swallow some *cidre* (hard apple cider) or *calvados* (apple brandy). *Trou Normand* is apple sorbet swimming in *calvados*.

Provence (Avignon): Sample the *soupe au pistou* (vegetable soup with garlic, cheese, and basil), *ratatouille* (eggplant, zucchini, tomatoes, onions, and green peppers), *brandade de morue* (salted cod in garlic cream), *tapenade* (a spread of pureed olives, garlic, and anchovies), *tians* (gratin-like vegetable dishes), *artichauts à la barigoule* (artichokes stuffed with garlic, ham, and herbs), and *riz de Camargue* (a reddish, chewy, nutty-tasting rice). *Tourte de blettes* is a confused "pie," made with Swiss chard, that's both savory and sweet.

Riviera (Nice): Dive into various fish stews: *bouillabaisse* (the classic, spicy fish stew), *soupe de poisson* (cheaper, simpler alternative to *bouillabaisse*), *bourride* (creamy fish soup), and *baudroie* (fishy soup cooked with vegetables and garlic). Other classics include *salade niçoise* (potatoes, tomatoes, olives, tuna, green beans, hard-boiled egg and anchovies) and *pan bagnat* (a *salade niçoise* on a bun).

French Cooking Styles

à l'anglaise ah lahn-glehz
boiled ("English")

au jus oh zhew
in its natural juices

basquaise bahs-kehz
with tomato, eggplant, red pepper, and garlic ("Basque-style")

bourguignon boor-geen-yohn
cooked in red wine ("Burgundy-style")

confit kohn-fee
any meat cooked in its own fat

fines herbes feen ehrb
with chopped fresh herbs

forestière foh-rehs-tee-yehr
with mushrooms

gratinée grah-tee-nay
topped with cheese, then broiled

jardinière zhar-deen-yehr
with vegetables

meunière muhn-yehr
coated with flour and fried in butter ("miller's wife")

nouvelle cuisine noo-vehl kwee-zeen
small portions of dishes from fresh ingredients; popular, relatively low-fat, and expensive

provençale proh-vahn-sahl
with tomatoes, garlic, olive oil, and herbs ("Provence-style")

roulade roo-lahd
anything "rolled" around a filling

savoyard sah-voy-ar
hearty alpine food, typically with melted cheese and / or potatoes

French Sauces

Sauces are a huge part of French cooking. In the early 20th century, the legendary French chef Auguste Escoffier identified five French "mother sauces" from which all others are derived: *béchamel* (milk-based white sauce), *espagnole* (veal-based brown sauce), *velouté* (stock-based white sauce), *hollandaise* (egg yolk-based white sauce), and *tomate* (tomato-based red sauce).

aïoli ah-ee-oh-lee
garlic mayonnaise

béchamel bay-shah-mehl
creamy, milk-based sauce

béarnaise bayr-nehz
sauce of egg yolks, butter, tarragon, white wine, and shallots

beurre blanc bur blahn
sauce of butter, white wine, and shallots

beurre noisette bur nwah-zeht
browned butter

crème fraîche krehm frehsh
"fresh cream" (similar to, but thinner than, sour cream)

crème normande krehm nor-mahnd
sauce of cream, cider, and spices

demi-glace duh-mee-glahs
"half-glazed" brown sauce

espagnole ehs-pahn-yohl
flavorful veal-based sauce

hollandaise oh-lahn-dayz
sauce of butter and egg yolks

marinière mah-reen-yehr
sauce of white wine, parsley, and shallots

mornay mor-nay
white sauce with grated Gruyère cheese

rouille roo-ee
thickened reddish mayonnaise heady with garlic and spicy peppers

soubise soo-beez
béchamel sauce (see above) with onion

tomate toh-maht
red sauce with tomato base

velouté vuh-loo-tay
light sauce, usually chicken or fish stock, thickened with flour

Flavors and Spices

spicy (hot)	piquant pee-kah<u>n</u>
spicy (flavorful)	épicée ay-pee-say
(too) salty	(trop) salé (troh) sah-lay
sour	aigre ay-gruh
sweet	doux doo
bitter	amer ah-mehr
cayenne	poivre de Cayenne pwah-vruh duh kah-yehn
cilantro	coriandre koh-ree-ah<u>n</u>-druh
cinnamon	cannelle kah-nehl
citrus fruits	agrumes ah-grewm
garlic	ail ī
herbs	herbes ehrb
horseradish	raifort ray-for
mint	menthe mah<u>n</u>t
paprika	paprika pah-pree-kah
parsley	persil pehr-seel
pepper	poivre pwah-vruh
saffron	safran sah-frah<u>n</u>
salt	sel sehl
sugar	sucre sew-kruh

You can look up more herbs and spices in the Menu Decoder (next chapter).

Veggies and Sides

vegetables	légumes	lay-gewm
mixed vegetables	légumes variés	lay-gewm vah-ree-ay
with vegetables	garni	gar-nee
artichoke	artichaut	ar-tee-shoh
arugula (rocket)	roquette	roh-keht
asparagus	asperges	ah-spehrzh
avocado	avocat	ah-voh-kah
beans	haricots	ah-ree-koh
beets	betterave	beh-tuh-rahv
broccoli	brocoli	broh-koh-lee
cabbage	chou	shoo
carrots	carottes	kah-roht
cauliflower	chou-fleur	shoo-flur
corn	maïs	mah-ees
cucumber	concombre	kohn-kohn-bruh
eggplant	aubergine	oh-behr-zheen
endive	endive	ahn-deev
fennel	fenouil	fuh-noo-ee
garlic	ail	ī
green beans	haricots verts	ah-ree-koh vehr
leeks	poireaux	pwah-roh
lentils	lentilles	lahn-teel
mushrooms	champignons	shahn-peen-yohn
olives	olives	oh-leev
onions	oignons	ohn-yohn
peas	petits pois	puh-tee pwah
pepper...	poivron...	pwah-vrohn
...green / red / yellow	...vert / rouge / jaune	vehr / roozh / zhohn
pickles	cornichons	kor-nee-shohn
potato	pomme de terre	pohm duh tehr

radish	radis rah-dee
rice	riz ree
spaghetti	spaghetti "spaghetti"
spinach	épinards ay-pee-nar
tomatoes	tomates toh-maht
truffles	truffes trewf
turnip	navet nah-vay
zucchini	courgette koor-zheht

In Provence, where olives are a specialty, you'll find several varieties. For example, *tanche* are plump, full-flavored, and black, while *picholine* are green and buttery.

There are also multiple types of mushrooms. The basic version is *champignon* (or *champignon de Paris*). Others include *chanterelle ou girolle* (big, yellow, wild chanterelle), *cèpe* (classic porcini-like boletus mushroom), *morille* (honeycomb-shaped morel mushroom), *mousseron* (meadow mushroom), and *pleurote* (oyster mushroom).

Fruits

fruit	fruit frwee
fruit cup	salade de fruits sah-lahd duh frwee
fruit smoothie	smoothie aux fruits smoo-zee oh frwee
apple	pomme pohm
apricot	abricot ah-bree-koh
banana	banane bah-nahn
berries	fruits rouges frwee roozh
blueberry	myrtille meer-tee
cantaloupe	melon muh-lohn
cherry	cerise suh-reez
cranberry	canneberge kah-nuh-behrzh
date	datte daht
fig	figue feeg

grapefruit	pamplemousse pahn-pluh-moos
grapes	raisins ray-zan
lemon	citron see-trohn
melon	melon muh-lohn
orange	orange oh-rahnzh
peach	pêche pehsh
pear	poire pwahr
pineapple	ananas ah-nah-nahs
plum	prune prewn
pomegranate	grenade gruh-nahd
prune	pruneau prew-noh
raisin	raisin sec ray-zan sehk
raspberry	framboise frahn-bwahz
strawberry	fraise frehz
tangerine	mandarine mahn-dah-reen
watermelon	pastèque pah-stehk

While *fraise* is a basic word for "strawberry," the French have more than 600 variations: *fraises des bois* are tiny, sweet, and less visually appealing strawberries found in nearby forests; other variations include *gariguettes* and *maras des bois*. Buy *une barquette* (small basket) to put them in, and suddenly your two-star hotel room is a three-star.

Likewise, the French have various names for watermelon: a *pastèque* is a particularly sweet one; a *citre* (also called a *gigérine*, *barbarine*, or *méréville*) is used only for making jams or pies.

Nuts to You

nuts	noix nwah
almond	amande ah-mahnd
chestnut	marron / châtaigne mah-rohn / shah-tehn-yuh
coconut	noix de coco nwah duh koh-koh

hazelnut	noisette nwah-zeht
peanut	cacahuète kah-kah-weht
pine nut	pignon de pin peen-yohn duh pan
pistachio	pistache pee-stahsh
seeds	graines grehn
sunflower	tournesol toor-nuh-sohl
walnut	noix nwah

Just Desserts

I'd like...	Je voudrais... zhuh voo-dray
We'd like...	Nous voudrions... noo voo-dree-ohn
dessert	dessert day-sehr
cookies	biscuits / petits gâteaux bees-kwee / puh-tee gah-toh
cake	gâteau gah-toh
ice cream...	glace... glahs
...scoop	...boule bool
...cone	...cornet kor-nay
...cup	...bol bohl
...vanilla	...vanille vah-nee
...chocolate	...chocolat shoh-koh-lah
...strawberry	...fraise frehz
sorbet	sorbet sor-bay
fruit cup	salade de fruits sah-lahd duh frwee
tart	tartelette tar-tuh-leht
pie	tarte tart
whipped cream	crème chantilly krehm shahn-tee-yee
pastry	pâtisserie pah-tee-suh-ree
crêpes	crêpes krehp
sweet crêpes	crêpes sucrées krehp sew-kray
candy	bonbon bohn-bohn

chocolates	chocolats	shoh-koh-lah
low calorie	bas en calories	bah ahn kah-loh-ree
homemade	fait maison	fay may-zohn
We'll split one.	Nous le partageons.	
	noo luh par-tah-zhohn	
Two forks / spoons, please.	Deux fourchettes / cuillères, s'il vous plaît.	
	duh foor-sheht / kwee-yehr see voo play	
I shouldn't, but...	Je ne devrais pas, mais...	
	zhuh nuh duh-vray pah may	
Magnificent!	Magnifique!	mahn-yee-feek
It's heavenly!	C'est divin!	say dee-van
Death by pleasure.	C'est à mourrir de plaisir.	
	say ah moo-reer duh play-zeer	
Orgasmic.	Orgasmique.	or-gahz-meek
A moment on the lips, forever on the hips.	Un moment sur les lèvres et pour toujours sur les hanches.	
	uhn moh-mahn sewr lay lehv-ruh ay poor too-zhoor sewr lay ahnsh	

Crème de la Crème

These are some of the desserts you'll likely see at restaurants.

baba au rhum bah-bah oh room
brioche-like cake drenched in rum and served with whipped cream

bavarois / crème bavaroise bah-var-wah / krehm bah-var-wahz
gelatin-thickened "Bavarian cream" pudding

café gourmand kah-fay goor-mahn
coffee served with an assortment of small desserts—a great way to sample several desserts and learn your favorite

clafoutis klah-foo-tee
baked fruit-custard pie

crème brûlée krehm brew-lay
rich caramelized custard

Crème de la Crème *(cont.)*

crème caramel krehm kah-rah-mehl
flan (solid custard) in caramel sauce

crêpes suzette krehp sew-zeht
crêpes flambéed with an orange brandy sauce

financier fee-nahns-yay
rectangular brown-butter sponge cake

fondant au chocolat / moelleux au chocolat
fohn-dahn oh shoh-koh-lah / mweh-luh oh shoh-koh-lah
molten chocolate cake with a runny (not totally cooked) center

fromage blanc froh-mahzh blahn
fresh white cheese eaten with sugar

gâteau gah-toh
cake, usually layered with pastry cream

île flottante eel floh-tahnt
meringues floating in cream sauce

mousse au chocolat moos oh shoh-koh-lah
ultra-light chocolate mousse

nougat de Montélimar noo-gah duh mohn-tay-lee-mar
rich, chewy confection made with nuts, honey, and sometimes
lavender

poires au vin rouge pwahr oh van roozh
pears poached in red wine and spices

profiterole proh-fee-tuh-rohl
cream puff, often filled with ice cream

riz au lait reez oh lay
rice pudding

soufflé au chocolat soo-flay oh shoh-koh-lah
chocolate soufflé

tarte tatin tart tah-tan
upside-down caramelized apple pie

tartes tart
narrow strips of fresh fruit, baked in a crust and served in thin slices

tourteau fromager toor-toh froh-mah-zhay
goat-cheese cake

You may also see *glaces* (ice creams) and *sorbets* (sorbets). For a wide range of pastries, see page 122.

If you order espresso, it will always come after dessert. To have coffee with dessert, ask for *café avec le dessert* (kah-fay ah-vehk luh day-sehr).

DRINKING

Every *café* or *bar* has a complete price list posted (and refills aren't free). In bigger cities, prices go up when you sit down. It's cheapest to stand at the *comptoir* (counter); drinks cost a bit more *en salle* (at a table indoors) or on the *terasse* (at a table outside). The outdoor seating is worth the extra cost in pleasant weather, with tidy sidewalk tables all set up facing the street, as if ready to watch a show.

Water

mineral water...	eau minérale... oh mee-nay-rahl
...carbonated	...gazeuse gah-zuhz
...not carbonated	...non gazeuse nohn gah-zuhz
tap water (in a restaurant)	une carafe d'eau ewn kah-rahf doh
(not) drinkable	(non) potable (nohn) poh-tah-bluh
Is the water safe to drink?	L'eau est potable? loh ay poh-tah-bluh

The French typically order *eau minérale* (and wine) with their meals. But if you want free tap water, ask for *une carafe d'eau, s'il vous plaît*. (The technical term for "tap water," *l'eau du robinet*, sounds crass to waiters.)

Milk

whole milk	lait entier lay ahnt-yay
skim milk	lait écrémé lay ay-kray-may
fresh milk	lait frais lay fray

Key Phrases: Drinking

drink	verre vehr
(mineral) water	eau (minérale) oh (mee-nay-rahl)
tap water (in a restaurant)	une carafe d'eau ewn kah-rahf doh
milk	lait lay
juice	jus zhew
coffee	café kah-fay
tea	thé tay
wine	vin van
beer	bière bee-ehr
Cheers!	Santé! sahn-tay

cold / warm	froid / chaud frwah / shoh
straw	paille pī-yuh

Juice and Other Drinks

fruit juice	jus de fruit zhew duh frwee
100% juice	cent pour cent jus sahn poor sahn zhew
orange juice	jus d'orange zhew doh-rahnzh
freshly squeezed	pressé preh-say
apple juice	jus de pomme zhew duh pohm
cranberry juice	jus de canneberge zhew duh kah-nuh-behrzh
grape juice	jus de raisin zhew duh ray-zan
grapefruit juice	jus de pamplemousse zhew duh pahn-pluh-moos
pineapple juice	jus d'ananas zhew dah-nah-nahs
fruit smoothie	smoothie aux fruits smoo-zee oh frwee

lemonade	citron pressé see-trohn preh-say
iced tea	thé glacé tay glah-say
(diet) soda	soda ("light") soh-dah ("light")
energy drink	boisson énergétique bwah-sohn ay-nehr-zhay-teek
with / without...	avec / sans... ah-vehk / sahn
...sugar	...sucre sew-kruh
...ice	...glaçons glah-sohn
25... (small)	Vingt-cinque... vant-sank
33... (medium)	Trente-trois... trahnt-trwah
50... (large)	Cinquante... san-kahnt
...centiliters.	...centilitres. sahn-tee-lee-truh

When you order a drink, state the size in centiliters (don't say "small," "medium," or "large," because the waiter might bring a bigger drink than you want). For something small, ask for 25 **centilitres** (about 8 ounces); for a medium drink, order 33 **centilitres** (about 12 ounces—a normal can of soda); a large is 50 **centilitres** (about 16 ounces); and a super-size is one **litre** (lee-truh; about a quart—which is more than I would ever order in France).

Coffee Talk

The French define various types of espresso drinks by how much milk is added. Here are the most common coffee drinks:

coffee (espresso)	café kah-fay
a shot of espresso with no milk	un café / un express uhn kah-fay / uhn ehk-sprehs
espresso shot with a "hazelnut"-size dollop of milk	une noisette ewn nwah-zeht
coffee with milk (similar to American latte)	un café crème uhn kah-fay krehm

coffee with lots of milk (in bowl-like cup)	un café au lait uhn kah-fay oh lay
coffee with whipped cream	un café avec chantilly uhn kah-fay ah-vehk shahn-tee-yee
a double espresso with milk	un grand crème uhn grahn krehm
espresso with a touch of apple brandy (calvados)	café-calva kah-fay-kahl-vah
espresso with water (like an Americano)	un café allongé / café longue uhn kah-fay ah-lohn-zhay / kah-fay lohng
instant coffee	Nescafé "Nescafé"
decaffeinated / decaf	décaféiné / déca day-kah-fay-nay / day-kah
sugar	sucre sew-kruh

To the French, milk is a delicate form of nutrition: You need it in the morning, but as the day goes on, too much can upset your digestion. Therefore, the amount of milk that's added to coffee decreases as the day goes on. A *café au lait*—espresso with milk in a bowl-like cup—is exclusively for breakfast time. You can get a *café crème* around midday, but getting one later might be frowned upon. If you want an after-dinner coffee, try a *café noisette* (literally "hazelnut")—a shot of espresso cut with just a hazelnut-sized dollop of cream. You're welcome to order a milkier coffee drink late in the day, but don't be surprised if you get a funny look.

Other Hot Drinks

hot water	l'eau chaude loh shohd
hot chocolate	chocolat chaud shoh-koh-lah shoh
tea	thé tay
lemon	citron see-trohn
tea bag	sachet de thé sah-shay duh tay
plain tea	thé nature tay nah-tewr

herbal tea	tisane tee-zahn
lemon tea	thé au citron tay oh see-trohn
orange tea	thé à l'orange tay ah loh-rahnzh
peppermint tea	thé à la menthe tay ah lah mahnt
fruit tea	thé de fruit tay duh frwee
green tea	thé vert tay vehr
chai tea	thé chai tay "chai"

You may see the word *infusion,* which means anything that's suspended in water to provide flavor (such as tea and herbal teas).

French Wine Lingo

These terms will help you navigate French wine—whether you're choosing from a wine list at a restaurant or sampling vintages at a winery. Winemakers and sommeliers are happy to work with you...*if* they can figure out what you want (which they expect you to already know). It helps to know what you like—study and use the terms below.

wine	vin van
house wine	vin de la maison van duh lah may-zohn
cheapest wine	vin ordinaire van or-dee-nair
I'd like / We'd like a wine that is _____ and _____.	Je voudrais / Nous voudrions un vin _____ et _____. zhuh voo-dray / noo voo-dree-ohn uhn van _____ ay _____
local	du pays dew pay-ee
of the region	de la région duh lah ray-zhee-ohn
red	rouge roozh
white	blanc blahn
rosé	rosé roh-zay
sparkling	pétillant / mousseux / bouché (for cider) pay-tee-yahn / moo-suh / boo-shay
light	léger lay-zhay

full-bodied (heavy)	robuste / costaud roh-bewst / koh-stoh
sweet	doux doo
semi-dry	demi-sec duh-mee-sehk
dry	sec sehk
very dry	brut brewt
tannic	tannique tah-neek
oaky	goût du fût de chêne goo duh foo duh shehn
fruity (jammy)	confituré kohn-fee-tew-ray
fine	fin / avec finesse fan / ah-vehk fee-nehss
ready to drink (mature)	prêt à boire preh ah bwahr
not ready to drink	fermé fehr-may
from old vines	de vieille vignes duh vee-yay-ee veen-yuh
chilled	bien frais / rafraîchi bee-an fray / rah-fray-shee
at room temperature	chambré shahn-bray
cork	bouchon boo-shohn
corkscrew	tire-bouchon teer-boo-shohn
corked (spoiled from a bad cork)	bouchonné boo-shoh-nay
vineyard	vignoble veen-yoh-bluh
harvest	vendange vahn-dahnzh

The French believe that the specific qualities of wine are a unique product of its place of origin (microclimate, soil, geology, culture, and so on). This uniquely French concept is known as *terroir* (tehr-wahr, literally "soil") and also applies to cheese and other foods.

Ordering Wine

I would like...	Je voudrais... zhuh voo-dray
We would like...	Nous voudrions... noo voo-dree-ohn
...the wine list.	...la carte des vins. lah kart day van
...a glass...	...un verre... uhn vehr
...a small pitcher...	...un pichet... uhn pee-shay
...a carafe...	...une carafe... ewn kah-rahf
...a half bottle...	...une demi-bouteille... ewn duh-mee-boo-tay
...a bottle...	...une bouteille... ewn boo-tay
...a barrel...	...un tonneau... uhn toh-noh
...of red wine.	...de vin rouge. duh van roozh
...of white wine.	...de vin blanc. duh van blahn
of the region	de la région duh lah ray-zhee-ohn
house wine	vin de la maison van duh lah may-zohn
What is a good vintage?	Quelles est un bon millésime? kehl ay uhn bohn mee-lay-zeem
What do you recommend?	Qu'est-ce que vous recommandez? kehs kuh voo ruh-koh-mahn-day
Choose for me, please.	Choisissez pour moi, s'il vous plaît. shwah-zee-say poor mwah see voo play
Around _____ euros.	Autour de _____ euro. oh-toor duh _____ uh-roh
Another, please.	Un autre, s'il vous plaît. uhn oh-truh see voo play

You can put yourself in the capable hands of your server to match a wine to your meal. Say **Choisissez pour moi, s'il vous plaît** (Choose for me, please). To avoid paying more than you'd like, add **Au tour de _____ euro** (Around _____ euros).

If all you want is a basic table wine, you can order **vin de la maison** (house wine). It might not be available by the glass, but a **pichet** (small pitcher) of a quarter-liter isn't much bigger than a generously poured

Regional Wines

In France, wine is a work of art. Each wine-growing region and each vintage has its own distinct personality. I prefer drinking wine from the region I'm in. Ask for *vin de la région,* available at reasonable prices.

While Americans think of wine in terms of the type of grape (Merlot, Cabernet Sauvignon, Riesling), the French usually think in terms of the place of origin—whether a region *(Côtes du Rhône),* a specific town or village *(Gigondas),* or even a particular winery *(Domaine du Grand Montmirail).*

Here's a rundown of what each region specializes in:

Alsace: The wines here (mostly whites) are German-influenced. This is one region where wines are named for their grapes: Try the Riesling, Sylvaner, Pinot Gris (formerly "Tokay"), Muscat, or Gewürztraminer.

Bordeaux: This region offers some of the world's most elegant, expensive red wines—such as Château Lafite Rothschild—along with Sauternes (a sweet dessert wine) and Graves (a fine white).

Burgundy: From Chablis to Beaujolais, you'll find great fruity reds, dry whites, and crisp rosés. For inexpensive but good reds, look for Bourgogne and Passetoutgrain. For whites, consider those from Mâcon and Chalon; St-Véran whites are also a good value. For rosé, try Marsannay.

Champagne: This hilly region pops the cork on the finest sparkling wine in the world.

glass. If you don't want a whole bottle of wine for the table, look on the menu for a section of *vins au verre* (wines sold by the glass).

Wine Labels

The information on a French wine label can give you a lot of details about the wine. Here are several terms to help you identify and choose a specific wine.

ordogne (Périgord): Wines to sample are Bergerac (red, white, and sé), Pecharmant (red, must be at least four years old), Cahors (a full-died red), and Monbazillac (sweet dessert wine).

anguedoc: Good-value reds include Corbières, Minervois, and Côtes Roussillon.

ire Valley: For whites, choose between the excellent, expensive ncerres and the cheaper but still tasty Touraine Sauvignons, the light uscadets, and the sweeter Vouvrays. The better reds come from Chin and Bourgueil.

on: Gamay Beaujolais grapes produce a light, fruity, easy-to-drink d wine; most big reds here are Syrahs. Look for Saint-Joseph, Crozes-ermitage, and the rich, perfumy whites from Condrieu.

ormandy and Brittany: Rather than wines, Normandy and Brittany ecialize in apple-based beverages—such as the powerful Calvados ple brandy and alcoholic apple cidre.

ovence: The three main growing areas are Côtes du Rhône, Côtes de ovence, and Côteaux d'Aix-en-Provence; all three produce rich, fruity ls and dry, fresh rosés. Some of the main options to look for include âteauneuf-du-Pape (velvety), Gigondas (spicy), Beaumes de Venise veet Muscat), Rasteau (robust), and Tavel (dry, crisp rosé).

AOC (appellation d'origine contrôlée): Meets nationwide laws for production of the highest-quality French wines

Appellation: Area in which a wine's grapes are grown

Cave: Cellar

Cépage: Grape variety (Syrah, Chardonnay, etc.)

Côte / Côteau: Hillside or slope

Cru: Superior growth

Domaine: Wine estate

Étiquette: Label
Fût: Wine barrel
Grand vin: Excellent wine
Millésime: Vintage (specific year)
Mis en bouteille au château / à la domaine: Estate-bottled (where it was made)
Mis en bouteille dans nos caves: Bottled in our cellars
Tonneau: Wine barrel
VDQS (vin délimité de qualité supérieure): Quality standards for specific regional wines
Vin de table: Table wine (can be a blend of several wines)
Vin du pays: Wine from a given area (a step up from *vin de table*)

Beer

I'd like / We'd like...	Je voudrais / Nous voudrions... zhuh voo-dray / noo voo-dree-ohn
a beer	une bière ewn bee-ehr
from the tap	pression preh-see-ohn
bottle	bouteille boo-tay
light / dark	blonde / brune blohnd / brewn
local / imported	régionale / importée ray-zhee-oh-nahl / an-por-tay
a small beer	un demi uhn duh-mee
a large beer	une chope ewn shohp
lager	blonde blohnd
pilsner	pils / pilsner peel / peels-nehr
ale	bière anglaise légère / ale bee-ehr ahn-glehz lay-zhehr / ehl
wheat	bière blanche bee-ehr blahnsh
porter	bière brune bee-ehr brewn
stout	bière de malte forte bee-ehr duh mahlt fort
microbrew	bière artisanale bee-ehr ar-tee-zah-nahl
low-calorie ("lite")	biere "light" bee-ehr "light"

EATING

Drinking

shandy	panaché pah-nah-shay
a non-alcoholic beer	une bière non-alcoolisée ewn bee-ehr nohn-ahl-koh-lee-zay
hard apple cider	cidre see-druh

American soft drinks can be far more expensive than wine or beer. If you want something refreshing, but don't want a whole glass of beer, consider a *panaché*—half lemon-lime soda, half beer.

Bar Talk

Would you like to go out for a drink?	Voulez-vous prendre un verre? voo-lay-voo prahn-druh uhn vehr
I'll buy you a drink.	Je vous offre un verre. zhuh voo oh-fruh uhn vehr
It's on me.	C'est moi qui paie. say mwah kee pay
The next one's on me.	Le suivant est sur moi. luh swee-vahn ay sewr mwah
What would you like?	Qu'est-ce que vous prenez? kehs kuh voo pruh-nay
I'll have a _____.	Je prends un _____. zhuh prahn uhn _____
I don't drink alcohol.	Je ne bois pas d'alcool. zhuh nuh bwah pah dahl-kohl
What is the local specialty?	Quelle est la spécialité régionale? kehl ay lah spay-see-ah-lee-tay ray-zhee-oh-nahl
Straight.	Sec. sehk
With / Without...	Avec / Sans... ah-vehk / sahn
...ice.	...glaçons. glah-sohn
One more.	Encore une. ahn-kor ewn
I'm a little drunk.	Je me sens pompette. zhuh muh sahn pohm-peht
Cheers!	Santé! sahn-tay

To your health!	À votre santé! ah voh-truh sah<u>n</u>-tay
Long live France!	Vive la France! veev lah frah<u>n</u>s
I'm hung over.	J'ai la gueule de bois. zhay lah guhl duh bwah

Spirits Specialties

An *apéritif* is served before dinner, and a *digestif* is served after dinner. Ask what's local.

Typical *apéritifs* are **Champagne, bière** (beer), and these:

kir keer
a thumb's level of crème de cassis (black currant liqueur) topped with white wine

kir royal keer roh-yahl
Champagne with cassis

pastis pahs-tees
sweet anise (licorice) drink that comes on the rocks with a glass of water—cut it to taste

pineau pee-noh
cognac and grape juice

port por
fortified wine

Here are some common *digestifs* (for after the meal):

armagnac ar-mahn-yahk
cognac's cheaper twin brother (from a different region)

B&B bay ay bay
brandy and Bénédictine

calvados kahl-vah-dohs
apple brandy from Normandy

Chambord shah<u>n</u>-bor
raspberry liqueur

Chartreuse / Bénédictine   shar-truhz / bay-nay-deek-teen
two distinct, herb-based liqueurs, made by monks with secret
formulas

cognac   kohn-yahk
wine-distilled brandy from the Charentes region; well-known brands
are Rémy Martin, Hennessy, and Martel

Cointreau   kwan-troh
orange liqueur

crème de cassis   krehm duh kah-sees
black currant liqueur

crème de menthe   krehm duh mahnt
mint liqueur

eaux de vie   oh duh vee
fruit brandy, literally "waters of life"; *framboise* (strawberry), *poire
williams* (pear), and *kirsch* (cherry) are best-known

Grand Marnier   grahn marn-yay
orange brandy

marc   mark
regional brandy, e.g., marc de Bourgogne

For a non-alcoholic alternative, try one of the many flavored syrups
mixed with bottled water (*sirops à l'eau*; see-roh ah loh). *Un diabolo
menthe* is 7-Up with mint syrup, and *un diabolo grenadine* is with
cherry syrup. *Orangina* is a carbonated orange juice with pulp, and
limonade (lee-moh-nahd) is Sprite or 7-Up.

PICNICKING

Gather supplies early for a picnic lunch; you'll probably visit several
small stores to assemble a complete meal, and many close at noon for
their lunch break. For convenience, you can assemble your picnic at a
supermarché or *hypermarché* (supermarket)—but smaller shops or
a *marché* (open-air market) are more fun and offer the best selection.
Look for a *boulangerie* (bakery), a *crémerie* or *fromagerie* (cheeses),
a *charcuterie* or *traiteur* (deli items, prepared salads, meats, and pâtés),
an *épicerie* or *magasin d'alimentation* (small grocery with fruit,

veggies, and so on), and a *pâtisserie* (delicious pastries). Late-night grocery stores are called *dépanneurs* (day-pah-nur).

Tasty Picnic Words

picnic	pique-nique peek-neek
sandwich	sandwich sahnd-weech
bread	pain pan
roll	petit pain puh-tee pan
ham	jambon zhahn-bohn
sausage	saucisse soh-sees
cheese	fromage froh-mahzh
mustard...	moutarde... moo-tard
mayonnaise...	mayonnaise... mah-yoh-nehz
...in a tube	...en tube ahn tewb
olives...	olives... oh-leev
pickles...	cornichons... kor-nee-shohn
...in a jar	...dans un pot dahnz uhn poh
yogurt	yaourt yah-oort
fruit	fruit frwee
juice	jus zhew
cold drinks	boissons fraîches bwah-sohn frehsh
container	barquette bar-keht
spoon / fork...	cuillère / fourchette... kwee-yehr / foor-sheht
...made of plastic	...en plastique ahn plah-steek
cup / plate...	gobelet / assiette... goh-blay / ahs-yeht
...made of paper	...en papier ahn pahp-yay

To weigh and price your produce at more modern stores, put it on the scale, push the photo or number (keyed to the bin it came from), and then stick your sticker on the food. When buying produce in a market or from a produce stand, resist the temptation to touch, and wait your turn to be served.

Picnic-Shopping Phrases

Meat and cheese are sold by the gram. One hundred grams is about a quarter pound, enough for two sandwiches.

Is it self-service?	C'est libre service? say lee-bruh sehr-vees
Fifty grams.	Cinquante grammes. san-kahnt grahm
One hundred grams.	Cent grammes. sahn grahm
More. / Less.	Plus. / Moins. plew / mwan
A piece.	Un morceau. uhn mor-soh
A slice.	Une tranche. ewn trahnsh
Four slices.	Quatre tranches. kah-truh trahnsh
Sliced.	Tranché. trahn-shay
Half.	La moitié. lah mwaht-yay
A few.	Quelques. kehl-kuh
A handful.	Une poignée. ewn pwahn-yay
A small bag.	Un petit sachet. uhn puh-tee sah-shay
A bag, please.	Un sachet, s'il vous plaît. uhn sah-shay see voo play
Ripe for today?	Pour manger aujourd'hui? poor mahn-zhay oh-joord-wee
Can I taste it?	Je peux goûter? zhuh puh goo-tay
Can you make me...?	Vous pouvez me faire...? voo poo-vay muh fair
Can you make us...?	Vous pouvez nous faire...? voo poo-vay noo fair
...a sandwich	...un sandwich uhn sahnd-weech
...two sandwiches	...deux sandwichs duh sahnd-weech
to take out	à emporter ah ahn-por-tay
Can you please slice it?	Pourriez-vous le couper en tranches, s'il vous plaît? poor-yay-voo luh koo-pay ahn trahnsh see voo play

Does it need to be cooked?	Il faut le faire cuire? eel foh luh fair kweer
Can I use the microwave?	Je peux utiliser le micro-onde? zhuh puh ew-tee-lee-zay luh mee-kroh-ohnd
Ready to eat?	Prêt à manger? preh ah mahn-zhay
May I borrow a...?	Je peux emprunter...? zhuh puh ahn-pruhn-tay
Do you have a...?	Vous avez...? vooz ah-vay
Where can I buy / find a...?	Où puis-je acheter / trouver un...? oo pwee-zhuh ah-shuh-tay / troo-vay uhn
...corkscrew	...tire-bouchon teer-boo-shohn
...can opener	...ouvre boîte oo-vruh bwaht
...bottle opener	...décapsuleur day-kahp-sew-lur
Is there a park nearby?	Il y a un parc près d'ici? eel yah uhn park preh dee-see
Where is a good place to picnic?	Il y a un coin sympa pour pique-niquer? eel yah uhn kwan san-pah poor peek-nee-kay
Is picnicking allowed here?	On peut pique-niquer ici? ohn puh peek-nee-kay ee-see

Don't forget the wine for your *pique-nique*. While public consumption is forbidden back home, the French see no problem with sipping a glass of wine *en plein air*—in parks, on benches or along the riverbank. In fact, on a balmy summer evening when Parisians line up along the Seine for picnics, the soundtrack is the popping of corks.

Deli Items

To get some prepared food for your picnic, drop by a *charcuterie*, a *traiteur*, or a *rôtisserie*. Note that a *traiteur* is literally a "caterer"— a place where someone might come to buy items they plan to serve at a party in their home. Much of the food can be eaten as-is, but other items might need to be heated or cooked. If you're not sure, ask *Il faut le faire cuire?* (Does this need to be cooked?) or *Prêt à manger?* (Ready to eat?).

Meat Dishes

The French slow-cook various meats to create meatloaf-like blocks that can be sliced or spread on a sandwich. Lined up in a case, they all look about the same: a block of meat and spices. But there's a lot of variety:

pâté pah-tay
a soft, spreadable meat dish; the most famous pâté is *foie gras* (made with duck or goose liver)

confit kohn-fee
meat that is slow-cooked, then preserved in its own fat

rillettes ree-yeht
meat that is stewed, shredded, then mixed with fat and packed into a brick

mousse moos
meat that has been whipped to become smooth and airy

jambon persillé zhahn-bohn pehr-see-yay
cold ham layered in a garlic-parsley gelatin

Don't confuse *pâté* (processed block of meat) with *pâtes* (pasta). And don't mistake *confit* (slow-cooked meat preserved in its own fat) for *confiture* (fruit jam).

   Foie gras—the famous French *pâté* of goose or duck liver—comes in several forms. The more expensive *entier* is a piece cut right from the product, whereas *bloc* has been blended to make it easier to spread; *mousse* has been whipped for an even creamier consistency.

Salads

You can order a *barquette* (bar-keht; small plastic container) of any *salade* to spiff up your picnic. Just see what looks good in the display case, and keep an eye out for these favorites.

carrottes râpées kah-roht rah-pay
grated carrots in vinaigrette

céleri remoulade say-luh-ree ruh-moo-lahd
celery root in a cream sauce, usually with mayonnaise and mustard

cervelas vinaigrette sehr-vuh-lah vee-nay-greht
pork sausage with vinaigrette sauce

salade piémontaise sah-lahd pee-ay-mohn-tehz
French potato salad, usually with sausage, pickles, and mayonnaise

museau de porc / boeuf mew-zoh duh por / buhf
the nose (and other assorted bits) of a pig / cow chopped up and
mixed in with parsley and vinaigrette (not for beginners)

betteraves rouges beh-tuh-rahv roozh
red beets

salade camarguaise sah-lahd kah-mar-gehz
salad with rice and veggies

taboulé tah-boo-lay
couscous salad

Produce Markets

It's considered rude for customers to touch produce; instead, tell the
clerk what you want. Pointing and gesturing go a long way. Pay care-
ful attention, as the unit of measure can differ. It could be *par* (per) *kg*
(for *kilogram,* which is the same as a kilo), *par kilo, par ½ kg, par ¼
kg, par 500 g, par 100 g,* and so on. *Un livre* is 500 grams (about a
pound in the US). You'll also see items priced by *la pièce* (piece), *la
botte* (bunch), *la barquette* (container), or *le pot* (for plants).

kilo (1,000 grams)	kilo kee-loh
½ kilo (500 grams)	demi-kilo / livre duh-mee-kee-loh / lee-vruh
¼ kilo (250 grams)	quart-kilo kar-kee-loh
100 grams	cent grammes sahn grahm
that	ça sah

this much	comme ça kohm sah
more / less	plus / moins plew / mwan
a little more / less	un peu plus / moins uhn puh plew / mwan
too much	trop troh
enough	suffisament sew-fee-zah-mahn
piece	la piéce lah pee-ehs
bunch	la botte lah boht
one / two	un / deux uhn / duh
container	la barquette lah bar-keht
pot (for plants)	le pot luh poh

MENU DECODER

This handy French-English decoder won't list every word on the menu, but it'll help you get *riz et veau* (rice and veal) instead of *ris de veau* (calf pancreas).

Note that decoding a menu can be particularly challenging in France, where ingredients are lovingly described in painstaking detail. For simplicity, I've listed the most prevalent terms and commonly seen variations, but this decoder is far from exhaustive when it comes to listing every melon or mushroom under the French sun.

Menu Categories

When you pick up a menu, you'll likely see these categories of offerings, and they'll generally appear in this order.

Petit déjeuner	Breakfast
Déjeuner	Lunch
Dîner	Dinner
Entrées	First course; appetizers
Chaud	Hot
Froid	Cold
Sandwichs	Sandwiches
Salades	Salads
Potages/Soupes	Soups
Menu	Fixed-price meal(s)
Spécialités	Specialties
Plats	Dishes
Plats principals	Main dishes
Viande	Meat
Porc	Pork
Volaille	Poultry
Poisson	Fish
Fruits de mer	Seafood
Garnitures	Side dishes
Légumes	Vegetables
Carte des consommations	Drink menu
Carte des vins	Wine list
Fromages	Cheeses
Desserts	Desserts

Enfants	Children
Suggestion du jour /	Daily special
Plat du jour	

And for the fine print:

Couvert	Cover charge
Service (non) compris	Service (not) included
Prix net	Tax included

Small Words

à la / à l'	in the style of
au / aux / avec	with
de / d' / des / du	of
et	and
ou	or
sans	without
sur	over

If you see *à la* or *à l'* on a menu, the next word might not appear in this decoder. That's because these phrases mean "in the style of," and often are followed by flowery, artsy, obscure descriptions. Even if you knew the exact meaning, it might not make things much clearer.

FRENCH / ENGLISH

abricot apricot

accompagné de accompanied by

acide sour; acidic

affiné aged

agneau lamb

agneau de pré salé lamb raised on salt-marsh lands

agrume citrus

ail / aillet garlic; garlic shoot

aile wing (poultry or fowl)

aïoli garlic mayonnaise

airelle wild cranberry

Aisy cendré soft cow cheese coated in ash

alcool alcohol

aligot mashed potatoes with cheese

aloyau sirloin

amande almond

amer bitter

amuse-bouche appetizer

ananas pineapple

anchoïade garlic and anchovy paste

anchois anchovies

(à l') ancienne in the old style

andouille pungent tripe sausage

anémone de mer anemone

aneth dill

anglaise "English" apple pastry

(à l') anglaise boiled

anis anise

AOC certified origin, designation for top-quality wine as well as cheese and butter

apéritif before-dinner drink

appellation area in which a wine's grapes are grown

araignée de mer spider crab

armagnac brandy produced in southwest France

artichaut artichoke

artichaut à la barigoule artichoke stuffed with garlic, ham, and herbs

artisanal from a small producer

asperge asparagus

assiette plate

assiette de charcuterie cold cuts

assiette d'enfant children's plate

au gratin topped with cheese and browned

au jus meat served in its natural juices

au vinaigre pickled

aubergine eggplant

Auvergne cow cheese sold in big wheels

avocat avocado

baba au rhum rum-soaked brioche

Baeckeoffe meat-and-potato stew

bagna cauda anchovy and butter sauce

baguette long loaf of bread

bain-marie water bath

ballon roll

banane banana

Banon soft goat cheese, wrapped in chestnut leaves

bar sea bass

barbarine watermelon used in pies and preserves

(à la) barigoule brown sauce with artichokes and mushrooms

barquette basket

basilic basil

basquaise Basque-style: cooked with tomato, eggplant, red pepper, and garlic

baudroie monkfish

bavarois rich "Bavarian cream" custard

bavette flank steak; skirt steak

Béarnaise sauce of egg and wine

Beaufort hard, sharp, aged cow cheese

béchamel creamy, milk-based sauce

beignet deep-fried doughnut

Bénédictine herb-based liqueur

betterave beet

beurre (doux / demi-sel / salé) butter (unsalted / salted / very salted)

beurre blanc sauce of butter, white wine, and shallots

beurre de cacahuètes peanut butter

beurre manié butter-and-flour thickening agent

beurre noisette browned butter

biche deer

bien cuit well-done (meat)

bien fait aged, mature (cheese)

bière beer

bière brune dark beer

bifteck steak (can be tough)

biologique / "bio" organic

bis, pain / bisse, pain dark-grain bread

biscuit cookie

biscuit de Savoie sponge cake

bisque shellfish chowder

blanc white

blanc (de volaille) breast (chicken)

blanc d'oeuf egg white

blanquette slow-cooked stew with rich white sauce

blette chard

bleu blue (cheese); very rare (meat)

bleu d'Auvergne pungent blue cow cheese from Auvergne

boeuf beef

(de) bois "of the woods" (wild)

boisson beverage

bonbon candy

bonite bonito (skipjack tuna)

bouché sparkling (cider)

bouchée bite-size ("mouthful"), usually describes a small puff pastry

bouchée à la reine pastry shell with creamed sweetbreads and mushroom

boudin blanc bratwurst-like sausage

boudin noir blood sausage

bouillabaisse seafood stew

bouilli boiled
bouillon broth
boulangerie / boulanger bakery
boule scoop (ice cream)
boulette de viande meatball
bouquet garni "bouquet" of herbs used to flavor soups, then removed
bourguignon cooked in red wine
bourride creamy fish soup
Boursin soft, creamy, herbed cow cheese
bouteille bottle
braisé braised
brandade de morue salted cod in garlic cream
brebis, fromage de sheep-milk cheese
brick fritter
Brie (de Meaux) mild, soft (almost runny) cow cheese
brié, pain dense, crusty bread
Brillat-Savarin buttery, slightly sour variant of Brie cheese
brioche buttery roll made with eggs
Brocciu sweet, fresh goat or ewe cheese
brochet pike
brochette skewer
brocoli broccoli
brouillé scrambled
Brousse du Rove fresh, creamy goat cheese
brune dark (beer)
brunoise finely chopped vegetables

brut very dry (wine or cider)
Cabécou pungent, nutty goat cheese
cabillaud cod
cacahuète peanut
café coffee
café allongé / café longue "long" coffee (espresso with water, like an Americano)
café au lait coffee with lots of milk
café avec chantilly coffee with whipped cream
café calva espresso with a touch of brandy
café crème coffee with milk
café décaféiné / café déca decaffeinated; decaf coffee
café gourmand coffee served with 2 or 3 small pastries
café noisette coffee with a dollop of milk
caille quail
caladon honey and almond cookie
calamar squid
calisson (d'Aix) marzipan cookie
calvados apple brandy
camarguaise, salade salad with rice and veggies
Camembert pungent, semi-creamy cow cheese
(de) campagne / campagnarde country-style; rustic
canapé appetizer; finger food
canard duck

cannelé "fluted" custard and caramel pastry

cannelle cinnamon

Cantal aged, semi-hard cow cheese

câpre caper

cardamome cardamom

cargolade snail, lamb, and sausage stew

carotte carrot

carpaccio thinly sliced raw meat or fish

carré (d'agneau / de porc) loin (lamb / pork)

carrelet plaice (flatfish)

carte menu

(à la) carte individual items on the menu

cassis black currant

cassonade brown sugar

cassoulet bean and meat stew

cavaillon, melon de small cantaloupe

cave wine cellar

céleri rave celery root

cendré with ashes

Cendré de Champagne Brie-like cheese covered in ash

(aux) cendres rolled in cinders (cheese)

cépage grape variety (wine)

cèpe boletus mushroom (similar to porcini)

cerf deer

cerise cherry

cervelas garlic pork sausage

cervelle brains

Chambord raspberry liqueur

chambré room temperature

champignon mushroom

chantilly / crème chantilly whipped cream

chapelure browned breadcrumbs

charbon de bois charcoal

charcuterie prepared meats such as sausages and pâtés

charentais, melon de yellow cantaloupe

Charolais high-quality beef; also a goat cheese from the Charolais region

Chartreuse herb-based liqueur

châtaigne chestnut

château wine bottled where it was made

chaud hot

chaud-froid cooked but served cold

chausson fruit-filled pastry

chausson aux pommes apple turnover

chêne, goût du fût de oaky (wine)

cheval horse

chèvre goat

chèvre chaud, salade au salad with warm goat cheese on toasted croutons

chevreuil, viande de venison

chiffonnade sliced into thin strips

chinois Chinese

chocolat chocolate

(le) choix de choice of

C

chope large beer
chorizo spicy sausage
chou cabbage
chou frisé kale
choucroute sauerkraut
choucroute garnie sauerkraut and sausage
chou-fleur cauliflower
chouquette eggy little baked doughnut
ciboulette chives
cidre hard apple cider
citre watermelon used in pies and preserves
citron lemon
clafoutis fruit tart made with egg batter
clou de girofle clove
cochon pig
cocotte casserole
cognac wine-distilled brandy
coing quince
Cointreau orange liqueur
colin hake (fish)
complet whole (whole grain); full
composée, salade "composed" salad with various ingredients
compote stewed fruit
compote de pommes applesauce
compris included
comptoir counter
Comté "Swiss cheese" from cow's milk
concassé coarsely chopped
concombre cucumber
confit a preserve, often fowl or pork cooked in its own fat

confiture preserves; jam
confituré jammy (wine)
consommé clear broth
copieux filling
coq rooster
coq au vin chicken braised in red wine
coque cockle
coquelet cockerel (young rooster)
coquille Saint-Jacques scallop
corbeille basket
coriandre cilantro; coriander
cornichon pickle
costaud full-bodied (wine)
côte rib or chop (meat)
côte de boeuf T-bone steak
côtelette cutlet
côtes chops (for meat); hillsides (for wine)
cou neck
coulis thick sauce, usually a purée of a single ingredient
Coulommiers soft, rich, creamy, Brie-like cow cheese
courge summer squash
courgette zucchini
couronne "crown," ring-shaped baguette
court-bouillon herbed liquid used to cook fish
couteau knife
couvert cover charge
crabe crab
cramique brioche bread with raisins
crème cream; custard

crème à l'anglaise custard sauce
crème bavaroise Bavarian
  cream pudding
crème brûlée caramelized
  custard
crème caramel custard with
  caramel sauce
crème chantilly whipped cream
crème de cassis black currant
  liqueur
crème de menthe mint liqueur
crème fraîche heavy, slightly
  soured cream
crème (velouté) d'asperges
  cream of asparagus soup
créole (ice cream) rum and
  tropical fruit (like rum raisin)
crêpe crêpe (thin pancake)
crêpe de froment sweet crêpe
  (made of wheat batter)
crêpe sucrées sweet crêpe
crêpe suzette crêpe flambéed
  with orange brandy sauce
cresson watercress
crevette shrimp
croissant classic French
  crescent roll
croque madame grilled ham,
  cheese, and egg sandwich
croque monsieur grilled ham
  and cheese sandwich
croquette deep-fried ball of
  potato and other ingredients
Crottin de Chavignol goat
  cheese from the Loire Valley
croustade pastry-wrapped dish
  (e.g., fruit filled)

croustillant crispy
croûte crust (bread); rind
  (cheese)
croûte au fromage cheese
  pastry
croziflette buckwheat pasta with
  melted cheese
cru raw; superior growth (wine)
crudité raw vegetable
cuillère spoon
cuisse thigh
cuisse de grenouille frog leg
cuit cooked
cuit au four baked
culotte rump (steak)
dariole small cylindrical mold
datte date
daube stew, usually meat
dauphine, pommes (de terre)
  fried puffs of mashed potatoes
décortiqué peeled; shelled
déglacé deglazed
dégustation tasting; sampling
déjeuner lunch
demi half; small beer
demi-baguette half-length
  baguette
demi-bouteille half bottle
demi-glace brown sauce
demi-sec medium-dry (wine)
désossé boned; boneless
diabolo grenadine lemon-lime
  soda with cherry syrup
diabolo menthe lemon-lime soda
  with mint syrup
digestif after-dinner drink
dinde turkey

dîner dinner
domaine wine estate
doré browned
doux mild, sweet (wine); mild, soft (cheese)
douze / douzaine dozen
droit de bouchon corkage fee
duchesse, pommes (de terre) baked puffs of mashed potatoes
duxelles chopped mushrooms, shallots, and cream
eau water
eau de vie fruit brandy ("water of life")
échalote shallot
Echourgnac cow cheese with brown rind
éclair oblong, iced custard-filled roll
écrivisse crayfish
édulcorant artificial sweetener
élevé en liberté / en plein air free-range
émincé chopped
Emmentaler "Swiss cheese"
(à) emporter to go
endive endive
entier whole
entrecôte rib-eye steak
entrée first course; appetizers
entremet small dish served between courses (sometimes dessert)
épaule shoulder (of beef, pork, lamb)
éperlan smelt
épice spice

épicée spicy (flavorful, well-seasoned)
épice, pain d' gingerbread
épinard spinach
Époisses (de Bourgogne) gooey, pungent, rich cow cheese
érable maple
escalope thin slice of meat
escalope normande turkey or veal in cream sauce
escargot snail
escargot raisins "snail"-shaped raisin pastry
espagnole flavorful veal-based sauce
estragon tarragon
étiquette label (wine)
express espresso
façon in the style or fashion of
fait, bien aged, mature (cheese)
fait maison homemade
(de) fantaisie fancy (can mean bread sold by the piece)
far breton baked flan, often with prunes
farce stuffing
farci stuffed
faux-filet sirloin
faux-sucre artificial sweetener
fenouil fennel
ferme farm; firm, young (cheese)
fermé not ready to drink (wine)
fermier / fermière farm-raised
feuille de vigne grape leaf
feuilleté flaky or puff pastry
fève fava bean

ficelle "string," super-thin baguette

figue fig

filet fillet

fin fine (wine)

fines herbes chopped fresh green herbs (chives, parsley, tarragon, etc.)

flambée flaming

flétan halibut

fleur de courgette stuffed and batter-fried zucchini flower

fleurie, croûte "bloomy" (soft, edible) rind (cheese)

flûte "flute," a slim baguette

foie liver

foie gras d'oie (de canard) liver from a fattened goose (duck)

fondant au chocolat molten chocolate cake

fondue small pieces of food dipped in hot liquid for cooking

fondue bourguignonne beef fondue (cooked in oil)

fondue savoyarde cheese fondue

forestière with mushrooms

fort sharp, strong (cheese)

fougasse bread with tasty tidbits baked in, often herbs

fougasse monégasque almond and anise pastry

four, cuit au baked

Fourme d'Ambert pungent cow's-milk blue cheese

frais fresh

fraise / fraise des bois strawberry / wild strawberry

framboise raspberry

friand (au fromage) cheese puff

fricadelle meatball

fricassée fricassee

frit fried; deep-fried

froid cold

fromage cheese

fromage à la crème cream cheese

fromage aux herbes cheese with herbs

fromage blanc fresh white cheese

fromage bleu blue cheese

fromage de la région cheese of the region

froment wheat

froment, pain au wheat bread

fruit fruit

fruit de la passion passion fruit

fruité fruity (wine)

fruits de mer seafood

fruits rouges berries

fumé smoked

fût wine barrel

galette a round pastry, pancake, or cake; also a buckwheat crêpe

galette de pommes de terre hash browns

gambas big prawn

Gana brand name of baguette

gariguette small strawberry

garni garnished; with vegetables

garniture side dish

gâteau cake

gâteau basque cherry and almond cake
gaufre waffle
gazeuse carbonated
gelée jelly; aspic
gésier gizzard
gibier game
gibier à plume game bird
gigérine watermelon used in pies and preserves
gigot (d'agneau) leg (of lamb)
gingembre ginger
girolle chanterelle mushroom
glace ice cream
glacé frozen; very cold (iced tea); glazed
glaçon ice cube
gougère savory cream puff with cheese
gourmandise sweet treat
goût du fût de chêne oaky (wine)
goûté snack
grain seed
grand large
Grand Marnier orange liqueur
gras fat
gratinée topped with cheese and browned
grenade pomegranate
grenouille frog
grillade grilled meat; mixed grill
grillé grilled
grillé pommes apple-filled pastry with "grill" pattern
griotte sour cherry (morello)
gros pain "large" baguette

groseille red currant
Gruyère "Swiss cheese"
haché minced
hachis hash
hachis Parmentier shepherd's pie
hareng herring
haricot (vert) bean (green)
herbes herbs
Hollandaise sauce of egg and butter
homard lobster
hors d'oeuvre appetizer
huile oil
huître oyster
île flottante meringue floating in cream sauce
importée imported
(à la) italienne Italian-style; grilled panini (for sandwiches)
izarra herbal brandy (Basque)
jambon de Bayonne dry-cured ham
jambon de Reims ham cooked in Champagne and wrapped in a pastry shell
jambon-mornay savory puff pastry with ham and cheese
jambon persillé ham and parsley preserved in gelatin
jardinière with vegetables
jarret shank; hock; knuckle
jaune (d'oeuf) egg yolk
jésuite triangular pastry filled with almond crème
joue cheek

julienne in matchstick-sized slices

jus juice (fruit juice, but also meat juices)

jus lié gravy

juteux juicy

kaki persimmon

kasher kosher

ker-y-pom shortbread and apple biscuit

kir white wine with black currant liqueur

kir royal champagne with black currant liqueur

kouign amann buttery, caramelized cake

Kuglehopf glacé raisin-and-almond cake with cherry liqueur

lait milk

lait demi-écrémé low-fat milk

lait écrémé nonfat milk

lait entier whole milk

lait ribot fermented milk drink; buttermilk

laitue lettuce

langoustine small, lobster-like shellfish

Langres soft cow cheese

langue tongue

lapin rabbit

lard / lardon bacon / slab bacon

laurier bay leaf

lavée, croûte washed rind (cheese)

léger light (not heavy)

légume vegetable

lentille lentil

levain, pain au sourdough ("yeast") bread

levure yeast

liaison thickening agent

light light (low-calorie)

limande dab (flatfish)

lit (sur un lit de) bed (on a bed of)

Livarot pungent, creamy cow cheese

lotte monkfish

loup sea bass

(à la) lyonnaise with onions

lyonnaise, salade salad with croutons, fried ham, and poached egg

macaron delicate sandwich cookie

macédoine mix of diced vegetables or fruit

mâche lamb's lettuce

madeleine buttery sponge cake

magret (de canard) breast (of duck)

maïs corn

maison house (specialty)

manchon wing (duck, chicken)

mandarine tangerine

mangue mango

mara des bois strawberry variety

marc regional brandy

(du) marché of the market (of the day)

mariné marinated

marinière white-wine and shallot sauce

M

marjolaine marjoram
marmitako Basque tuna stew
marmite stew pot
marron chestnut
médaillon tenderloin
mélangé mixed
melon cantaloupe
melon charentais yellow cantaloupe
(de) ménage homemade
mendiant chocolate with nuts and dried fruit ("beggar")
menthe mint
menu fixed-price meal
menu de dégustation tasting menu
menu du jour menu of the day
méréville watermelon used in pies and preserves
merlan whiting (cod-like fish)
mesclun mixed greens
meunière fried in butter
meurette red wine sauce
miche large round loaf of bread
mie, pain de sandwich bread
miel honey
mignardise miniature petit four
mille-feuille puff pastry with many layers; Napoleon
millésime vintage (wine)
mirepoix diced mix of celery, onions, and carrots
mixte mixed
moelleux moist, creamy, sometimes not fully cooked; sweet (wine)

moelleux au chocolat molten chocolate cake
moisi / moisi noble mold / "noble mold" that makes cheese and wine delicious
molle, à pâte gooey cheese with edible rind
Montrachet soft, tangy goat cheese, often covered in ash
Morbier semi-soft cow cheese with a charcoal streak
morceau piece
morille morel mushroom
mornay white sauce with Gruyère cheese
Morteau smoked pork sausage
morue salty cod
moule mussel
mousse mousse
mousseron meadow mushroom
mousseux sparkling
moutarde mustard
mouton mutton
multicéréales multigrain
Munster stinky, soft, aged cow cheese
mûre blackberry
muscade nutmeg
museau snout
myrtille blueberry
naturelle, croûte hard rind (cheese)
navarin lamb stew
navet turnip
Nescafé instant coffee

niçoise, salade with tomatoes, green beans, anchovies, olives, hard-boiled eggs, and tuna
noir black
noisette hazelnut; espresso with a dollop of milk
noix walnut; nuts
noix de beurre a pat of butter
noix de coco coconut
noix de Saint-Jacques scallop
Normande cream sauce
nougat de Montélimar honey and nut nougat
nouille noodle
nouvelle new
oeuf egg
oeuf à la coque (mollet / dur) boiled egg (soft / hard)
oeuf au plat fried egg
oeuf brouillé scrambled egg
oeuf mayonnaise hard-boiled egg topped with mayo
oeufs de poisson fish roe
oie goose
oignon onion
olive olive
omelette montoise puffy omelet (Mont Saint-Michel)
onglet hanger steak
oranais apricot danish
Orangina carbonated orange juice with pulp
ordinaire ordinary
origan oregano
os à moelle marrowbone
oseille sorrel

Ossau-Iraty smooth, firm, buttery ewe's cheese
pain bread
pain au chocolat flaky pastry filled with chocolate
pain au froment wheat bread
pain au lait "milk bread"; smaller, less sweet brioche
pain au levain sourdough bread
pain aux raisins spiral, glazed raisin pastry
pain bis / pain bisse dark-grain bread
pain brié dense, crusty bread
pain complet whole-wheat bread
pain de campagne rustic country loaf
pain de mie sandwich bread
pain de seigle rye bread
pain d'épices gingerbread ("spice bread")
pain doré French toast
pain pavé "cobblestone"-shaped rye bread
pain perdu French toast
pain salé bacon, olive, and cheese roll
pain viennois soft, shiny, slightly sweeter baguette
paleron chuck (beef)
palmier "palm"-shaped buttery pastry
palourde clam
pamplemousse grapefruit
pan bagnat tuna salad sandwich (Riviera)

panaché half beer, half lemon-lime soda
pané breaded
panier basket
papaye papaya
(en) papillote cooked in parchment
paprika paprika
paquets, pieds et sheep's feet and tripe
parfumé flavored
pastèque watermelon
pastis sweet anise (licorice) drink, cut with water
pâté seasoned ground meat shaped into a loaf, can also be made of fish
pâte pastry; dough
pâte à choux eggy butter-and-flour pastry
pâte à tartiner spread (like Nutella or peanut butter)
pâte molle gooey cheese with edible rind
pâtes pasta
paupiette meat beaten thin, then rolled
pavé thick hunk of meat
Pavé d'Auge spicy, tangy, square-shaped cow cheese
pavé, pain "cobblestone"-shaped rye bread
paysanne country style
paysanne, salade salad with potatoes, walnuts, tomatoes, ham, and egg
PDT (pomme de terre) potato

pêche peach
Pélardon nutty goat cheese
pépin seed
perdrix partridge
périgourdine, salade mixed green salad with foie gras and gizzards
persil parsley
pétillant sparkling (wine, water)
petit small
petit déjeuner breakfast
petit four miniature cake
petit gâteau cookie
petit pain bread roll
petit pois pea
petit salé salt pork
pichet pitcher
picholine green, buttery olive
Picodon spicy goat cheese
pied (de cheval / de mouton) foot (horse / sheep)
pieds et paquets sheep's feet and tripe
piémontaise, salade potato salad with tomato and egg
pigeon squab (pigeon)
pignon pine nut
piment d'Espelette spicy red pepper
pineau cognac and grape juice
pintade guinea hen
piperade omelet with tomatoes and peppers
piquant spicy (hot)
pissaladière onion, olive, and anchovy bread
pissenlit dandelion leaf

pistache pistachio
pithivier spiral-shaped puff pastry pie
planche wooden board for cutting or serving
plat dish
plat du jour special of the day
plat principal main course
plateau platter
plateau de charcuterie platter of cured meats
plateau de fromages cheese platter
plateau mixte platter of both cheese and cured meats
pleurote oyster mushroom
poché poached
poêlée pan-fried
Poilâne big, round loaf of rustic bread
(à) point medium (meat)
poire pear
poire au vin rouge pear poached in red wine and spices
poireau leek
pois, petit pea
poisson fish
poitrine de boeuf brisket (beef)
poitrine de porc pork belly
poivre / au poivre pepper / pepper sauce
poivre de Cayenne cayenne pepper
poivron bell pepper
pomme apple
pomme de terre potato

pommes (de terre) dauphine fried puffs of mashed potatoes
pommes (de terre) duchesse baked puffs of mashed potatoes
pommes (de terre) sarladaise potatoes fried in duck fat
pommes frites French fries
Pont l'Evêque flavorful, smooth, earthy cow cheese
porc pork
Port Salut soft, sweet cow cheese
porto fortified wine
potage soup, usually thick
potage de légumes thick vegetable soup
potée prepared in earthenware pot
potée champenoise meat, potato, and vegetable stew
potiron winter squash
poulet chicken
poulet rôti roast chicken
poulpe octopus
pour emporter to go
poussin young chicken
pré salé raised on salt-marsh lands
pression draft (beer)
prêt à boire ready to drink; mature (wine)
prix fixe fixed price
profiterole cream puff (sometimes with ice cream)
provençale with garlic and tomatoes
prune plum

pruneau prune
pur pure
purée mashed
purée de pomme de terre mashed potatoes
quatre-quarts pound cake
quenelle meat or fish dumpling
quenelle de brochet fish dumpling in a creamy sauce
queue de boeuf oxtail
quiche quiche
quiche lorraine quiche with bacon, cheese, and onions
quotidien everyday
racine root
raclette melted cheese over potatoes and meats
radis radish
ragoût stew
raie sting ray
raifort horseradish
raisin grape
raisin sec raisin
râpée grated
ratatouille tomato stew with vegetables (often eggplant, zucchini, etc.)
ravioli de Royans ravioli with goat cheese filling
Reblochon soft, gooey, mild, creamy, Brie-like cow cheese
réchauffée reheated
régionale local
réglisse licorice
religieuse round éclair (shaped like a nun)

rémoulade mayonnaise sauce (often mustard-flavored)
rillette cold, shredded pork
rillon belly (pork)
ris (d'agneau / de veau) sweetbreads (lamb / veal)
riz rice
riz au lait rice pudding
riz basmati basmati rice
riz complet brown rice
riz de Camargue nutty, chewy rice
riz jasmin jasmine rice
robuste full-bodied (wine)
rognon kidney
rognon blanc testicle
romarin rosemary
Roquefort powerful, blue-veined, tangy sheep cheese
roquette arugula (rocket)
rosbif roast beef
rosé rosé (wine)
rösti hash browns
rôti roasted
rouge red
rouget red mullet
rouille mayo with garlic and spicy peppers
roulade "rolled" around a filling
roulé aux noix sweet walnut roll with nutty filling
roux butter and flour thickening agent
sablé shortcrust pastry
safran saffron
saignant rare (meat)

Saint-Jacques, coquille / noix de scallop

Saint-Marcellin soft cow cheese

Saint-Nectaire semi-soft, nutty cow cheese

Saint-Pierre John Dory (fish)

Sainte-Maure soft, creamy goat cheese

saison, de seasonal

salade salad

salade au chèvre chaud salad with warm goat cheese on toasted croutons

salade camarguaise rice and veggie salad

salade composée "composed" salad with various ingredients

salade de pissenlit warm dandelion greens with bacon

salade lyonnaise salad with croutons, fried ham, and poached egg

salade niçoise salad with tuna, green beans, tomatoes, anchovies, olives, and hard-boiled eggs

salade paysanne potato, walnut, tomato, ham, and egg salad

salade périgourdine salad with foie gras and gizzards

salade piémontaise potato, tomato, and ham salad

salé savory, salty

salé cake savory loaf, often with ham and cheese or olives

sandre freshwater fish, like pike or perch

sanglier wild boar

sapeur, tablier de tripe dish

sarladaise, pommes (de terre) potatoes fried in duck fat

sauce verte tarragon-flavored mayo (sometimes with parsley)

saucisse sausage

saucisse-frites hot dog and fries

saucisson dried sausage; salami

sauge sage

saumon salmon

sauté sautéed

sauvage wild

savoyarde with melted cheese and/or potatoes

scampi prawns

scarole escarole

sec dry

seigle, pain de rye bread

sel salt

Selles-sur-Cher mild goat cheese

selon arrivage market price

semoule semolina (grain)

service compris service included

service non compris service not included

sole sole (fish)

sorbet sorbet

soubise onion-cream sauce

soufflé soufflé

soufflé au chocolat chocolate soufflé

soupe soup

soupe à l'oignon onion soup

soupe à l'ognion gratinée French onion soup

soupe au pistou Provençal vegetable soup with pesto

sous-vide vacuum-sealed and very slow-cooked in heated water (therefore very tender)

Spätzle soft egg noodles

spécialité specialty

spéculoos molasses cookie

steak haché gourmet hamburger patty

steak tartare raw minced beef

sucre sugar

tablier de sapeur tripe dish

taboulé couscous salad

tanche plump black olive

tannique tannic (wine)

tapenade olive spread

tarte pie; tart

tarte à l'oignon onion tart

tarte alsacienne fruit tart from Alsace

tarte au fromage cheese tart

tarte flambée thin-crust pizza with onion and bacon

tarte salée savory tart; quiche

tarte tatin upside-down apple pie

tartelette small tart

tartiflette scalloped potatoes with melted cheese

tartine bread (sometimes toasted) with sweet or savory toppings

tasse cup

taureau bull meat

terrine pressed, chilled loaf of chopped meat or vegetables

tête head

thé tea

thon tuna

thym thyme

tian gratin-like vegetable dish

tiède lukewarm

tilapia tilapia

tire-bouchon corkscrew

tisane herbal tea

tomate tomato

Tomme (de Savoie) mild, semi-soft cow cheese

tonneau wine barrel

torchon cheese cloth

tourin garlic soup

tournedos steak tenderloin

tournée cut into a football shape, often potatoes or carrots

tournesol sunflower

tourte de blettes sweet and savory Swiss chard pie

tourteau crab (similar to Dungeness crab)

tourteau fromager sweet goat-cheese cake

tranche / tranché slice / sliced

tresse "braid"-shaped brioche

trévise radicchio

tripes tripe

trou Normand apple sorbet in apple brandy

truffe truffle

truite trout

ttoro Basque seafood stew

turbot turbot (flatfish)

unilatéral, (grillé) à l' (grilled) on one side

vache cow

Valençay firm, nutty, goat cheese

vanille vanilla

(à la) vapeur steamed

varié assorted

VDQS quality standards for regional wines

veau veal

végétarien vegetarian

velouté smooth sauce or soup

venaison venison

vendange harvest (wine)

verre glass

verrine small glass serving dish

vert green

viande meat

viande de chevreuil venison

viandes fumées smoked meats

viandes salées salt-cured meats

vichyssoise potato and leek soup

(de) vieille vignes from old vines (wine)

viennoise coated with egg and breadcrumbs

(de) vigne from the vine

vignoble vineyard

vin wine

vin de la maison house wine

vin du pays wine from a given area

vin ordinaire cheapest house wine

vinaigre vinegar

vinaigrette vinaigrette

volaille poultry

vol-au-vent cylindrical, filled pastry

yaourt yogurt

ENGLISH / FRENCH

aged affiné; bien fait (cheese)
alcohol alcool
almond amande
anchovy anchois
anemone anémone de mer
anise anis
appetizer hors d'oeuvre
apple pomme
apple cider, hard cidre
apple pie, upside-down tarte
  tatin
applesauce compote de pommes
apricot abricot
artichoke artichaut
artificial sweetener faux-sucre
arugula (rocket) roquette
asparagus asperge
assorted varié
avocado avocat
bacon / slab bacon lard / lardon
baked cuit au four
banana banane
basil basilic
bay leaf laurier
bean / green bean haricot /
  haricot vert
beef boeuf
beef steak bifteck
beer (small / large) bière
  (demi / chope)
beer, draft bière pression
beet betterave
bell pepper poivron
belly (pork) poitrine (de porc)
berries fruits rouges

beverage boisson
bitter amer
black noir
black currant cassis
blackberry mûre
blood sausage boudin noir
blue cheese fromage bleu
blueberry myrtille
boar sanglier
boiled à l'anglaise; bouilli
boiled egg (soft / hard) oeuf à la
  coque (mollet / dur)
boletus mushroom cèpe
boneless / deboned désossé
bottle bouteille
brains cervelle
braised braisé
brandy cognac
bread pain...
    dark-grain ...bisse
    rye ...de seigle
    sandwich ...de mie
    sourdough ...au levain
    wheat ...au froment
    whole wheat ...complet
breaded pané
breakfast petit déjeuner
breast (chicken) blanc (de
  volaille)
brioche brioche
brisket (beef) poitrine (de
  boeuf)
broccoli brocoli
broth bouillon; consommé
browned doré

butter (unsalted / salted / very salted) beurre (doux / demi-sel / salé)

cabbage chou

cake gâteau

candied confit

candy bonbon

cantaloupe melon

caper câpre

carafe carafe

carbonated gazeuse

cardamom cardamome

carrot carotte

casserole cocotte

cauliflower chou-fleur

cayenne pepper poivre de Cayenne

celery root céleri rave

chanterelle mushroom chanterelle; girolle

chard blette

cheek joue

cheese fromage

cheese, blue fromage bleu

cheese, cream fromage à la crème; fromage à tartiner

cheese of the region fromage de la région

cheese pastry croûte au fromage

cheese platter plateau de fromages

cheese puff gougère

cheese tart tarte au fromage

cheese with herbs fromage aux herbes

cheese-topped gratinée; au gratin

cherry / sour cherry cerise / griotte

chestnut châtaigne; marron

chicken / roast chicken poulet / poulet rôti

children's plate assiette d'enfant

chilled rafraîchi

Chinese chinois

chive ciboulette

chocolate chocolat

chocolate soufflé soufflé au chocolat

choice of le choix de

chop (meat) côte

chuck (beef) paleron

cilantro coriandre

cinnamon cannelle

citrus agrume

clam palourde

clove clou de girofle

cockle coque

coconut noix de coco

cod / rock cod / salt cod cabillaud / morue de roche / morue

coffee (espresso) café...
 with water (like an Americano) ...allongé; ...longue
 with lots of milk ...au lait
 with some milk ...crème
 with a dollop of milk ...noisette

coffee, decaf café déca

coffee, instant Nescafé

cold froid

cold cuts assiette de charcuterie

cooked cuit
cooked in its own fat confit
cooked in red wine Bourguignon
cookie petit gâteau; biscuit
coriander coriandre
corkage fee droit de bouchon
corked (wine) bouchonné
corkscrew tire-bouchon
corn maïs
course, first entrée
course, main plat principal
couscous couscous
cover charge couvert
cow vache
crab crabe; tourteau
crab, spider araignée de mer
cranberry (wild) airelle
crayfish écrivisse
cream crème
cream cheese fromage à la crème
cream puff (with ice cream) chou à la crème; profiterole
cream sauce Normande
crêpe crêpe
crêpe, savory buckwheat galette
crêpes flambéed with orange brandy sauce crêpes suzette
crêpes, sweet crêpes sucrées
crescent roll croissant
crisp / crispy croustillant
cucumber concombre
cumin cumin
cup tasse
custard crème
custard sauce crème à l'anglaise

custard with caramel sauce crème caramel
custard with caramelized top crème brulée
cutlet côtelette
dab (flatfish) limande
dark (beer) brune
dark-grain bread pain bisse; pain de seigle
date datte
deep-fried frit
deer biche; cerf; chevreuil
delicatessen charcuterie
diet (drinks) light
dill aneth
dinner dîner
doughnut beignet; merveille
dozen douzaine
draft beer pression
drink menu carte des consommations
dry / very dry (wine) sec / brut
duck / duck breast canard / magret de canard
dumpling (meat or fish) quenelle
egg(s) œuf(s)...
  boiled (soft / hard) ...à la coque (mollet / dur)
  fried ...au plat
  scrambled ...brouillé
egg white blanc d'oeuf
egg yolk jaune d'oeuf
eggplant aubergine
endive endive
escarole scarole
espresso express

espresso with brandy café-calva
fat gras
fava bean fève
fennel fenouil
fig figue
fillet filet
first course entrée
fish poisson
fixed-price meal prix fixe; menu
flaming flambée
flank steak bavette
flavored parfumé
fork fourchette
free-range élevé en liberté; en plein air
French fries pommes frites; frites
French toast pain perdu; pain doré
fresh frais
fricassee fricassée
fried frit
fried eggs oeufs au plat
fried in butter meunière
fritter beignet
frog / frog leg grenouille / cuisse de grenouille
fruit fruit
fruit-filled pastry chausson
fruity (wine) fruité
full-bodied (wine) robuste; costaud
game gibier
game bird gibier à plume
garlic / garlic shoot ail / aillet
garlic mayonnaise aïoli
garnish garniture

ginger gingembre
gingerbread pain d'épices
gizzard gésier
glass verre
goat chèvre
goat cheese fromage de chèvre
goose oie
grape raisin
grape leaf feuille de vigne
grapefruit pamplemousse
grated râpée
gravy sauce
green vert
green bean haricot vert
grill, mixed grillade
grilled grillé
guinea hen pintade
half demi
half bottle demi-bouteille
halibut flétan
ham (de Bayonne) jambon (dry-cured)
ham and cheese sandwich (grilled) croque monsieur
ham, cheese, and egg sandwich (grilled) croque madame
hamburger hamburger; steak haché
harvest (wine) vendange
hash hachis
hash browns rösti; galette de pommes de terre
hazelnut noisette
herbal tea tisane
herring hareng
hock jarret

homemade fait maison; de ménage
honey miel
horse cheval
hot chaud
hot dog and fries saucisse-frites
house maison
house wine vin de la maison
ice cream glace
ice cube glaçon
imported importée
intestines tripes
jam confiture
juice / juicy jus / juteux
kidney rognon
knife couteau
kosher kasher
lamb agneau
lamb, leg of gigot d'agneau
lamb stew navarin
large grand
leek poireau
lemon citron
lentil lentille
lettuce laitue; mâche; mesclun: salade
licorice réglisse
light (beer) blonde
light (not heavy) léger
liver foie
lobster homard
lobster (small) langoustine
local régionale; du pays
loin (lamb / pork) carré (d'agneau / de porc)
lukewarm tiède
lunch déjeuner

mango mangue
maple érable
marinated mariné
marjoram marjolaine
market price selon arrivage
marrow / marrowbone moelle / os à moelle
mayonnaise / garlic mayonnaise mayonnaise / aïoli
meat viande
meat stew ragoût
meatball boulette (de viande); fricadelle
medium (meat) à point
medium (wine) demi-sec
menu carte
menu of the day menu du jour
mild, soft (cheese) doux
mild, sweet (wine) doux
milk lait
minced haché; hachis
mint menthe
mixed mixte
mixed grill grillades
monkfish lotte; baudroie
morel mushroom morille
multigrain multicéréales
mushroom champignon
(with) mushrooms forestière
mussel moule
mustard moutarde
mutton mouton
new nouvelle
noodle (pasta) nouille; pâtes
nutmeg muscade
octopus poulpe
oil huile

olive olive; picholine; tanche
onion oignon
onion tart tarte à l'oignon
orange orange
organic biologique
oyster huître
oyster mushroom pleurote
oxtail queue de boeuf
pan fried poêlée
papaya papaye
paprika paprika
parsley persil
partridge perdrix
passion fruit fruit de la passion
pasta pâtes
pâté pâté; terrine
peach pêche
peanut cacahuète
peanut butter beurre de
  cacahuètes
pea petit pois
pear poire
peeled décortiqué
pepper (bell) poivron
pepper (spice) poivre
pepperoni pepperoni
persimmon kaki
pickle cornichon
pickled au vinaigre
pie tarte
piece morceau
pike brochet
pine nut pignon
pineapple ananas
pistachio pistache
plate assiette
platter plateau

plum prune
poached poché
pomegranate grenade
pork porc
pork sausage (with garlic)
  cervelas
potato pomme de terre
potatoes, mashed purée de
  pommes de terre
poultry volaille
pound cake quatre-quarts
prawn scampi; gambas
preserves confiture
prune pruneau
puff pastry feuilleté
pure pur
quail caille
quiche quiche; tarte salée
quince coing
rabbit lapin
radicchio trévise
radish radis
raisin raisin sec
rare / very rare (meat)
  saignant / bleu
raspberry framboise
raw cru
raw hamburger steak tartare
raw vegetables crudités
red rouge
red currant groseille
rib-eye steak entrecôte
rice riz...
  basmati ...basmati
  brown ...complet
  pudding ...au lait
roast beef rosbif

roasted rôti

roe (fish eggs) oeufs de poisson

room temperature chambré

rooster coq

root racine

rosé (wine) rosé

rosemary romarin

rump (steak) culotte

saffron safran

sage sauge

salad salade

salmon saumon

salt sel

salt pork petit salé

sauce sauce...
  butter, white wine, and
  shallots ...beurre blanc
  cream ...normande
  egg and butter ...hollandaise
  egg and wine ...béarnaise
  white ...béchamel
  white, with Gruyère
  cheese ...mornay

sauerkraut choucroute

sausage saucisse

sausage, blood boudin noir

sautéed sauté

scallop coquille Saint-Jacques;
  noix de Saint-Jacques

scoop (ice cream) boule

scrambled / scrambled
  eggs brouillé / oeufs brouillés

sea bass loup

seafood fruits de mer

seafood stew bouillabaisse

seasonal de saison

seed grain; pépin

semi-dry (wine) demi-sec

semolina (grain) semoule

shallot échalote

shank (leg meat) jarret

sharp (cheese) fort

shepherd's pie hachis
  Parmentier

shelled décortiqué

shellfish chowder bisque; soupe
  de poisson

shoulder (of beef, pork, lamb)
  épaule

shrimp crevette

side dishes garnitures

sirloin aloyau; faux-filet

skewer brochette

slice / sliced tranche / tranché

small petit

smelt éperlan

smoked fumé

snack amuse-bouche; goûté

snails escargots

sole (fish) sole

sorbet sorbet

sorrel oseille

soufflé soufflé

soufflé, chocolate soufflé au
  chocolat

soup soupe; potage
  cream of asparagus crème
  (velouté) d'asperges
  onion (French-onion) soupe à
  l'oignon (gratinée)
  potato and leek vichyssoise
  Provençal vegetable soupe
  au pistou
  vegetable potage de légumes

sour acide
sour cream crème aigre; crème fraîche
sparkling mousseux
special of the day plat du jour
specialty spécialité
spice épice
spicy (flavorful) épicée
spicy (hot) piquant
spinach épinards
sponge cake biscuit de Savoie
spoon cuillère
squab pigeon
squash, summer courge
squash, winter potiron
squid calamar
steak steak; bifteck; entrecôte; côte de boeuf
steamed à la vapeur
stew daube; ragout; blanquette
stew, bean and meat cassoulet
stew, seafood bouillabaisse
strawberry / wild strawberry fraise / fraise des bois
stuffed / stuffing farci / farce
sugar sucre
sugar, brown cassonade
sunflower tournesol
sweet doux
sweetbreads (lamb / veal) ris (d'agneau / de veau)
sweetener, artificial faux-sucre
Swiss cheese Gruyère; Emmentaler
tangerine mandarine
tarragon estragon

tart / small tart tarte / tartelette
tea thé
tenderloin médaillon; tournedos
testicle rognon blanc
thigh (poultry) cuisse
thyme thym
tilapia tilapia
"to go" pour emporter; à emporter
tomato tomate
tongue langue
toothpick cure-dent
tripe tripes
trout truite
truffles truffes
tuna thon
turbot (fish) turbot
turkey dinde
turnip navet
vanilla vanille
veal veau
vegetable légume
vegetables, raw crudités
(with) vegetables jardinière; garni
vegetarian végétarien
venison viande de chevreuil
vinaigrette vinaigrette
vinegar vinaigre
vineyard vignoble
vintage date (wine) millésime
waffle gaufre
walnut noix
water eau
  carbonated gazeuse
  not carbonated non gazeuse

water bath   bain-marie
watercress   cresson
watermelon   pastèque
well done / very well done
  (meat)   bien cuit / très bien cuit
wheat   froment; blé
whipped cream   crème chantilly
white   blanc
whiting (fish)   merlan
whole (entire)   entier
whole (full)   complet
whole-grain bread   pain complet
wild game   gibier

wine   vin...
  red   ...rouge
  rosé   ...rosé
  sparkling   ...pétillant
  white   ...blanc
wine, house   vin de la maison
wine of the region   vin de la
  région
yeast   levure
yogurt   yaourt
yolk (egg)   jaune (d'oeuf)
zucchini   courgette

SIGHTSEEING

Whether you're touring a museum, going on a city walking tour, visiting a church, or conquering a castle, these phrases will help you make the most of your sightseeing time.

WHERE?

Where is / are the...?	Où est / sont...? oo ay / sohn
tourist information office	l'office de tourisme loh-fees duh too-reez-muh
toilets	les toilettes lay twah-leht
main square	la place principale lah plahs pran-see-pahl
old town center	la vieille ville lah vee-yay veel
entrance	l'entrée lahn-tray
exit	la sortie lah sor-tee
museum	le musée luh mew-zay
cathedral	la cathédrale lah kah-tay-drahl
church	l'église lay-gleez
castle	le château luh shah-toh
palace	le palais luh pah-lay
ruins	les ruines lay rween
amusement park	le parc d'attractions luh park dah-trahk-see-ohn
aquarium	l'aquarium lah-kwah-ree-uhm
zoo	le zoo (le jardin zoologique) luh zoh (luh zhar-dan zwoh-loh-zheek)
best view	la meilleure vue lah meh-yur vew
viewpoint	le point de vue luh pwan duh vew
Is there a fair nearby?	Il y a une fête foraine dans les environs? eel yah ewn feht foh-rehn dahn layz ahn-vee-rohn
Is there a festival nearby?	Il y a une festival dans les environs? eel yah ewn fehs-tee-vahl dahn layz ahn-vee-rohn

Key Phrases: Sightseeing

ticket	billet bee-yay
How much is it?	C'est combien? say kohn-bee-an
price	prix pree
Is there a guided tour (in English)?	Il y a une visite guidée (en anglais)? eel yah ewn vee-zeet gee-day (ahn ahn-glay)
When?	Quand? kahn
What time does this open / close?	À quelle heuere c'est ouvert / fermé? ah kehl ur say oo-vehr / fehr-may

AT SIGHTS

Tickets and Discounts

ticket office	billetterie bee-yeh-teh-ree
ticket	billet bee-yay
combo-ticket	billet combiné bee-yay kohn-bee-nay
reservation	réservation ray-zehr-vah-see-ohn
price	prix pree
Is there a discount for...?	Il y a une réduction pour...? eel yah ewn ray-dewk-see-ohn poor
...children	...les enfants layz ahn-fahn
...youths	...les jeunes lay juhn
...students	...les étudiants layz ay-tew-dee-ahn
...families	...les familles lay fah-mee
...seniors	...les gens âgés lay zhahn ah-zhay
...groups	...les groupes lay groop
I am...	J'ai... zhay
He / She is...	Il / Elle a... eel / ehl ah
... _____ years old.	... _____ ans. _____ ahn
I am extremely old.	Je suis très âgé. zhuh swee trehz ah-zhay

Is the ticket good all day?	Le billet est valable toute la journée? luh bee-yay ay vah-lah-bluh toot lah zhoor-nay
Can I get back in?	Je peux rentrer? zhuh puh rahn-tray

For some very crowded museums it's wise to book tickets in advance.

Information and Tours

information	les renseignements lay rahn-sehn-yuh-mahn
tour	une visite ewn vee-zeet
in English	en anglais ahn ahn-glay
Is there a...?	Il y a...? eel yah
...city walking tour	...une promenade guidée de la ville ewn proh-muh-nahd gee-day duh lah veel
...guided tour	....une visite guidée ewn vee-zeet gee-day
...audioguide	...un audioguide uhn oh-dee-oh-geed
...local guide (who is available)	...un guide local (qui est disponible) uhn geed loh-kahl (kee ay dee-spoh-nee-bluh)
...city guidebook (for Paris)	...un guide touristique (de Paris) uhn geed too-rees-teek (duh pah-ree)
...museum guidebook	...un guide de musée uhn geed duh mew-zay
Is it free?	C'est gratuit? say grah-twee
How much is it?	C'est combien? say kohn-bee-an
How long does it last?	Ça dure combien de temps? sah dewr kohn-bee-an duh tahn
When is the next tour in English?	La prochaine visite en anglais est à quelle heure? lah proh-shehn vee-zeet ahn ahn-glay ay ah kehl ur

Some sights are tourable only by groups with a guide *(un guide)*. Individuals usually end up with the next French tour. To get an English tour, call in advance to see if one's scheduled; individuals can often tag along with a large tour group.

Visiting Sights

opening times	horaires d'ouverture oh-rair doo-vehr-tewr
last entry	la dernière entrée lah dehrn-yehr ahn-tray
At what time does this open / close?	À quelle heuere c'est ouvert / fermé? ah kehl ur say oo-vehr / fehr-may
What time is the last entry?	La dernière entrée est à quelle heure? lah dehrn-yehr ahn-tray ay ah kehl ur
Do I have to check this bag?	Est-ce que je dois déposer ce sac à la consigne? ehs kuh zhuh dwah day-poh-zay suh sahk ah lah kohn-seen-yuh
bag check	consigne kohn-seen-yuh
floor plan	plan plahn
floor	étage ay-tahzh
collection	collection koh-lehk-see-ohn
exhibition...	exposition... ehks-poh-zee-see-ohn
...temporary / special	...temporaire / spéciale tahn-poh-rair / spay-see-ahl
...permanent	...permamente pehr-mah-nahnt
café	café kah-fay
elevator	ascenseur ah-sahn-sur
toilet	toilette twah-leht
Where is _____?	Où est _____? oo ay _____
I'd like to see _____.	Je voudrais voir _____. zhuh voo-dray vwahr _____
Photo / Video OK?	Photo / Vidéo OK? foh-toh / vee-day-oh "OK"

(No) flash.	(Pas de) flash. (pah duh) flahsh
(No) tripod.	(Pas de) trépied. (pah duh) tray-pee-yay
Will you take my / our photo?	Vous pouvez prendre ma / notre photo? voo poo-vay prah<u>n</u>-druh mah / noh-truh foh-toh
Please let me in. (if room or sight is closing)	S'il vous plaît, laissez-moi entrer. see voo play leh-say-mwah ah<u>n</u>-tray
I promise I'll be fast.	Je promets d'aller vite. zhuh proh-may dah-lay veet
It was my mother's dying wish that I see this.	C'était le dernier souhait de ma mère que je voies ça. say-tay luh dehrn-yay soo-way duh mah mehr kuh zhuh vwah sah

Once at the sight, get your bearings by viewing *le plan* (floor plan). *Vous êtes ici* means "You are here." Many museums have an official, one-way route that all visitors take—just follow signs for *Sens de la visite.*

Signs at Sights

First figure out which line is for buying tickets (*billets d'entrée* or *caisse individuelle*), and which is for the entrance (*entrée*). Some larger museums have separate entrances for individuals (*entrée individuels*), for groups (*entrée groupe*), and for people who already have tickets reserved (*entrée billets coupe-file*).

Entrée	Entrance
Resérvations	Reservations
Guichet / Billetterie	Ticket office
Billets	Tickets
Adultes	Adults
Enfants	Children
Jeunes	Youths
Étuidants	Students
Gens âgés	Seniors
Billet combiné	Combo-ticket

Réduction	Discount
Visite guidée	Guided tour
Exposition	Exhibition
Plan (d'orientation)	Map (orientation)
Vous êtes ici	You are here (on map)
Vestiaire	Cloakroom
Consigne	Bag check
Obligatoire	Required
Consigne automatique	Lockers
Audioguide	Audioguide
Ascenseurs	Elevators
Vers l'exposition	To the exhibition
Sens de la visite	Direction of visit ("this way")
Photos interdites	No photography
Flash / trépied interdit	No flash / tripod
Défense de toucher	Do not touch
Nourriture / boissons interdite	No eating / drinking
Non autorisé	Not allowed
Interdit	Forbidden
Travaux (de restauration) en cours	Work in restoration
En dépôt	Work on loan
Salle d'étude	Classroom
Accès réservé au personel autorisé	Staff only
Sortie interdite	Exit not allowed
Sortie	Exit
Sortie de secours	Emergency exit

Toilets can be marked *toilettes* or *WC.*

MUSEUMS

Types of Museums

Many of France's national museums close on Tuesdays. For efficient sightseeing in Paris, buy a Museum Pass. It'll save you money and time (because you can bypass ticket-buying lines).

museum	musée mew-zay
gallery	galerie gah-luh-ree
art gallery	galerie d'art gah-luh-ree dar
painting gallery	galerie de peinture gah-luh-ree duh pan-tewr
modern art	art moderne ar moh-dehrn
contemporary art	art contemporain ar kohn-tahn-poh-ran
folk	art populaire ar poh-pew-lair
history	histoire ees-twahr
town / city	village / ville vee-lahzh / veel
children's	pour les enfants poor layz ahn-fahn
Jewish	juif zhweef
memorial	mémorial may-moh-ree-ahl

Art Appreciation

I like it.	Ça me plaît. sah muh play
It's so...	C'est si... say see
...beautiful.	...beau. boh
...ugly.	...laid. lay
...strange.	...bizarre. bee-zar
...boring.	...ennuyeux. ahn-nuh-yuh
...interesting.	...intéressant. an-tay-reh-sahn
...thought-provoking.	...provocateur. proh-voh-kah-tur
It's B.S.	C'est con. say kohn
I don't get it.	Je n'y comprends rien. zhuh nee kohn-prahn ree-an
Is it upside down?	C'est à l'envers? say ah lahn-vehr
Who did this?	Qui a fait ça? kee ah fay sah
How old is this?	C'est vieux? say vee-uh
Wow!	Sensass! sahn-sahs
My feet hurt!	J'ai mal aux pieds! zhay mahl oh pee-yay

Art and Architecture Terms

art	art ar
artist	artiste ar-teest
painting	peinture pan-tewr
portrait	portrait por-tray
sculptor	sculpteur skewlp-tur
sculpture	sculpture skewlp-tewr
architect	architecte ar-shee-tehkt
architecture	architecture ar-shee-tehk-tewr
original	original oh-ree-zhee-nahl
restored	restauré rehs-toh-ray
B.C. / A.D.	avant J.-C. / après J.-C. ah-vahn zhay-say / ah-preh zhay-say
century	siècle see-eh-kluh
style	style steel
prehistoric	préhistorique pray-ees-toh-reek
ancient	ancien ahn-see-an
classical	classique klah-seek
Roman	romain roh-man
Byzantine	byzantin bee-zahn-tan
Islamic	islamique ees-lah-meek
medieval	médiéval may-day-vahl
Romanesque	romanesque roh-mah-nehsk
Gothic	gothique goh-teek
Renaissance	Renaissance ruh-nay-sahns
Baroque	baroque bah-rohk
Neoclassical	néoclassique nay-oh-klah-seek
Romantic	romantique roh-mahn-teek
Impressionist	impressionniste an-preh-see-oh-neest
Art Nouveau	art nouveau ar noo-voh
Modern	moderne moh-dehrn

| abstract | abstrait ahb-stray |
| contemporary | contemporaire kohn-tahn-poh-rair |

Historical Terms

Roman	Romain roh-man
Gauls / Franks	Gaulois / Francs goh-lwah / frahn
Middle Ages	le Moyen Âge luh moy-ahn ahzh
Hundred Years' War	la Guerre de Cent Ans lah gehr duh sahnt ahn
Joan of Arc	Jeanne d'Arc zhahn dark
Renaissance	la Renaissance lah ruh-nay-sahns
Louis XIV (Sun King)	Louis Quatorze (le Roi-Soleil) loo-ee kah-torz (luh rwah-soh-lay)
Enlightenment	les Lumières lay lew-mee-ehr
Pre-Revolutionary France	l'Ancien Régime lahn-see-an ray-zheem
French Revolution	la Révolution française lah ray-voh-lew-see-ohn frahn-sehz
Reign of Terror	la Terreur lah tehr-ur
First Empire (Napoleon I)	le Premier Empire luh pruhm-yay ahn-peer
Second Empire (Napoleon III)	le Second Empire luh suh-gohnd ahn-peer
Gilded Age (1871-1914)	la Belle Époque lah behl ay-pohk
turn of 20th century	fin de siècle fan duh see-eh-kluh
World War I	la Première Guerre mondiale lah pruhm-yehr gehr mohnd-yahl
World War II	la Seconde Guerre mondiale lah suh-gohnd gehr mohnd-yahl
Nazi-Collaborationist France	Vichy France vee-shee frahns

resistance	la Résistance	lah ray-zees-tahns
D-Day	Jour J	zhoor zhee
postwar	l'après-guerre	lah-preh-gehr
Fifth Republic (current French government)	la Cinquième République	lah san<u>k</u>-yehm ray-pew-bleek
European Union (EU)	l'Union Européenne (UE)	lew<u>n</u>-yoh<u>n</u> ur-oh-pay-ehn (ew uh)

CHURCHES

cathedral	cathédrale	kah-tay-drahl
church	église	ay-gleez
chapel	chapelle	shah-pehl
altar	autel	oh-tehl
bells	cloches	klohsh
carillon	carillon	kah-ree-yoh<u>n</u>
chapter house (meeting room)	chapitre	shah-pee-truh
choir	choeur	kur
cloister	cloître	klwah-truh
cross	croix	krwah
crypt	crypte	kreept
dome	dôme	dohm
organ	orgue	org
pulpit	chaire	shair
relic	relique	ruh-leek
sacristy	sacristie	sah-kree-stee
stained glass	vitraux	vee-troh
steeple / bell tower	clocher	kloh-shay
treasury	trésorerie	tray-zoh-ree
pope	Le Pape	luh pahp

Mass	messe mehs
When is the Mass?	La messe est quand? lah mehs ay kah<u>n</u>
Are there church concerts?	Il y a des concerts à l'église? eel yah day koh<u>n</u>-sehr ah lay-gleez
Can I climb the tower?	Puis-je monter le tour? pweezh moh<u>n</u>-tay luh toor

CASTLES AND PALACES

castle	château shah-toh
palace	palais pah-lay
royal residence	résidence royale ray-zee-dah<u>n</u>s roh-yahl
fortified castle	château-fort shah-toh-for
kitchen	cuisine kwee-zeen
dungeon	cachot kah-shoh
moat	fossé foh-say
fortified walls	remparts rah<u>n</u>-par
tower	tour toor
fountain	fontaine foh<u>n</u>-tehn
garden	jardin zhar-da<u>n</u>
king	roi rwah
queen	reine rehn
knight	chevalier shuh-vahl-yay
fair maiden	épouse fidèle ay-pooz fee-dehl
dragon	dragon drah-goh<u>n</u>

ANCIENT SITES

ancient sites	sites anciens seet ah<u>n</u>-see-a<u>n</u>
Gauls	Gaulois goh-lwah
Roman	Romain roh-man

walls	murailles mew-rī
forum (main square)	forum foh-ruhm
temple	temple tah<u>n</u>-pluh
column	colonne koh-lohn
mosaic	mosaïque moh-zī-eek
theater	théâtre tay-ah-truh
arena	arène ah-rehn
aqueduct	aqueduc ahk-dew

RECREATION AND ENTERTAINMENT

This chapter offers phrases for your recreational pleasure, whether you're going to the park or beach, swimming, biking, hiking, or enjoying other sports. It also covers your options for nightlife and entertainment.

RECREATION

Outdoor Fun

Where is the best place for...?	Où est le meilleur endroit pour...? oo ay luh meh-yur ah<u>n</u>-drwah poor
...biking	...faire du vélo fair dew vay-loh
...walking	...marcher mar-shay
...hiking	...faire de la randonnée fair duh lah rah<u>n</u>-doh-nay
...running	...courrir / faire du jogging koo-reer / fair dew zhoh-geeng
...picnicking	...pique-niquer peek-nee-kay
...sunbathing	...se bronzer suh brohn-zay
Where is a...?	Où est...? oo ay
...park	...un parc uh<u>n</u> park
...playground	...une aire de jeux ewn air duh juh
...snack shop	...un snack uh<u>n</u> "snack"
...toilet	...une toilette ewn twah-leht
Where can I rent...?	Où puis-je louer...? oo pweezh loo-ay
...a bike	...un vélo uh<u>n</u> vay-loh
...that	...ça sah
What's fun to do...?	Qu'est-ce qu'il y a d'amusant à faire...? kehs keel yah dah-mew-zah<u>n</u>t ah fair
...for a boy / a girl...	...pour un garçon / une fille... poor uh<u>n</u> gar-soh<u>n</u> / ewn fee
... _____ years old	...de _____ ans duh _____ ah<u>n</u>

At nearly any park, people (usually men) play **boules** (pronounced "bool," also called **pétanque**). Each player takes turns tossing an iron ball, with the goal of getting it as close as possible to the small, wooden target ball **(cochonnet)**.

At bigger parks, you can sometimes rent toy sailboats **(voiliers de bassin)** or see puppet shows **(guignols)**—fun to watch in any language.

Swimming and Water Sports

swimming	natation nah-tah-see-ohn
to swim	nager nah-zhay
Where's a...?	Où est...? oo ay
...swimming pool	...une piscine ewn pee-seen
...water park	...un parc aquatique uhn park ah-kwah-teek
...(good) beach	...une (belle) plage ewn (behl) plahzh
...nude beach	...une plage naturiste ewn plahzh nah-tewr-eest
Is it safe for swimming?	On peut nager en sécurité? ohn puh nah-zhay ahn say-kew-ree-tay
Where can I buy / rent...?	Où puis-je acheter / louer...? oo pweez ah-shuh-tay / loo-ay
swimsuit	un maillot de bain uhn mī-yoh duh ban
towel	une serviette ewn sehrv-yeht
sunscreen	une crème solaire ewn krehm soh-lair
sunglasses	des lunettes de soleil day lew-neht duh soh-lay
flip-flops	des tongues day tohn-guh
water shoes	des chaussons étanches day shoh-sohn ay-tahnsh
umbrella (for sun)	un parasol uhn pah-rah-sohl
umbrella (for rain)	un parapluie uhn pah-rah-plwee
lounge chair	une chaise longue ewn shehz lohng

Renting

Whether you're renting a bike or a boat, here's what to ask.

Where can I rent a...?	Où puis-je louer...?	oo pweezh loo-ay
Can I rent a...?	Je peux louer...?	zhuh puh loo-ay
...bike	...un vélo	uhn vay-loh
...boat	...une bâteau	ewn bah-toh
How much per...?	C'est combien par...?	say kohn-bee-an par
...hour	...heure	ur
...half-day	...demie-journée	duh-mee-zhoor-nay
...day	...jour	zhoor
Is a deposit required?	Une caution est obligatoire?	ewn koh-see-ohn ay oh-blee-gah-twahr

inner tube	une chambre à air ewn shahn-bruh ah air
goggles	des lunettes de natation day lew-neht duh nah-tah-see-ohn
snorkel and mask	un tuba et une masque uhn tew-bah ay ewn mahsk
surfing	surf sewrf
surfboard	une planche de surf ewn plahnsh duh sewrf
windsurfing	planche à voile plahnsh ah vwahl
waterskiing	ski nautique skee noh-teek
jet ski	un jet ski uhn "jet ski"
paddleboard	un paddleboard uhn "paddleboard"
boat	un bâteau uhn bah-toh
rowboat	une barque ewn bark
paddleboat	un pédalo uhn pay-dah-loh

canoe / kayak	un canoë / un kayak
	uhn kah-noh-ay / uhn "kayak"
sailboat	un voilier uhn vwahl-yay

In France, nearly any beach is topless. For a nude beach, look for a *plage naturiste.* At some French beaches (especially along the Atlantic), be wary of *grandes marées*—high tides.

Bicycling

bicycle / bike	bicyclette / vélo bee-see-kleht / vay-loh
mountain bike	VTT (vélo tout-terrain)
	vay tay tay (vay-loh too-tuh-ran)
I'd like to rent a bike.	Je voudrais louer un vélo.
	zhuh voo-dray loo-ay uhn vay-loh
two bikes	deux vélos duh vay-loh
kid's bike	vélo d'enfant vay-loh dahn-fahn
helmet	casque kahsk
map	carte kart
lock	antivol ahn-tee-vohl
chain	chaîne shehn
pedal	pédale pay-dahl
wheel	roue roo
tire	pneu pnuh
air / no air	air / pas d'air air / pah dair
pump	pompe pohmp
brakes	les freins lay fran
How does this work?	Ça marche comment?
	sah marsh koh-mahn
How many gears?	Combien de vitesses?
	kohn-bee-an duh vee-tehs
Is there a bike path?	Il y a une piste cyclable?
	eel yah ewn peest see-klah-bluh

I don't like hills or traffic.	Je n'aime pas les côtes ni la circulation. zhuh nehm pah lay koht nee lah seer-kew-lah-see-ohn
I brake for bakeries.	Je m'arrête à chaque boulangerie. zhuh mah-reht ah shahk boo-lahn-zhuh-ree

Hiking

go hiking	faire de la randonnée fair duh lah rahn-doh-nay
a hike	une randonnée ewn rahn-doh-nay
a trail	un sentier uhn sahn-tee-ay
Where can I buy a...?	Où puis-je acheter...? oo pweezh ah-shuh-tay
...hiking map	...une carte de randonnée / carte IGN ewn kart duh rahn-doh-nay / kart ee zhay ehn
...compass	...une boussole ewn boo-sohl
Where's the trailhead?	Où commence le sentier? oo koh-mahns luh sahn-tee-ay
How do I get there?	Comment est-ce que j'y arrive? koh-mahn ehs kuh zhee ah-reev
Show me?	Vous pouvez me montrer? voo poo-vay muh mohn-tray
How is the trail marked?	Comment le sentier est-il balisé? koh-mahn luh sahn-tee-ay ay-teel bah-lee-zay

Most hiking trails are well-marked with signs listing the destination and the duration in hours *(parcours de ____ heures)* and minutes *(parcours de ____ minutes).*

To reach the best views, consider taking advantage of the network of *chemin de fer de montagne* or *trains de montagne* (mountain railways).

Way to Go!

Whether you're biking or hiking, you'll want to know the best way to go.

Can you recommend a route / a hike that is...?	Pouvez-vous recommander un itinéraire / une randonnée qui est...? poo-vay-voo ruh-koh-mahn-day uhn ee-tee-nay-rair / ewn rahn-doh-nay kee ay
...easy	...facile fah-seel
...moderate	...modéré moh-day-ray
...strenuous	...difficile dee-fee-seel
...safe	...sans danger sahn dahn-zhay
...scenic	...panoramique / beau pah-noh-rah-meek / boh
...about _____ kilometers	...environ _____ kilomètres ahn-vee-rohn _____ kee-loh-meh-truh
How many hours / minutes?	Combien d'heures / de minutes? kohn-bee-an dur / duh mee-newt
uphill / level / downhill	montée / plat / descente mohn-tay / plah / day-sahnt

There are various types: **train à crémaillère** (cogwheel train—rack-and-pinion railway), **funicular** (an incline railway), **téléphérique** (cable car—one large car pulled up by cable), and **télécabine** (gondola—smaller compartments pulled up by cable).

Sports Talk

sports	sport spor
sports bar	un bar avec des sports à la télé uhn bar ah-vehk day spor ah lah tay-lay
game	match mahtch
team	équipe ay-keep
championship	championnat shahn-pee-oh-nah

field	terrain tuh-ra<u>n</u>
court	court koor
fitness club	club de fitness kluhb duh feet-nehs
I like to play...	J'aime jouer à... zhehm zhoo-ay ah
I like to watch...	J'aime regarder... zhehm ruh-gar-day
American football	football américain foot-bohl ah-may-ree-ka<u>n</u>
baseball	baseball bayz-bohl
basketball	basket bah-skeht
ice skating	patin sur glace pah-ta<u>n</u> sewr glahs
golf	golf "golf"
miniature golf	golf miniature "golf" mee-nee-ah-tewr
rugby	rugby roog-bee
skiing	ski "ski"
snowboarding	snowboard "snowboard"
soccer	football foot-bohl
tennis	tennis tehn-ees
volleyball	volleyball voh-lay-bohl
Where can I play?	Où puis-je jouer? oo pweez zhoo-ay
Where can I rent / buy equipment?	Où puis-je louer / acheter de l'équipment? oo pweez loo-ay / ah-shuh-tay duh lay-keep-mah<u>n</u>
Where can I see a game?	Où puis-je voir un match? oo pweez vwahr uh<u>n</u> mahtch

ENTERTAINMENT

What's Happening

event guide	guide des événements geed dayz ay-vay-nuh-mah<u>n</u>
What's happening tonight?	Qu'est-ce qui ce passe ce soir? kehs kee suh pahs suh swahr

What do you recommend?	Qu'est-ce que vous recommandez? kehs kuh voo ruh-koh-mahn-day
Where is it?	C'est où? say oo
How do I get there?	Comment est-ce que j'y arrive? koh-mahn ehs kuh zhee ah-reev
How do we get there?	Comment est-ce que nous y arrivons? koh-mahn ehs kuh nooz ee ah-ree-vohn
Is it free?	C'est gratuit? say grah-twee
Are there seats available?	Il y a des places disponibles? eel yah day plahs dee-spoh-nee-bluh
Where can I buy a ticket?	Où puis-je acheter un billet? oo pweez ah-shuh-tay uhn bee-yay
Do you have tickets for today / tonight?	Avez-vous des billets pour aujourd'hui / ce soir? ah-vay-voo day bee-yay poor oh-zhoor-dwee / suh swahr
When does it start?	Ça commence à quelle heure? sah koh-mahns ah kehl ur
When does it end?	Ça se termine à quelle heure? sah suh tehr-meen ah kehl ur
Where do people stroll?	Les gens se balladent où? lay zhahn suh bah-lahd oo

For concerts and special events, ask at the local tourist office. Cafés, very much a part of the French social scene, are places for friends to spend the evening together. To meet new friends, the French look for **pubs** or **bars américains.**

Music and Dance

Where's a good place for...?	Où se trouve un bon endroit pour...? oo suh troov uhn bohn ahn-drwah poor
...dancing	...danser dahn-say
...(live) music	...musique (en directe) mew-zeek (ahn dee-rehkt)

rock	rock rohk
jazz	jazz zhahz
blues	blues "blues"
classical	classique klah-seek
choir	de choeur duh kur
folk	folklorique fohk-loh-reek
folk dancing	danse folklorique dah<u>n</u>s fohk-loh-reek
disco	disco dee-skoh
karaoke	karaoké kah-rah-oh-kay
singer	chanteur shah<u>n</u>-tur
band	groupe groop
bar with live band	bar avec un groupe musical bar ah-vehk uh<u>n</u> groop mew-zee-kahl
nightclub	boîte bwaht
cabaret	caberet kah-buh-ray
cover charge	admission ahd-mee-see-oh<u>n</u>
concert	concert koh<u>n</u>-sehr
opera	d'opéra doh-pay-rah
symphony	symphonie sa<u>n</u>-foh-nee
show	spectacle spehk-tah-kluh
performance	séance say-ah<u>n</u>s
theater	théâtre tay-ah-truh
best seats	les meilleures places lay meh-yur plahs
cheap seats	les places bon marché lay plahs boh<u>n</u> mar-shay
sold out	complet koh<u>n</u>-play

Movies

movie	film feelm
Where is a movie theater?	Où est le cinema? oo ay luh see-nay-mah
Is this movie in English?	Est-ce que ce film est en anglais? ehs kuh suh feelm ayt ahn ahn-glay
original version	version originale (V.O.) vehr-see-ohn oh-ree-zhee-nahl (vay oh)
with subtitles	avec sous-titres ah-vehk soo-tee-truh
dubbed / "French version"	doublé / version française (V.F.) doo-blay / vehr-see-ohn frahn-sayz (vay "f")
3D	3D trwah-day
show times	l'horaire des séances loh-rair day say-ahns
matinee	matinée mah-tee-nay
ticket	billet bee-yay
discount	réduction ray-dewk-see-ohn
popcorn	popcorn "popcorn"
I liked it.	Je l'ai aimé. zhuh lay eh-may
The book is better.	Le roman est beaucoup mieux. luh roh-mahn ay boh-koo mee-uh

Paris has a great cinema scene, especially on the Champs-Élysées. Films listed as *V.O.* are in their original language; *V.F. (version française)* means dubbed in French.

SHOPPING

These phrases will give you the basics on browsing and bargaining; help you shop for various items, including souvenirs, clothes, and jewelry; and assist you in shipping items home.

SHOP TILL YOU DROP

Bargain hunters keep an eye out for *soldes* (sales), *liquidation de stock* (liquidation sale), *tout doit disparaître* (everything must go), *prix choc* (a shockingly good price), or *réductions* (reduced). When the French go window shopping, they call it *lèche-vitrines* (window licking).

Shop Talk

opening hours	les heures d'ouverture layz ur doo-vehr-tewr
sale	solde sohld
discounted	prix réduit pree ray-dwee
big discounts	prix choc pree shohk
cheap	bon marché bohn mar-shay
affordable	abordable ah-bor-dah-bluh
(too) expensive	(trop) cher (troh) shehr
good value	bon rapport qualité prix bohn rah-por kah-lee-tay pree
window shopping	lèche-vitrines lehsh-vee-treen
Pardon me (for bothering you).	Excusez-moi (de vous déranger). ehk-skew-zay-mwah (duh voo day-rahn-zhay)
Where can I buy ____?	Où puis-je acheter ____? oo pweezh ah-shuh-tay ____
How much is it?	C'est combien? say kohn-bee-an
I'm just browsing.	Je regarde. zhuh ruh-gard
We're just browsing.	Nous regardons. noo ruh-gar-dohn
I'd like ____.	Je voudrais ____. zhuh voo-dray ____
Do you have...?	Vous avez...? vooz ah-vay
...more	...plus plew

Key Phrases: Shopping

How much is it?	C'est combien? say kohn-bee-an
I'm just browsing.	Je regarde. zhuh ruh-gard
Can I see more?	Je peux en voir d'autres? zhuh puh ahn vwahr doh-truh
I'll think about it.	Je vais réfléchir. zhuh vay ray-flay-sheer
I'll take it.	Je le prends. zhuh luh prahn
Do you accept credit cards?	Vous prenez les cartes? voo pruh-nay lay kart
Can I try it on?	Je peux l'essayer? zhuh puh lay-say-yay
It's too expensive / big / small.	C'est trop cher / grand / petit. say troh shehr / grahn / puh-tee

...something cheaper	...quelque chose de moins cher kehl-kuh shohz duh mwan shehr
...something nicer	...quelque chose plus agréable kehl-kuh shohz plew ah-gray-ah-bluh
Can I see more?	Je peux en voir d'autres? zhuh puh ahn vwahr doh-truh
May I see this more closely?	Pourrais-je voir de plus près? poo-rayzh vwahr duh plew preh
This one.	Celui ci. suhl-wee see
I'll think about it.	Je vais réfléchir. zhuh vay ray-flay-sheer
I'll take it.	Je le prends. zhuh luh prahn
What time do you close?	Vous fermez à quelle heure? voo fehr-may ah kehl ur
What time do you open tomorrow?	Vous allez ouvrir à quelle heure demain? vooz ah-lay oo-vreer ah kehl ur duh-man

Except in department stores, ask first before you pick up an item: ***Pourrais-je voir de plus près?*** (May I see this more closely?).

Pay Up

Where do I pay?	Où se trouve la caisse? oo suh troov lah kehs
cashier	caisse kehs
Do you accept credit cards?	Vous prenez les cartes? voo pruh-nay lay kart
VAT (Value-Added Tax)	TVA (Taxe sur la Valeur Ajoutée) tay vay ah (tahks sewr lah vah-lur ah-zhoo-tay)
Can I get...?	Je peux avoir...? zhuh puh ah-vwahr
I need the paperwork for...	J'ai besoin de remplir un formulaire pour... zhay buh-zwan duh rahn-pleer uhn for-mew-lair poor
...a VAT refund	...la détaxe lah day-tahks
Can you ship this?	Vous pouvez l'envoyer? voo poo-vay lahn-voy-ay

When you're ready to pay, look for a ***caisse*** (cashier). The cashier might ask you something like ***Auriez-vous quinze centimes?*** (Do you have 15 cents?), or ***Voulez-vous un sac?*** (Do you want a bag?).

If you make a major purchase from a single store, you may be eligible for a VAT refund; for details, see www.ricksteves.com/vat.

WHERE TO SHOP

Types of Shops

Where is a...?	Où est...? oo ay
antique shop	un magasin d'antiquités uhn mah-gah-zan dahn-tee-kee-tay
art gallery	une gallerie d'art ewn gah-luh-ree dar
bakery	une boulangerie ewn boo-lahn-zhuh-ree

barber shop	un salon de coiffeur pour hommes uhn sah-lohn duh kwah-fur poor ohm
beauty salon	un salon de coiffeur pour dames uhn sah-lohn duh kwah-fur poor dahm
bookstore...	une librairie... ewn lee-bray-ree
used bookstore...	une boutique de livres d'occasion... ewn boo-teek duh lee-vruh doh-kah-zee-ohn
...with books in English	...avec des livres en anglais ah-vehk day lee-vruh ahn ahn-glay
camera shop	un magasin de photo uhn mah-gah-zan duh foh-toh
cheese shop	une fromagerie ewn froh-mah-zhuh-ree
clothing boutique	une boutique de vêtements ewn boo-teek duh veht-mahn
coffee shop	un café uhn kah-fay
crafts shop	un magasin d'artisanat uhn mah-gah-zan dar-tee-zahn-ah
delicatessen	une charcuterie-traiteur ewn shar-kew-tuh-ree-tray-tur
department store	un grand magasin uhn grahn mah-gah-zan
electronics store	un magasin d'équipements électroniques uhn mah-gah-zan day-keep-mahn ay-lehk-troh-neek
fabric store	un magasin de tissu uhn mah-gah-zan duh tee-sew
flea market	un marché aux puces uhn mar-shay oh pews
flower market	un marché aux fleurs uhn mar-shay oh flur
grocery store	une épicerie ewn ay-pee-suh-ree
hardware store	une quincaillerie ewn kan-kī-yuh-ree
jewelry shop (fine)	une boutique de joaillerie ewn boo-teek duh zhoh-ī-ree

SHOPPING Where to Shop

jewelry shop (cheap)	une bijouterie bon marché ewn bee-zhoo-tuh-ree bohn mar-shay
launderette (self-service)	une laverie automatique ewn lah-vuh-ree oh-toh-mah-teek
laundry (full-service)	une blanchisserie ewn blahn-shee-suh-ree
liquor store	une caviste ewn kah-veest
mobile phone shop	un magasin de portables uhn mah-gah-zan duh por-tah-bluh
newsstand	une maison de la presse ewn may-zohn duh lah prehs
office supply shop	une papeterie ewn pah-peh-tuh-ree
open-air market	un marché en plein air uhn mar-shay ahn plan air
optician	un opticien uhn ohp-tee-see-an
pastry shop	une pâtisserie ewn pah-tee-suh-ree
pharmacy	une pharmacie ewn far-mah-see
photocopy shop	un magasin de photocopie uhn mah-gah-zan duh foh-toh-koh-pee
shoe store	un magasin de chaussures uhn mah-gah-zan duh shoh-sewr
shopping mall	un centre commercial uhn sahn-truh koh-mehr-see-ahl
souvenir shop	une boutique de souvenirs ewn boo-teek duh soo-vuh-neer
supermarket	une supermarché ewn sew-pehr-mar-shay
sweets shop	une confiserie ewn kohn-fee-suh-ree
toy store	un magasin de jouets uhn mah-gah-zan duh zhoo-ay
travel agency	une agence de voyages ewn ah-zhahns duh voy-yahzh
wine store	une caviste ewn kah-veest

SHOPPING

Where to Shop

In France, most small shops close for a long lunch (noon until about 2 p.m.), and all day on Sundays and Mondays. For tips and phrases on shopping for a picnic—at grocery stores or open-air markets—see page 173.

Shoppers in Paris enjoy browsing the characteristic stalls along the Seine riverbank called *bouquinistes* (boo-kan-neest), which sell used books, art, cards, and more.

Department Stores

department store	grand magasin grahn mah-gah-zan
floor	étage ay-tazh
Pardon me (for bothering you).	Excusez moi (de vous déranger). ehks-kew-say mwah (duh voo day-rahn-zhay)
Where is ___?	Où se trouve ___? oo suh troov
clothing for...	les vêtement de... lay veht-mahn duh
...men / women	...hommes / femmes ohm / fahm
...children	...enfants ahn-fahn
accessories	accessoires ahk-seh-swahr
books	livres lee-vruh
electronics	électroniques ay-lehk-troh-neek
fashion	mode mohd
footwear	chaussures shoh-sewr
groceries	épicerie ay-pee-suh-ree
housewares / kitchenware	bricolage / matériel de cuisine bree-koh-lahzh / mah-tay-ree-ehl duh kwee-zeen
intimates	lingerie lan-zhuh-ree
jewelry	bijoux bee-zhoo
maternity (wear)	(vêtements de) femmes enceinte (veht-mahn duh) fahm ahn-sant
mobile phones	portables por-tah-bluh

Department stores, like the popular Printemps chain, sell nearly everything and are a good place to get cheap souvenirs and postcards. Most have a directory (often with English) by the escalator or elevator.

Street Markets

There are two types of street markets. The more common and colorful *les marchés* feature products from local farmers and artisans. *Les marchés brocantes* specialize in quasi-antiques and flea-market bric-a-brac.

Did you make this?	C'est vous qui l'avez fait?	say voo kee lah-vay tay
Is this made in France?	C'est fabriqué en France?	say fah-bree-kay ahn frahns
How much is it?	C'est combien?	say kohn-bee-añ
Cheaper?	Moins cher?	mwañ shehr
Will you take ___?	Est-ce que vous prendriez ___?	ehs kuh voo prahñ-dree-ay
(name price)		
Is it cheaper if I buy several?	C'est moins cher si j'en achète plusieurs?	say mwañ shehr see zhahñ ah-sheht plewz-yur
It's a good price.	C'est un bon prix.	say uñ bohñ pree
My last offer.	Ma dernière offre.	mah dehrn-yehr oh-fruh
I'll take it.	Je le prends.	zhuh luh prahñ
We'll take it.	Nous le prenons.	noo luh pruh-nohñ
I'm nearly broke.	Je suis presque fauché.	zhuh swee prehsk foh-shay
We're nearly broke.	Nous sommes presque fauché.	noo suhm prehsk foh-shay
My friend...	Mon ami...	mohñ ah-mee

stationery (office supplies, cards)	papeterie	pah-peh-tuh-ree

My husband...	Mon mari...	mohn mah-ree
My wife...	Ma femme...	mah fahm
...has the money.	...a l'argent.	ah lar-zhahn

It's OK to bargain at street markets, though not every vendor will drop prices. Expect to pay cash and be wary of pickpockets. For help with numbers, see page 26.

WHAT TO BUY

Here are some of the items you might buy, ranging from souvenirs to clothing to jewelry. For personal care items, see page 290. For electronics, see page 254.

Souvenirs

Do you have a...?	Vous avez...?	vooz ah-vay
I'd like a...	Je voudrais...	zhuh voo-dray
book	un livre	uhn lee-vruh
guidebook	un guide	uhn geed
children's book	un livre d'enfant	uhn lee-vruh dahn-fahn
bookmark	un marque-page	uhn mark-pahzh
calendar	un calendrier	uhn kah-lahn-dree-ay
candle	une bougie	ewn boo-zhee
doll	une poupée	ewn poo-pay
journal	un journal	uhn zhoor-nahl
magnet	un aimant	uhn eh-mahn
notecards	des fiches	day feesh
ornament	un ornement	uhn or-nah-mahn
pen / pencil	un stylo / un crayon	uhn stee-loh / uhn kray-ohn
postcard	une carte postale	ewn kart poh-stahl
poster	une affiche	ewn ah-feesh

print	une estampe / gravure ewn ehs-tah<u>n</u>p / grah-vewr
toy	un jouet uh<u>n</u> zhoo-ay
umbrella	un parapluie uh<u>n</u> pah-rah-plwee

Clothing

clothing	vêtement veht-mah<u>n</u>
This one.	Celui-ci. suhl-wee-see
Can I try it on?	Je peux l'essayer? zhuh puh lay-say-yay
Do you have a...?	Vous avez...? vooz ah-vay
...mirror	...un miroir uh<u>n</u> meer-wahr
...fitting room	...une salle d'essayage ewn sahl day-say-ahzh
It's too...	C'est trop... say troh
...expensive.	...cher. shehr
...big / small.	...grand / petit. grah<u>n</u> / puh-tee
...short / long.	...court / long. koor / loh<u>n</u>
...tight / loose.	...serré / grand. suh-ray / grah<u>n</u>
...dark / light.	...foncé / clair. foh<u>n</u>-say / klair
Do you have a different color / a different pattern?	Avez-vous une couleur différente / un motif différent? ah-vay-voo ewn koo-lur dee-fay-rah<u>nt</u> / uh<u>n</u> moh-teef dee-fay-rah<u>n</u>
What's this made of?	C'est en quoi ça? say ah<u>n</u> kwah sah
Is it machine washable?	C'est lavable en machine? say lah-vah-bluh ah<u>n</u> mah-sheen
Will it shrink?	Ça va rétrécir? sah vah ray-tray-seer
Will it fade in the wash?	Ça va déteindre au lavage? sah vah day-ta<u>n</u>-druh oh lah-vahzh
Dry clean only?	Nettoyage à sec seulement? neh-twah-yahzh ah sehk suhl-mah<u>n</u>

For a list of colors, see page 248, and for fabrics, see page 249.

Types of Clothes and Accessories

For a...	Pour... poor
...man.	...un homme. uhn ohm
...woman.	...une femme. ewn fahm
...male teen.	...un adolescent. uhn ah-doh-luh-sahn
...female teen.	...une adolescente. ewn ah-doh-luh-sahnt
...male child.	...un petit garçon. uhn puh-tee gar-sohn
...female child.	...une petite fille. ewn puh-teet fee
...baby boy / girl.	...un bébé garçon / fille. uhn bay-bay gar-sohn / fee
I'm looking for a...	Je cherche... zhuh shehrsh
I want to buy a...	Je veux acheter... zhuh vuh ah-shuh-tay
bathrobe	un peignoir de bain uhn pehn-wahr duh ban
bib	un bavoir uhn bah-vwahr
belt	une ceinture ewn san-tewr
bra	un soutien-gorge uhn soo-tee-an-gorzh
dress	une robe ewn rohb
flip-flops	des tongs day tohn-guh
gloves	des gants day gahn
handbag	un sac à main uhn sahk ah man
hat	un chapeau uhn shah-poh
jacket	une veste ewn vehst
jeans	un jean uhn "jean"
leggings	un caleçon uhn kahl-sohn
nightgown	une chemise de nuit ewn shuh-meez duh nwee
nylons	des bas nylon day bah nee-lohn

pajamas	un pyjama uhn pee-zhah-mah
pants	un pantalon uhn pahn-tah-lohn
raincoat	un imperméable uhn an-pehr-may-ah-bluh
sandals	des sandales day sahn-dahl
scarf	un foulard uhn foo-lar
shirt...	une chemise... ewn shuh-meez
...long-sleeved	...à manches longues ah mahnsh lohn-guh
...short-sleeved	...à manches courtes ah mahnsh koort
...sleeveless	...sans manche sahn mahnsh
shoelaces	des lacets day lah-say
shoes	des chaussures day shoh-sewr
shorts	un short uhn short
skirt	une jupe ewn zhewp
sleeper (for baby)	une grenouillière / un pyjama (pour bébé) ewn gruh-noo-yehr / uhn pee-zhah-mah (poor bay-bay)
slip	un jupon uhn zhew-pohn
slippers	des chaussons day shoh-sohn
socks	des chaussettes day shoh-seht
sweater	un pull uhn pewl
swimsuit	un maillot de bain uhn mī-yoh duh ban
tank top	un débardeur uhn day-bar-dur
tennis shoes	des baskets day bahs-keht
tie	une cravate ewn krah-vaht
tights	un collant uhn koh-lahn
T-shirt	un T-shirt uhn "T-shirt"
underwear	des sous vêtements day soo veht-mahn
vest	un gilet uhn zhee-lay
wallet	un portefeuille uhn por-tuh-fuh-ee

Clothing Sizes

extra-small	"xs" eeks-ehs"
small	"s" ehs
medium	"m" ehm
large	"l" ehl
extra-large	"xl" eeks-ehl
I need a bigger / smaller size.	J'ai besoin d'une plus grande / plus petite taille. zhay buh-zwan dewn plew grahnd / plew puh-teet tī
What's my size?	Quelle est ma taille? kehl ay mah tī

US-to-European Comparisons

When shopping for clothing, use these US-to-European comparisons as general guidelines (but note that no conversion is perfect).

Women's pants and dresses: Add 32 (US 10 = European 42)

Women's blouses and sweaters: Add 8 for most of Europe (US 32 = European 40)

Men's suits and jackets: Add 10 (US 40 regular = European 50)

Men's shirts: Multiply by 2 and add about 8 (US 15 collar = European 38)

Women's shoes: Add 30-31 (US 7 = European 37/38)

Men's shoes: Add 32-34 (US 9 = European 41; US 11 = European 45)

Children's clothing: Clothing is sized by height--in centimeters (2.5 cm = 1 inch), so a US size 8 roughly equates to 132-140. Juniors, subtract 4 (US 14 = European 10)

Children's shoes: For shoes up to size 13, add 16-18, and for sizes 1 and up, add 30-32

Sew What?

Traveling is hard on clothes.

I need...	J'ai besoin... zhay buh-zwan
...a button.	...d'un bouton. duhn boo-tohn
...a needle.	...d'une aiguille. dewn ay-gwee
...thread.	...de fil. duh feel
...scissors.	...de ciseaux. duh see-zoh
...stain remover.	...d'un détachant. duhn day-tah-shahn
...a new zipper.	...d'une nouvelle fermeture à glissière. dewn noo-vehl fehr-muh-tewr ah glees-yehr
Can you fix it?	Pouvez-vous le réparer? poo-vay-voo luh ray-pah-ray

Colors

black	noir nwahr
blue	bleu bluh
brown	marron mah-rohn
gray	gris gree
green	vert vehr
orange	orange oh-rahnzh
pink	rose rohz
purple	violet vee-oh-lay
red	rouge roozh
white	blanc blahn
yellow	jaune zhohn
dark(er)	(plus) foncé (plew) fohn-say
light(er)	(plus) clair (plew) klair
bright(er)	(plus) coloré (plew) koh-loh-ray

Fabrics

What's this made of?	C'est en quoi ça? say ahn kwah sah
A mix of...	Un mélange de... uhn may-lahnzh duh
cashmere	cachemire kahsh-meer
cotton	cotton koh-tohn
denim	denim deh-neem
flannel	flanelle flah-nehl
fleece	laine polaire lehn poh-lair
lace	dentelle dahn-tehl
leather	cuir kweer
linen	lin lan
nylon	nylon nee-lohn
polyester	polyester poh-lee-ehs-tehr
silk	soie swah
velvet	velours vuh-loor
wool	laine lehn

Jewelry

jewelry	bijoux bee-zhoo
fine jewelry shop	une boutique de joaillerie ewn boo-teek duh zhoh-ī-ree
cheap fashion jewelry shop	une bijouterie bon marché ewn bee-zhoo-tuh-ree bohn mar-shay
bracelet	bracelet brahs-lay
brooch	broche brohsh
cuff links	des boutons de manchette day boo-tohn duh mahn-sheht
earrings	boucles d'oreille boo-kluh doh-ray
necklace	collier kohl-yay
ring	bague bahg
watch	montre mohn-truh

watch battery	pile de montre peel duh mohn-truh
silver / gold	argent / or ar-zhahn / or
Is this...?	C'est...? say
...sterling silver	...de l'argent duh lar-zhahn
...real gold	...de l'or véritable duh lor vay-ree-tah-bluh
...handmade	...fabriqué à la main fah-bree-kay ah lah man
...made in France	...fabriqué en France fah-bree-kay ahn frahns
...stolen	...volé voh-lay

SHIPPING AND MAIL

If you need to ship packages home, head for *la Poste* (post office), which is often marked *PTT* (for its old name, *Postes, Télégraphes et Téléphones*). Otherwise, you can often get stamps at a *tabac* (tobacco shop).

At the Post Office

post office	la Poste / PTT lah pohst / pay tay tay
Where is the post office?	Où est la Poste? oo ay lah pohst
stamps	timbres tan-bruh
postcard	carte postale kart poh-stahl
letter	lettre leht-ruh
package	colis koh-lee
window / line	guichet / file gee-shay / feel
Which window for _____?	Quel guichet pour _____? kehl gee-shay poor _____
Is this the line for _____?	C'est la file pour _____? say lah feel poor _____
I need...	J'ai besoin... zhay buh-zwan

...to buy stamps.	...d'acheter des timbres. dah-shuh-tay day tan-bruh
...to mail a package.	...d'envoyer un colis. dahn-vwah-yay uhn koh-lee
to the United States	pour les Etats-Unis poor layz ay-tah-zew-nee
by air mail	par avion par ah-vee-ohn
by express mail	par express par ehk-sprehs
by surface mail	par surface par sewr-fahs
slow and cheap	lent et pas cher lahn ay pah shehr
How much is it?	C'est combien? say kohn-bee-an
How much to send a letter / postcard to ____?	Combien pour envoyer une lettre / carte postale pour ____? kohn-bee-an poor ahn-voh-yay ewn leht- ruh / kart poh-stahl poor ____
Pretty stamps, please.	De jolis timbres, s'il vous plaît. duh zhoh-lee tan-bruh see voo play
Can I buy a box?	Puis-je acheter une boîte? pweezh ah-shuh-tay ewn bwaht
This big.	De cette taille. duh seht tī
Do you have tape?	Avez-vous du scotch? ah-vay-voo dew skohtch
How many days will it take?	Ça va prendre combien de jours? sah vah prahn-druh kohn-bee-an duh zhoor
I always choose the slowest line.	Je choisis toujours la file la plus lente. zhuh shwah-zee too-zhoor lah feel lah plew lahnt

SHOPPING Shipping and Mail

Bigger post offices may have windows labeled **Timbres** or **Affranchisse-
ment** for stamps, **Envoi de Colis** for packages, and **Toutes Opérations**
for all services. If you need to **prenez un numéro** (take a number),
watch the board listing the **numéro appelé** (number currently being
served) and **guichet** (window) to report to.

Licking the Postal Code

to / from	à / de ah / duh
address	adresse ah-drehs
zip code	code postal kohd poh-stahl
envelope	enveloppe ahn-vuh-lohp
package	colis koh-lee
box	boîte bwaht
packing material	matériaux d'emballage mah-tay-ree-oh dahn-bah-lahzh
tape	scotch skohtch
string	ficelle fee-sehl
mailbox	boîte aux lettres bwaht oh leht-ruh
book rate	tarif-livres tah-reef-lee-vruh
weight limit	poids limite pwah lee-meet
registered	enregistré ahn-ruh-zhee-stray
insured	assuré ah-sew-ray
fragile	fragile frah-zheel
contents	contenu kohn-tuh-new
customs	douane doo-ahn
tracking number	numéro de suivi new-may-roh duh swee-vee

Post offices sell sturdy boxes, which you can assemble, fill with souvenirs, and mail home...so you can keep packing light.

TECHNOLOGY

his chapter covers phrases for your tech needs—from buying headphones to taking photos, from making phone calls to getting online.

TECH TERMS

Portable Devices and Accessories

I need a...	J'ai besoin de... zhay buh-zwa<u>n</u> duh
Do you have a...?	Avez-vous...? ah-vay-voo
Where can I buy a...?	Où puis-je acheter...? oo pweezh ah-shuh-tay
battery (for my _____)	une pile (pour mon _____) ewn peel (poor moh<u>n</u> _____)
battery charger	un chargeur de piles uh<u>n</u> shar-zhur duh peel
charger	un chargeur uh<u>n</u> shar-zhur
computer	un ordinateur uh<u>n</u> or-dee-nah-tur
convertor	un convertisseur uh<u>n</u> koh<u>n</u>-vehr-tee-sur
ebook reader	un ereader uh<u>n</u> ee-ree-dehr
electrical adapter	un adaptateur électrique uh<u>n</u> ah-dahp-tah-tur ay-lehk-treek
flash drive	une carte mémoire flash ewn kart may-mwahr flahsh
headphones / earbuds	un casque / les écouteurs uh<u>n</u> kahsk / layz ay-koo-tur
laptop	un ordinateur portable / laptop uh<u>n</u> or-dee-nah-tur por-tah-bluh / "laptop"
memory card	une carte mémoire ewn kart may-mwahr
mobile phone	un portable uh<u>n</u> por-tah-bluh
SIM card	une carte SIM ewn kart seem
speakers (for my _____)	des haut-parleurs (pour mon _____) dayz oh-par-lur (poor moh<u>n</u> _____)

tablet	une tablette ewn tah-bleht
(mini) USB cable	un (petit) câble USB uhn (puh-tee) kah-bluh ew ehs bay
USB key	clé USB klay ew ehs bay
video game	un jeu vidéo uhn zhuh vee-day-oh
Wi-Fi	Wi-Fi wee-fee

Familiar brands (like iPad, Facebook, YouTube, Instagram, or whatever the latest craze is) are just as popular in Europe as they are back home. Invariably, these go by their English names (sometimes with a French accent).

Cameras

camera	un appareil-photo uhn ah-pah-ray-foh-toh
digital camera	un appareil-photo numérique uhn ah-pah-ray-foh-toh new-may-reek
video camera	une caméra vidéo ewn kah-may-rah vee-day-oh
lens cap	un bouchon d'objectif uhn boo-shohn dohb-zhehk-teef
Will you take my / our photo?	Vous pouvez prendre ma / notre photo? voo poo-vay prahn-druh mah / noh-truh foh-toh
Can I take a photo of you?	Je peux prendre votre photo? zhuh puh prahn-druh voh-truh foh-toh
Smile!	Souriez! soo-ree-ay

You'll find words for batteries, chargers, and more in the previous list.

TELEPHONES

Travelers have several phoning options. Public pay phones are increasingly rare (and often require buying an insertable phone card). The simplest solution is to bring your own device and use it just as you would at home (by getting an international plan or connecting to free Wi-Fi whenever possible). Another option is to buy a European SIM card for your US mobile phone. As this is a fast-changing scene, check my latest tips at www.ricksteves.com/phoning.

Telephone Terms

telephone	téléphone	tay-lay-fohn
phone call...	appel... ah-pehl	
...local	...local	loh-kahl
...domestic	...national	nah-see-oh-nahl
...international	...international a<u>n</u>-tehr-nah-see-oh-nahl	
...toll-free	...gratuit	grah-twee
...with a credit card	...avec une carte de crédit ah-vehk ewn kart duh kray-dee	
...collect	...en PCV	ah<u>n</u> pay say vay
mobile phone	un portable	uh<u>n</u> por-tah-bluh
mobile number	numéro de portable new-may-roh duh por-tah-bluh	
landline	numéro fixe	new-may-roh feeks

For tips on calling in France, see page 422.

Making Calls

Where is the nearest phone?	Où est le téléphone le plus proche? oo ay luh tay-lay-fohn luh plew prohsh

Key Phrases: Telephones

telephone	téléphone tay-lay-fohn
phone call	appel téléphonique ah-pehl tay-lay-foh-neek
mobile phone	un portable uhn por-tah-bluh
What is the phone number?	Quel est le numéro de téléphone? kehl ay luh new-meh-roh duh tay-lay-fohn
May I use your phone?	Je peux téléphoner? zhuh puh tay-lay-foh-nay
Where is a mobile phone shop?	Où est un magasin de portables? oo ay uhn mah-gah-zan duh por-tah-bluh

What is the phone number?	Quel est le numéro de téléphone? kehl ay luh new-meh-roh duh tay-lay-fohn
May I use your phone?	Je peux téléphoner? zhuh puh tay-lay-foh-nay
Can you talk for me?	Vous pouvez parler pour moi? voo poo-vay par-lay poor mwah
It's busy.	C'est occupé. say oh-kew-pay
This doesn't work.	Ça ne marche pas. sah nuh marsh pah
out of service	hors service or sehr-vees
Try again?	Essayez de nouveau? ay-say-yay duh noo-voh

If the number you're calling is out of service, you'll likely hear this recording: *Le numéro que vous demandez n'est pas attribué.*

On the Phone

Hello, this is ___.	Âllo, c'est ___.	ah-loh say ___
My name is ___.	Je m'appelle ___.	zhuh mah-pehl ___
My phone number is ___.	Mon numéro de téléphone est ___. mohn new-may-roh duh tay-lay-fohn ay ___	
Do you speak English?	Parlez-vous anglais? par-lay-voo ahn-glay	
Sorry, I speak only a little French.	Désolé, je parle seulement un petit peu de français. day-zoh-lay zhuh parl suhl-mahn uhn puh-tee puh duh frahn-say	
Speak slowly, please.	Parlez lentement, s'il vous plaît. par-lay lahnt-mahn see voo play	
Wait a moment.	Un moment. uhn moh-mahn	

The French answer a call by saying simply **Allô** (Hello).

In this book, you'll find the phrases you need to reserve a hotel room (page 80) or a table at a restaurant (page 105). To spell your name over the phone, refer to the code alphabet on page 17. To provide your phone number, see the numbers on page 24.

Mobile Phones

It's easy and convenient to use your US mobile phone in Europe. Alternatively, you can buy a phone when you get there.

mobile phone	un portable uhn por-tah-bluh
roaming	itinérance / roaming ee-tee-nay-rahns / "roaming"
text message	SMS / texto "SMS" / tehk-stoh
Where is a mobile phone shop?	Où est un magasin de portables? oo ay uhn mah-gah-zan duh por-tah-bluh
I'd like to buy...	Je voudrais acheter... zhuh voo-dray ah-shuh-tay

...a (cheap) mobile phone.	...un portable (pas cher). uhn por-tah-bluh (pah shehr)
...a SIM card.	...une carte SIM. ewn kart seem
prepaid credit	unités prépayées ew-nee-tay pray-pay-ay
calling time	temps d'appel tahn dah-pehl
contract	abonnement ah-buhn-mahn
locked	bloqué bloh-kay
unlocked	debloqué day-bloh-kay
Is this phone unlocked?	Est-ce que ce téléphone est débloqué? ehs kuh suh tay-lay-fohn ay day-bloh-kay
Can you unlock this phone?	Pouvez-vous débloquer ce téléphone? poo-vay-voo day-bloh-kay suh tay-lay-fohn
How do I...?	Comment puis-je...? koh-mahn pweezh
...make calls	...appeler ah-puh-lay
...receive calls	...recevoir les appels ruh-suh-vwahr layz ah-pehl
...send a text message	...envoyer un SMS / texto ahn-vwoh-yay uhn "SMS" / tehk-stoh
...check my voicemail	...vérifier ma boîte vocale vehr-ee-fee-ay mah bwaht voh-kahl
...set the language to English	...paramétrer la langue en anglais pah-rah-may-tray lah lahng ahn ahn-glay
...mute the ringer	...appuyer sur la touche sourdine ah-pwee-yay sewr lah toosh soor-deen
...change the ringer	...changer la sonnerie shahn-zhay lah suhn-ree
...turn it on	...allumer ah-lew-may
...turn it off	...éteindre ay-tan-druh

Buying a Mobile Phone SIM Card

The simplest (but potentially most expensive) solution is to roam with your US phone in Europe. If your phone is unlocked *(debloqué)*, you can save money by buying a cheap European SIM card at a mobile-phone shop or a newsstand. There are no roaming charges for EU citizens using a domestic SIM card in other EU countries. When you buy your SIM card, ask if non-EU citizens also have this "roam-like-at-home" pricing.

Where can I buy...?	Où puis-je acheter...? oo pweezh ah-shuh-tay
I'd like to buy...	Je voudrais acheter... zhuh voo-dray ah-shuh-tay
...a SIM card.	...une carte SIM. ewn kart seem
...more calling time.	...plus de temps. plew duh tah<u>n</u>
Will this SIM card work in my phone?	Est-ce que cette carte SIM va fonctionner avec mon téléphone? ehs kuh seht kart seem vah foh<u>n</u>k-see-oh-nay ah-vehk moh<u>n</u> tay-lay-fohn
Which SIM card is best for my phone?	Quelle carte SIM est la meilleure pour mon téléphone? kehl kart seem ay lah meh-ur poor moh<u>n</u> tay-lay-fohn
How much per minute for...?	Combien par minute pour...? koh<u>n</u>-bee-a<u>n</u> par mee-newt poor
...making...	...émettre... ay-meh-truh
...receiving...	...recevoir... ruh-suh-vwahr
...domestic calls	...appels nationaux ah-pehl nah-see-oh-noh
...international calls	...appels internationaux ah-pehl a<u>n</u>-tehr-nah-see-oh-noh
...calls to the US	...appels vers les Etats-Unis ah-pehl vehr layz ay-tah-zew-nee
How much for text messages?	Combien par SMS / texto? koh<u>n</u>-bee-a<u>n</u> par "SMS" / tehk-stoh

How much credit is included?	Combien y-a-til d'unités incluses? kohn-bee-an yah-teel dew-nee-tay an-klewz
Can I roam with this card in another country?	Puis-je passer des appels depuis un pays étranger? pweezh pah-say dayz ah-pehl duh-pwee uhn pay-ee ay-trahn-zhay
Do you have a list of rates?	Avez-vous une liste des tarifs? ah-vay-voo ewn leest day tah-reef
How do I...?	Comment puis-je...? koh-mahn pweezh
...insert this into the phone	...insérer ceci dans mon téléphone an-say-ray suh-see dahn mohn tay-lay-fohn
...check the credit balance	...vérifier le nombre d'unités restantes vehr-ee-fee-ay luh nohn-bruh dew-nee-tay rehs-tahnt
...buy more time	...acheter des unités ah-shuh-tay dayz ew-nee-tay
...change the language to English	...paramétrer la langue sur anglais pah-rah-may-tray lah lahng sewr ahn-glay

Hotel-Room Phones

Most hotels charge a fee for placing calls—ask for rates before you dial.
Prepaid international phone cards *(cartes international)* are not widely
used in France, but can be found at some newsstands, tobacco shops,
and train stations. Dial the toll-free access number, enter the card's PIN
code, then dial the number.

Can I call from my room?	Est-ce que je peux appeler depuis ma chambre? ehs kuh zhuh puh ah-peh-lay duh-pwee mah shahn-bruh
How do I dial out?	Comment puis-je passer un appel vers l'extérieur? koh-mahn pweezh pah-say uhn ah-pehl vehr lehks-tay-ree-ur

How much per minute for a...?	Combien la minute pour un...? kohn-bee-an lah mee-newt poor uhn
...local call	...appel local ah-pehl loh-kahl
...domestic call	...appel national ah-pehl nah-see-oh-nahl
...international call	...appel international ah-pehl an-tehr-nah-see-oh-nahl
Can I dial this number for free?	Puis-je appeler ce numéro gratuitement? pweezh ah-puh-lay suh new-may-roh grah-tweet-mahn

GETTING ONLINE

To get online in Europe, you can bring your own mobile device or use public computers (such as at a library or your hotel).

Internet Terms

Internet access	accès à l'internet ahk-seh ah lan-tehr-neht
Wi-Fi	Wi-Fi wee-fee
email	email ee-mehl
computer	ordinateur or-dee-nah-tur
username	nom d'utilisateur nohn dew-tee-lee-zah-tur
password	mot de passe moh duh pahs
network key	mot de passe pour le réseau moh duh pahs poor luh ray-zoh
secure network	un réseau sûr / un réseau en sécurité uhn ray-zoh sewr / uhn ray-zoh ahn say-kew-ree-tay
website	site web seet wehb
download	télécharger tay-lay-shar-zhay
print	imprimer an-pree-may

| My email address is _____. | Mon adresse email est _____.
mohn ah-drehs ee-mehl ay _____ |
| What's your email address? | Quelle est votre adresse email?
kehl ay voh-truh ah-drehs ee-mehl |

Note that a few terms look the same as in English, but are pronounced differently: **www** (doo-bluh-vay, doo-bluh-vay, doo-bluh-vay); **Wi-Fi** (wee-fee); **CD** (say day); **DVD** (day vay day); and **USB** (ew ehs bay).

Tech Support

Help me, please.	Aidez-moi, s'il vous plaît. eh-day-mwah see voo play
How do I...?	Comment je...? koh-mahn zhuh
...start this	...démarre ça day-mar sah
...get online	...me connecte muh koh-nehkt
...get this to work	...fais marcher ça fay mar-shay sah
...stop this	....arrête ça ah-reht sah
...send this	...envoie ça ahn-vwah sah
...print this	...imprime ça an-preem sah
...make this symbol	...fais ce symbole fay suh san-bohl
...copy and paste	...fais un copier-coller fay uhn kohp-yay-koh-lay
...type @	...tape arobase tahp ah-roh-bahz
This doesn't work.	Ça ne marche pas. sah nuh marsh pah

Using Your Own Mobile Device

You can get online at hotels, cafés, train stations, TIs, and many other places. While Wi-Fi is often free, sometimes you'll have to pay.

laptop	ordinateur portable / laptop or-dee-nah-tur por-tah-bluh / "laptop"
mobile phone	un portable uhn por-tah-bluh
tablet	tablette tah-bleht

Key Phrases: Getting Online

Where is a Wi-Fi hotspot?	Où se trouve un point Wi-Fi?
	oo suh troov uhn pwan wee-fee
Where can I get online?	Où puis-je me connecter?
	oo pweezh muh koh-nehk-tay
Can I check my email?	Je peux regarder mon email?
	zhuh puh ruh-gar-day mohn ee-mehl

Where is a Wi-Fi hotspot?	Où se trouve un point Wi-Fi?
	oo suh troov uhn pwan wee-fee
Do you have Wi-Fi?	Avez-vous le Wi-Fi?
	ah-vay-voo luh wee-fee
What is the...?	C'est quoi le...? say kwah luh
...network name	...nom du réseau nohn dew ray-zoh
...username	...nom d'utilisateur
	nohn dew-tee-lee-zah-tur
...password	...mot de passe moh duh pahs
Do you have a...?	Vous avez un...? vooz ah-vay uhn
Can I borrow a...?	Je peux emprunter un...?
	zhuh puh ahn-pruhn-tay uhn
...charging cable	...câble pour charger
	kah-bluh poor shar-zhay
...USB cable	...câble USB kah-bluh ew ehs bay
Free?	Gratuit? grah-twee
How much?	Combien? kohn-bee-an
Do I have to buy something to use the Internet?	J'ai besoin d'acheter quelque chose pour utiliser l'internet?
	zhay buh-zwan dah-shuh-tay kehl-kuh shohz poor ew-tee-lee-zay lan-tehr-neht

Using a Public Computer

Some hotels have a computer in the lobby for guests to get online. Otherwise you may find a public computer at a library or TI.

Where can I get online?	Où puis-je me connecter? oo pweezh muh koh-nehk-tay
Can I use this computer to...?	Je peux utiliser cet ordinateur pour...? zhuh puh ew-tee-lee-zay seht or-dee-nah-tur poor
...get online	...me connecter muh koh-nehk-tay
...check my email	...regarder mon email ruh-gar-day mohn ee-mehl
...download photos	...télécharger des photos tay-lay-shar-zhay day foh-toh
...print (something)	...imprimer (quelque chose) an-pree-may (kehl-kuh shohz)
boarding passes	cartes d'embarquement kart dahn-bar-kuh-mahn
tickets	billets bee-yay
reservation confirmation	confirmer une réservation kohn-feer-may ewn ray-zehr-vah-see-ohn
Free?	Gratuit? grah-twee
How much (for... minutes)?	C'est combien (pour... minutes)? say kohn-bee-an (poor... mee-newt)
...10	...dix dees
...15	...quinze kanz
...30	...trente trahnt
...60	...soixante swah-sahnt
I have a...	J'ai... zhay
Do you have a...?	Avez-vous...? ah-vay-voo
...webcam	...une webcam ewn "webcam"
...headset	...des écouteurs dayz ay-koo-tur
...USB cable	...un câble USB uhn kah-bluh ew ehs bay

...memory card	...une carte mémoire ewn kart may-mwahr
...flash drive	...une carte mémoire flash ewn kart may-mwahr flahsh
...USB key	...une clé USB ewn klay ew ehs bay
Can you switch the keyboard to American?	Vous-pourriez changer le clavier au format américain? voo-poo-ree-ay shah<u>n</u>-zhay luh klahv-yay oh for-maht ah-may-ree-ka<u>n</u>

If you're using a public computer, the keyboard, menus, and on-screen commands will likely be designed for French speakers. Some computers allow you to make the French keyboard work as if it were an American one (ask if it's possible).

French Keyboards

On French keyboards, most command keys differ, and some keys are in a different location. For example, the **M** key is where the semicolon is on American keyboards. The **A** and **Q** keys and the **Z** and **W** keys are reversed from American keyboards. Here's a rundown of how major commands are labeled on a French keyboard:

YOU'LL SEE...	IT MEANS...	YOU'LL SEE...	IT MEANS...
Entrée	Enter	**Suppr**	Delete
Maj	Shift	←	Backspace
Ctrl	Ctrl	**Inser**	Insert
Alt	Alt	↖	Home
Verr Maj	Shift Lock	**Fin**	End
Verr Num	Num Lock	**Page Haut**	Page Up
Tab	Tab	**Page Bas**	Page Down
Echap	Esc		

The Alt key to the right of the space bar is actually a different key, called **Alt Gr** (for "Alternate Graphics"). Press this key to insert the extra symbol that appears on some keys (such as the € in the corner of the E key).

A few often-used keys look the same, but have different names in French:

@ **sign**	signe	seen-yuh
	arobase	ah-roh-bahz
dot	point	pwan
hyphen (-)	tiret	tee-ray
underscore (_)	souligne	soo-leen-yuh
slash (/)	barre oblique / "slash"	bar oh-bleek / "slahsh"

French speakers have several names for the @ sign, but the most common is **_arobase._** When saying an email address, you say **_arobase_** in the middle.

To type @, press **Alt Gr** and the **à/0** key. Belgian keyboards may require pressing **Alt Gr** and the **é/2** key. If that doesn't work, try copying-and-pasting the @ sign from elsewhere on the page.

On Screen

YOU'LL SEE...	IT MEANS...	YOU'LL SEE...	IT MEANS...
Réseau	Network	**Aperçu**	View
Utilisateur (nom)	User (name)	**Insérer**	Insert
Mot de passe	Password	**Format**	Format
Clef / Clé	Key	**Outils**	Tools
Dossier	Folder	**Aide**	Help
Fichier	File	**Options**	Options
Nouveau	New	**Mail**	Mail
Ouvrir	Open	**Message**	Message
Fermer	Close	**Répondre à tous**	Reply All
Sauver	Save	**CC**	CC
Imprimer	Print	**Réexpédier**	Forward
Annuler	Delete	**Envoyer**	Send
Rechercher	Search	**Recevoir**	Receive
Éditer	Edit	**Boîte de réception**	Inbox

YOU'LL SEE...	IT MEANS...	YOU'LL SEE...	IT MEANS...
Couper	Cut	Pièces jointes / Document joints / Joindre	Attach
Copier	Copy	Expédier	Upload
Coller	Paste	Télécharge	Download
Paramétres	Settings		

HELP!

or any emergency service—ambulance, police, or fire—call 112 from a mobile phone or landline. Operators, who in most countries speak English, will deal with your request or route you to the right emergency service. *SOS Médecins* are doctors who make emergency house calls. If you need help, someone will call an *SOS médecin* for you. If you're lost, see the phrases on page 72.

EMERGENCIES

Medical Help

Help!	Au secours! oh suh-koor
Help me, please.	Aidez-moi, s'il vous plaît. eh-day-mwah see voo play
emergency	urgence ewr-zhahns
accident	accident ahk-see-dahn
medical clinic / hospital	clinique médicale / hôpital klee-neek may-dee-kahl / oh-pee-tahl
Call...	Appelez... ah-puh-lay
...a doctor.	...un docteur. uhn dohk-tur
...the police.	...la police. lah poh-lees
...an ambulance.	...le SAMU. luh sah-mew
I need / We need...	J'ai besoin / Nous avons besoin... zhay buh-zwan / nooz ah-vohn buh-zwan
...a doctor.	...un docteur. uhn dohk-tur
...to go to the hospital.	...d'aller à l'hôpital. dah-lay ah loh-pee-tahl
It's urgent.	C'est urgent. say ewr-zhahn
injured	blessé bleh-say
bleeding	saigne sehn-yuh
choking	étouffe ay-toof
unconscious	inconscient an-kohn-see-ahn
not breathing	ne respire pas nuh rehs-peer pah

ey Phrases: Help!

lelp!	Au secours! oh suh-koor
mergency	urgence ewr-zhahns
linic / hospital	clinique médicale / hôpital klee-neek may-dee-kahl / oh-pee-tahl
all a doctor.	Appelez un docteur. ah-puh-lay uhn dohk-tur
mbulance	SAMU sah-mew
olice	police poh-lees
hief	voleur voh-lur
top, thief!	Arrêtez, au voleur! ah-reh-tay oh voh-lur

Thank you for your help.	Merci pour votre aide. mehr-see poor voh-truh ehd
You are very kind.	Vous êtes très gentil. vooz eht treh zhahn-tee

If you need someone to come and get you because you're having a heart attack, you need the *SAMU,* which stands for *Service d'Aide Médicale Urgente. Ambulance* is also a word in French, but not for emergencies. *Les ambulances* are for transporting people without cars to doctor's visits. For other health-related words, see the Personal Care and Health chapter.

Theft and Loss

thief	voleur voh-lur
pickpocket	pickpocket peek-poh-keht
police	police poh-lees
embassy	ambassade ahn-bah-sahd

Stop, thief!	Arrêtez, au voleur! ah-reh-tay oh voh-lur
Call the police!	Appelez la police! ah-puh-lay lah poh-lees
I've been robbed.	On m'a volé. ohn mah voh-lay
We've been robbed.	Nous avons été volé. nooz ah-vohn ay-tay voh-lay
A thief took...	Un voleur à pris... uhn voh-lur ah pree
Thieves took...	Des voleurs ont pris... day voh-lur ohn pree
I've lost my...	J'ai perdu mon... zhay pehr-dew mohn
We've lost our...	Nous avons perdu nos... nooz ah-vohn pehr-dew noh
money	argent ar-zhahn
credit card	carte de crédit kart duh kray-dee
passport	passeport pahs-por
ticket	billet bee-yay
railpass	passe Eurail pahs "Eurail"
baggage	bagages bah-gahzh
purse	sac sahk
wallet	portefeuille por-tuh-fuh-ee
watch	montre mohn-truh
jewelry	bijoux bee-zhoo
camera	appareil-photo ah-pah-ray-foh-toh
mobile phone	téléphone portable tay-lay-fohn por-tah-bluh
iPod / iPad	iPod / iPad "iPod" / "iPad"
tablet	tablette tah-bleht
computer	ordinateur or-dee-nah-tur
laptop	ordinateur portable / laptop or-dee-nah-tur por-tah-bluh / "laptop"
faith in humankind	foi en l'humanité fwah ahn lew-mah-nee-tay

I want to contact my embassy.	Je veux contacter mon ambassade. zhuh vuh koh<u>n</u>-tahk-tay moh<u>n</u> ah<u>n</u>-bah-sahd
I need to file a police report (for my insurance).	Je veux porter plainte à la police (pour mon assurance). zhuh vuh por-tay plah<u>nt</u> ah lah poh-lees (poor moh<u>n</u> ah-sewr-rah<u>n</u>s)
Where is the police station?	Où se trouve la gendarmerie? oo suh troov lah zhah<u>n</u>-dar-muh-ree

To replace a passport, you'll need to go in person to your embassy (see page 423). Cancel and replace your credit and debit cards by calling your credit-card company (as of this printing, these are the 24-hour US numbers that you can call collect: Visa—tel. 303/967-1096, Master-Card—tel. 636/722-7111, American Express—tel. 336/393-1111). If you'll want to submit an insurance claim for lost or stolen gear, be sure to file a police report, either on the spot or within a day or two. For more info, see www.ricksteves.com/help. Precautionary measures can minimize the effects of loss—back up your photos and other files frequently.

Fire!

fire	feu fuh
smoke	fumée few-may
exit	sortie sor-tee
emergency exit	sortie de secours sor-tee duh suh-koor
fire extinguisher	extincteur ehks-ta<u>n</u>k-tur
Call the fire department.	Appelez les pompiers. ah-puh-lay lay poh<u>n</u>-pee-yay

HELP FOR WOMEN

Generally the best way to react to unwanted attention is loudly and quickly.

No!	Non! nohn
Stop it!	Arrêtez! ah-reh-tay
Enough!	Ça suffit! sah sew-fee
Don't touch me.	Ne me touchez pas. nuh muh too-shay pah
Leave me alone.	Laissez-moi tranquille. lay-say-mwah trahn-keel
Go away.	Allez-vous en. ah-lay-vooz ahn
Get lost!	Dégagez! day-gah-zhay
Drop dead!	Foutez-moi la paix! foo-tay-mwah lah pay
Police!	Police! poh-lees

Safety in Numbers

If a guy is bugging you, approach a friendly-looking couple, family, or business for a place to stay safe.

A man is bothering me.	Un homme est en train de me harceler. uhn ohm ayt ahn tran duh muh ar-suh-lay
May I...?	Est-ce que je peux...? ehs kuh zhuh puh
...join you	...vous joindre voo zhwan-druh
...sit here	...m'asseoir ici mah-swahr ee-see
...wait here until he's gone	...attendez ici jusqu'à ce qu'il parte ah-tahn-day ee-see zhew-skah skeel part

You Want to Be Alone

I want to be alone.	Je veux être seule. zhuh vuh eh-truh suhl
I'm not interested.	Ça ne m'intéresse pas. sah nuh ma<u>n</u>-tay-rehs pah
I'm married.	Je suis mariée. zhuh swee mah-ree-ay
I'm waiting for my husband.	J'attends mon mari. zhah-tah<u>n</u> moh<u>n</u> mah-ree
I'm a lesbian.	Je suis lesbienne. zhuh swee lehz-bee-ehn
I have a contagious disease.	J'ai une maladie contagieuse. zhay ewn mah-lah-dee koh<u>n</u>-tah-zhee-uhz

SERVICES

Whether you're getting a haircut, going to a spa, getting something fixed, or doing laundry, you'll find the phrases you need in this chapter.

HAIR AND BODY

At the Hair Salon

haircut	une coupe ewn koop
Where is...?	Où se trouve...? oo suh troov
...a hair salon	...un salon de coiffure pour femmes uhn sah-lohn duh kwah-fur poor fahm
...a barber	...un salon de coiffure pour hommes uhn sah-lohn duh kwah-fur poor ohm
...the price list	...la liste des prix lah leest day pree
I'd like...	J'aimerais... zheh-may-ray
...a haircut.	...une coupe. ewn koop
...a shampoo.	...un shampooing. uhn shahn-pwan
...a wash and dry.	...un brushing. uhn "brushing"
...highlights.	...des mèches. day mehsh
...my hair colored.	...mes cheveux colorés. may shuh-vuh koh-loh-ray
...a permanent.	...une permanente. ewn pehr-mah-nahnt
...just a trim.	...juste rafraîchir. zhewst rah-freh-sheer
How much?	Combien? kohn-bee-an
Cut about this much off.	Coupez ça à peu près. koo-pay sah ah puh preh
Here. (gesturing)	Ici. ee-see
Short.	Court. koor
Shorter.	Plus court. plew koor
Shave it all off.	Rasez les tous. rah-zay lay too